Quiet Water

MID-ATLANTIC

AMC's Canoe and Kayak Guide to the Best Ponds, Lakes, and Easy Rivers, from Pennsylvania to Virginia

BY RACHEL COOPER

Appalachian Mountain Club Books
Boston, Massachusetts

AMC is a nonprofit organization, and sales of AMC Books fund our mission of protecting the Northeast outdoors. If you appreciate our efforts and would like to become a member or make a donation to AMC, visit outdoors.org, call 800-372-1758, or contact us at Appalachian Mountain Club, 10 City Square, Boston, MA 02129.

outdoors.org/books-maps

Distributed by National Book Network.

Front cover photograph of Catfish Pond at Mohican Outdoor Center © Dan Klempa
Back cover photograph of Sinepuxent Bay, Assateague Island National Seashore, © Marc Chalufour
Interior photographs © Rachel Cooper except where noted
Maps by Ken Dumas © Appalachian Mountain Club
Book design by Eric Edstam

Library of Congress Cataloging-in-Publication Data
Names: Cooper, Rachel Q., 1963- author. | Appalachian Mountain Club.
Title: Quiet water Mid-Atlantic : AMC's canoe and kayak guide to the best ponds, lakes, and easy rivers, from
    Pennsylvania to Virginia / by Rachel Cooper.
Description: Boston, Massachusetts : Appalachian Mountain Club Books, [2018] | Series: Quiet Water series |
    "Distributed by National Book Network"--T.p. verso. | Includes index. | Identifiers: LCCN 2018010387 (print) |
    LCCN 2018022435 (ebook) | ISBN 9781628420883 (ePub) | ISBN 9781628420890 (mobi) | ISBN 9781628420876
    (paperback)
Subjects: LCSH: Canoes and canoeing--New Jersey--Guidebooks. | Canoes and canoeing--Pennsylvania--
    Guidebooks. | Canoes and canoeing--Delaware--Guidebooks. | Canoes and canoeing--Maryland--Guidebooks. |
    Canoes and canoeing--Washington, D.C.--Guidebooks. | Canoes and canoeing--Virginia--Guidebooks. | Canoes
    and canoeing--Mid-Atlantic--Guidebooks. | Kayaking--New Jersey--Guidebooks. | Kayaking--Pennsylvania--
    Guidebooks. | Kayaking--Delaware--Guidebooks. | Kayaking--Maryland--Guidebooks. | Kayaking--Washington,
    D.C.--Guidebooks. | Kayaking--Virginia--Guidebooks. | Kayaking--Mid-Atlantic--Guidebooks. | Hiking--Mid-
    Atlantic--Guidebooks. | Camping--Mid-Atlantic--Guidebooks. | New Jersey--Guidebooks. | Pennsylvania--
    Guidebooks. | Delaware--Guidebooks. | Maryland--Guidebooks. | Washington, D.C.--Guidebooks. | Virginia--
    Guidebooks. | Mid-AtlanVc--Guidebooks.
Classification: LCC GV776.A2 (ebook) | LCC GV776.A2 C59 2018 (print) | DDC 797.122/40975--dc23
LC record available at hbps://lccn.loc.gov/2018010387

The paper used in this publication meets the minimum requirements of the American National Standard for Information Sciences-Permanence of Paper for Printed Library Materials, ANSI Z39.48-1984. ∞

Interior pages and cover are printed on responsibly harvested paper stock certified by The Forest Stewardship Council®, an independent auditor of responsible forestry practices.
Printed in the United States of America, using vegetable-based inks.

5 4 3 2 1   18 19 20 21 22

MIX
Paper from
responsible sources
FSC® C005010
www.fsc.org

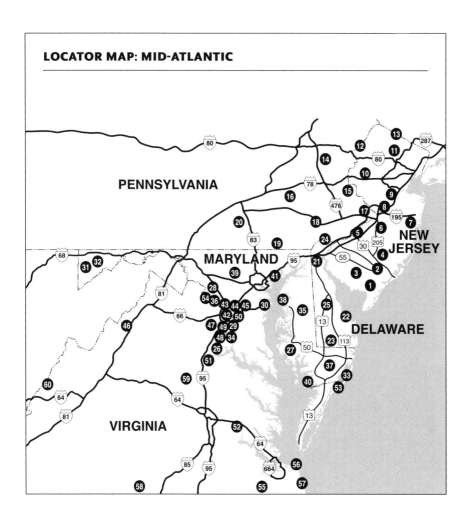

LOCATOR MAP: MID-ATLANTIC

Numbers on map correspond to trips; see also "Contents," beginning on page v.

Contents

SECTION 1: NEW JERSEY

SECTION 2: PENNSYLVANIA

At-a-Glance Trip Planner

#	Trip Name	Page	Access Location	Area/ One-Way Length	Estimated Time (round-trip)
NEW JERSEY					
1	Lake Nummy and East Creek Pond: Belleplain State Forest	3	Woodbine	26 acres; 62 acres	1 hour; 1–1.5 hours
2	Lake Lenape and Great Egg Harbor River	7	Mays Landing	350 acres	2.5–3.5 hours; 1.5–2 hours
3	Union Lake	10	Millville	898 acres	3–4 hours
4	Mullica River	14	Pleasant Mills	7.5 miles	3–4 hours
5	Cooper River Lake and Newton Lake	18	Collingswood	150 acres; 40 acres	2–2.5 hours; 1.5–2 hours
6	Rancocas Creek	22	Pemberton	6.6 miles	2.5 hours
7	Lakes Carasaljo and Shenandoah	26	Lakewood	67 acres; 50 acres	2 hours each
8	Lake Mercer	30	West Windsor	275 acres	2.5–3 hours
9	Farrington Lake	34	New Brunswick	290 acres	2.5–3.5 hours
10	Spruce Run Reservoir	38	Clinton	1,300 acres	5–5.5 hours

Hiking Trails	Swimming	Rentals On-Site	Motor Boats	Fee	Trip Highilghts
Y	Y	N	Electric only	Y	Very remote, raptors, white cedar wetlands, plentiful birdlife
Y	Y	N	10 horse-power limit	Y	Eagles, ospreys, islands, nationally ranked scenic river
Y	N	N	10 horse-power limit	N	Huge lake with islands, hawks, raptors, wildlife, good fishing
N	N	N	Unlimited	Y	Eagles, ospreys, cedar bogs, wading birds, river otters, beavers
Y	N	Y	Electric only	N	Two nice lakes, close to town, waterfowl, turtles
Y	N	Y	Electric only	N	Turtles, beavers, scenic waterway, abundant birdlife
Y	N	N	Electric only	N	Islands, waterfowl, freshwater marshes, scenic, close to town
Y	N	Y	Electric only	N	Nice lake in large park on the outskirts of Trenton
N	N	N	Electric only	N	Large, long scenic lake with abundant wildlife near town
Y	Y	Y	10 horse-power limit	Y	Serpentine lake, a few islands, abundant birdlife

#	Trip Name	Page	Access Location	Area/ One-Way Length	Estimated Time (round-trip)
11	Splitrock Reservoir	41	Rockaway	625 acres	4–5 hours
12	Appalachian Mountain Club's Mohican Outdoor Center: Catfish Pond	45	Millbrook	31 acres	1 hour
13	Wawayanda Lake	48	Vernon Township	255 acres	2.5–3 hours
PENNSYLVANIA					
14	Beltzville Lake	53	Lehighton	949 acres	4–4.5 hours
15	Lake Nockamixon	56	Quakertown	1,450 acres	4–4.5 hours
16	Blue Marsh Lake	62	Leesport	1,147 acres	2 hours or more
17	Lake Luxembourg: Core Creek Park	66	Newtown	166 acres	2–3 hours
18	Marsh Creek Reservoir	70	Downingtown	535 acres	3.5–4 hours
19	Susquehanna River: Conowingo Reservoir and Lake Aldred	73	Slab and Pequea	15,875 acres 2,400 acres	3–5 hours; 3–4 hours
20	Pinchot Lake: Gifford Pinchot State Park	79	Lewisberry	340 acres	4–4.5 hours
DELAWARE					
21	Lums Pond	84	Bear	200 acres	2–3 hours
22	Prime Hook National Wildlife Refuge	87	Milton	7 miles	3 hours or more

Hiking Trails	Swimming	Rentals On-Site	Motor Boats	Fee	Trip Highlights
Y	N	N	Electric only	N	Maine-like rock islands, clear water, remote location, beavers, abundant birdlife
Y	Y	Y	None	N	Remote, pristine lake high in the Kittatinny Mountains
Y	Y	Y	Electric only	Y	Islands, beautiful scenery, abundant waterfowl and wildlife
Y	Y	Y	Unlimited with no-wake zones	N	Steep wooded cliffs, rock faces, clear water, waterfall, beavers, otters, birds
Y	Y	Y	20 horse-power limit with no-wake zones	N	Ospreys, waterfowl, beavers, views of Haycock Mountain
Y	Y	Y	Unlimited with no-wake zones	N	Steep wooded hillsides, long coves, abundant waterfowl and birdlife
Y	N	Y	Electric only	Y	Pleasant paddling on nice lake near town
Y	N	Y	Electric only	N	Ospreys, forested rolling hillsides, good fishing
Y	N	N	Unlimited	N	Petroglyphs, eagles, ospreys, wonderful rock islands, abundant waterfowl
Y	N	Y	Electric only	N	Rocky shores, forested hillsides, mergansers, woodpeckers
Y	N	Y	Electric only	Y	Scenic park with lots of amenities, bird and wildlife viewing
Y	N	N	30 horse-power limit	N	Quiet and scenic water trail, variety of habitats, waterfowl, amphibians

#	Trip Name	Page	Access Location	Area/ One-Way Length	Estimated Time (round-trip)
23	Trap Pond	94	Laurel	90 acres	2 hours
24	Brandywine Creek	98	Wilmington	6–7 miles	2–3 hours
25	Killens Pond	101	Felton	2–4 miles	1.5–2 hours

MARYLAND

#	Trip Name	Page	Access Location	Area/ One-Way Length	Estimated Time (round-trip)
26	Mallows Bay	106	Nanjemoy	1.5 miles	1–2 hours
27	Blackwater National Wildlife Refuge	112	Cambridge	3.5–4 miles	2–3 hours
28	Little Seneca Lake: Black Hill Regional Park	116	Boyds	5 miles	3–5 hours
29	Piscataway Creek	120	Fort Washington	5 miles	2–3 hours
30	Spa Creek	125	Annapolis	3 miles	1–2 hours
31	Deep Creek Lake	129	Swanton	3,900 acres	2–3 hours or more
32	Savage River Reservoir: Big Run State Park	132	Swanton	360 acres	2 hours or more
33	Sinepuxent Bay: Assateague Island National Seashore	136	Berlin	3 miles or more	2–3 hours
34	Mattawoman Creek	140	Indian Head	up to 20 miles	2.5 hours or more
35	Tuckahoe Creek	144	Denton	2–3 miles or more	2 hours or more
36	Potomac River and Seneca Creek: Riley's Lock	147	Poolesville	5–7 miles or more	2–3 hours
37	Corker's Creek: Pocomoke River State Park	151	Snow Hill	2 miles	1–2 hours
38	Eastern Neck National Wildlife Refuge	157	Rock Hall	up to 10 miles	2 hours or more

Hiking Trails	Swimming	Rentals On-Site	Motor Boats	Fee	Trip Highlights
Y	N	Y	Electric only	Y	Large stands of bald cypress trees, forested scenery, wildlife
Y	N	Y	None	Y	Narrow creek, waterfowl
Y	N	Y	Electric only	Y	Aquatic plants, turtles, birds, scenic destination
Y	N	N	Unlimited	N	Graveyard of sunken ships from World War I
Y	N	Y	Electric only	Y	Scenic views, bald and golden eagles, ospreys, river otters, waterfowl
Y	N	Y	Electric only	Y	Water trail, birds, turtles, beaver dams
Y	N	Y	Unlimited	Y	Ospreys, herons, ducks, and other waterfowl
Y	N	Y	Unlimited	Y	Views of Annapolis and a variety of waterfront property
Y	Y	Y	Unlimited	Y	Beautiful mountain scenery with a lot of activity, narrow coves
Y	N	N	Electric only	N	Breathtaking scenery, mountain views, clear water, waterfowl
Y	Y	Y	Electric only	Y	Salt marshes, variety of waterfowl, wild ponies
Y	N	Y	Electric only	Y	Ospreys, herons, ducks, and other waterfowl, American lotus, scenic
N	N	N	Electric only	Y	Quiet creek, abundant wildlife
Y	N	N	Electric only	N	Two waterways, waterfowl, scenic views
Y	N	Y	Electric only	N	Cypress swamp, river otters, waterfowl, turtles
Y	N	N	Electric only	N	Water trail, scenic, variety of birds and other wildlife

#	Trip Name	Page	Access Location	Area/ One-Way Length	Estimated Time (round-trip)
39	Piney Run Reservoir	161	Sykesville	300 acres	2 hours
40	Daugherty Creek: Janes Island State Park	164	Crisfield	30 miles	2 hours or more
41	Dundee Creek	168	Middle River	2–3 miles or more	2 hours

WASHINGTON, D.C.

#	Trip Name	Page	Access Location	Area/ One-Way Length	Estimated Time (round-trip)
42	Potomac River: Key Bridge and Georgetown	173	Washington, D.C.	4–6 miles	2.5–3 hours
43	Potomac River: Fletcher's Boathouse	179	Washington, D.C.	2–4 miles	2–3 hours
44	Anacostia River: Anacostia Park	183	Washington, D.C.	3.5 miles	2 hours
45	Anacostia River: Bladensburg Waterfront Park	187	Bladensburg/ Washington, D.C.	6 miles or more	2.5–3 hours

VIRGINIA

#	Trip Name	Page	Access Location	Area/ One-Way Length	Estimated Time (round-trip)
46	Shenandoah River: North Fork	193	Mount Jackson	3–6 miles	2 hours or more
47	Occoquan Reservoir	197	Lake Ridge	2,100 acres	2.5 hours or more
48	Powell's Creek: Leesylvania State Park	201	Woodbridge	3 miles	1–2 hours
49	Pohick Bay	205	Lorton	4–5 miles or more	2–3 hours
50	Dyke Marsh Wildlife Preserve	209	Alexandria	4.5 miles	2.5–3 hours
51	Rappahannock River	213	Fredericksburg	3–5 miles	2–3 hours
52	Diascund Creek Reservoir	216	Lanexa	1,100 acres	2–3 hours or more

Hiking Trails	Swimming	Rentals On-Site	Motor Boats	Fee	Trip Highilghts
Y	N	Y	Electric only	Y	Scenic views, ducks, geese, wading birds
Y	Y	Y	Electric only	N	Multiple water trails, birds, fish, crabs, salt marshes, scenic vistas
Y	N	Y	Unlimited	N	Mix of marshland and an open bay, scenic views, waterfowl
Y	N	Y	Unlimited	Y	Views of urban skylines and forested areas, abundant waterfowl
Y	N	Y	Electric only	N	Scenic views, variety of birds, turtles
Y	N	N	Electric only	N	Wetlands, abundant waterfowl, reptiles, scenic views
N	N	Y	Electric only	N	Scenic views, aquatic gardens, abundant waterfowl
N	N	N	None	N	Historic covered bridge, scenic views, waterfowl
Y	N	Y	Electric only	Y	Great blue herons, hawks, turkey vultures, geese, turtles, other wildlife
Y	N	Y	Unlimited	Y	Scenic views, abundant aquatic plants, birds, fish, other wildlife
Y	N	Y	Unlimited	Y	Bald eagles, herons, ospreys, fish, other wildlife
Y	N	Y	Unlimited	Y	Scenic views, abundant aquatic plants, birds, fish, other wildlife
N	N	Y	Electric only	N	River otters, great blue heron, ospreys, other waterfowl
N	N	N	Electric only	N	Scenic views, great fishing, variety of birds

#	Trip Name	Page	Access Location	Area/One-Way Length	Estimated Time (round-trip)
53	Chincoteague National Wildlife Refuge	220	Chincoteague Island	7 miles	2–3 hours
54	Potomac River: Algonkian Regional Park	224	Sterling	2–3 miles or more	2 hours
55	Lake Drummond: Great Dismal Swamp	228	Suffolk	3,100 acres	2 hours
56	First Landing State Park	233	Virginia Beach	5 miles or more	2–3 hours or more
57	Back Bay National Wildlife Refuge	236	Virginia Beach	2 miles or more	2 hours or more
58	John H. Kerr Lake: Occoneechee State Park	240	Clarksville	48,000 acres	2–3 hours or more
59	Lake Anna	244	Spotsylvania	13,000 acres	2 hours or more
60	Lake Moomaw	247	Hot Springs	2,530 acres	2–3 hours or more

Hiking Trails	Swimming	Rentals On-Site	Motor Boats	Fee	Trip Highilghts
N	N	Y	Unlimited	Y	Scenic views, abundant variety of birds, wild ponies
Y	N	N	None	Y	River views, waterfowl, amphibians
Y	N	N	None	Y	Panoramic views, bald cypress, variety of birds
Y	N	Y	Unlimited	Y	Mix of habitats, beach, saltwater marsh and lake, waterfowl, crabs
Y	N	N	Electric only	N	Scenic vistas, birds, good fishing
Y	N	Y	Unlimited	Y	Large lake with many scenic vistas, butterflies, waterfowl
Y	Y	N	Unlimited	Y	Large lake with many scenic vistas, creeks, waterfowl
Y	Y	Y	Unlimited	Y	Breathtaking mountain scenery, good fishing, waterfowl

Acknowledgments

First and foremost, I would like to thank my husband, Brian, for his adventurous spirit and dedication to assisting me in the production of this book. In his own words, he served as my "Sherpa, photographer, and tech-support guru." He accompanied me on most of the trips and spent many hours driving, hauling gear, processing photographs, and reviewing content. His companionship and enthusiastic wildlife viewing kept me inspired and entertained.

Thanks to AMC for the opportunity to write this book and to author Kathy Kenley for agreeing to the use and modifications of content from *Quiet Water: New Jersey and Eastern Pennsylvania* (AMC Books, 2010). My thanks go to Shannon Smith, editor, for her guidance and kind words along the way; to Jennifer Wehunt, editorial director, for selecting me for this project; to Kenneth Dumas for the creation of the waterway maps; and to other members of the AMC staff involved in the publishing process.

I am grateful to my colleagues and contacts from the Mid-Atlantic Tourism Public Relations Alliance, who helped me gather information, as did many people I met and consulted with during this adventure. The list would be too long to singly name and thank all the park rangers, birders, naturalists, and paddling guides who gave their assistance. I also met many local kayakers, canoeists, and anglers who extended their time and gave me insider information about their favorite places.

A special thanks to Danielle Emerson, deputy director of communications at the Virginia Tourism Corporation, for connecting me with several Virginia Tourism representatives who were especially accommodating in providing insight about the paddling destinations within their jurisdictions. I am indebted to Evelyn Shotwell, executive director at the Chincoteague Chamber of Commerce; John and Basia Shields, owners of Snug Harbor Cottages; Nancy

Heltman, visitor services director of Virginia State Parks; and Teresa Hammond, executive director of the Alleghany Highlands Chamber of Commerce and Tourism, for their time and extra attention. Also, thanks to Judy Lathrop, owner of Atlantic Kayak Company, for sharing her knowledge and experience.

Finally, warm love and appreciation to my family and friends who accompanied me on different trips and made them more enjoyable.

Preface

This book profiles 60 of the best quietwater paddling destinations in the Mid-Atlantic region. To cover the region within a reasonable time frame, I personally kayaked 40 sites in Delaware; Maryland; Washington, D.C.; and Virginia. With permission from author Kathy Kenley, I revised and updated twenty trip descriptions from *Quiet Water: New Jersey and Eastern Pennsylvania* (AMC Books, 2010). Beginners and serious kayakers will find inspiration and detailed information to seek out new paddling destinations. This guide includes descriptions of each lake, pond, or river, with paddling routes, local flora and fauna, and seasonal highlights; driving, parking, and put-in instructions; safety tips; and local hiking, picnicking, and camping spots.

As a native of Maryland and a freelance writer with a focus on the Washington, D.C., metropolitan area for more than a decade, I have traveled the region extensively and am continuously surprised by the new places that I discover. My love for the outdoors has given me a great appreciation for the region's scenic landscapes, as well as its natural and human history. Paddling along dozens of waterways throughout the Mid-Atlantic awarded me a refreshing view and a fascination with the diverse and beautiful ecosystems of this region. I hope you, too, will enjoy exploring these sites and all that they offer.

Introduction

Something magical, almost spiritual, happens when I am out on the water. I feel a peaceful solitude when I sit still and take in the scenery on a pond, lake, or easy river. Quietwater paddling allows me to tune out the noisy world and focus on my surroundings, to meander through wetlands and spy an osprey diving for a silvery fish or wood ducks swimming through early-morning mists.

I am grateful for the opportunity to write this book and share my experiences, as well as for the many things I learned during the writing process. Over the years, my passion for outdoor recreation and travel has taken me to a wide range of beautiful destinations across the world. Surprisingly, I have seen more wildlife while kayaking in the Mid-Atlantic region than while participating in any other recreational activity—including my travels to seemingly more exotic places. Paddling takes you up close to explore the habitats that support a diverse assortment of fish, amphibians, reptiles, mammals, birds, and invertebrates. I have tried to learn to identify the creatures that are most common in the Mid-Atlantic region, and I got so excited by some of my newest discoveries that my daughter affectionately started calling me "the bird lady." It may take a lifetime to learn about all the species out there; some of the best sources of information are the naturalists employed by our region's parks and the exhibits in the visitor centers.

The Mid-Atlantic region is a relatively compact area with diverse geography and ecosystems within a few hours' drive. As I explored the waterways, I was amazed by the unique characteristics of each destination. While there are many common flora and fauna in the area, each body of water has something special to offer. The places that are most abundant in wildlife can be a delightful surprise. For example, urban waterways often offer more opportunities to watch birds than some of the remote locations. A large lake may be surrounded by beautiful scenery, but deep and open waters can be hard to paddle along, and often those large lakes have limited opportunities to view wildlife. The best paddling experiences are along the shorelines of narrow and shallow creeks and coves where large swaths of aquatic plants attract a variety of birds and amphibians. You can easily linger in these areas to listen to the symphony of nature songs and watch waterfowl stalk the shallow shores.

As I explored destinations with boat rental facilities, I discovered that many of these sites do not necessarily make it easy to launch your own kayak. Public boat ramps are often located at different parts of a park or lake from the rental operations. It is important to consult a map before heading out so that you can plan your route in advance. I also learned that you can get disoriented and even lost on a large body of water, but Google Maps works pretty well to help you navigate. Be sure to use a dry bag or a Ziploc bag to keep your cell phone from getting wet.

Today, more than 150 "water trails" have been designated throughout the United States. These routes often link bodies of water and identify public access points for canoes, kayaks, and small motorized watercraft. A note of caution: Water trails are not necessarily geared to the novice or quiet paddler. Some, with wide-open sections of water and strong currents, are better for motorized boats. When you look at a water trail map, be sure to note information about the waterway. Check out the distances, and know your limits and abilities. Follow safe practices and always check the tide chart and weather forecast before heading out on the water.

One more tip: At the end of the day, it is a good idea to remove your wet clothes and shoes from the car. Moldy odors can last for days, annoying you and your passengers.

WHY QUIET WATERS?

Quiet waters offer a special excursion for those who enjoy the tranquility of nature or want a respite, however brief, from hectic city life. Open skies over ponds, lakes, and easy rivers draw a variety of wildlife, such as ospreys, eagles, ducks, and certain hawks. This book will take you to some of the loveliest, most serene bodies of water in the Mid-Atlantic region and will help you prepare for what you'll find there. It is designed to allow paddlers of all experience levels to enjoy peaceful journeys on the water. Through the experience of writing this book, I became more determined than ever to help preserve and protect our waterways and public lands. Some absolutely delightful destinations are covered in this book, and I encourage you to visit them.

THE SELECTION PROCESS

This guide covers only a small percentage of the lakes, ponds, and slow-moving rivers in New Jersey; Pennsylvania; Delaware; Maryland; Washington, D.C.; and Virginia. How did I make selections? I looked for great scenery and opportunities to view wildlife, including places with lots of coves and interesting plants, animals, and geological formations. I consulted with other kayakers, paddling outfitters, and regional tourism bureaus. I chose locations near populated areas, as well as some remote places that make nice excursions for a weekend or even a weeklong vacation. A number of the sites may seem less than ideal for someone who wants to spend a day in the wilderness, but they are convenient for a quick trip by those living or working in nearby urban areas. Although I tried to include the very best places, I am sure there are some I missed. If you have suggestions of other lakes, ponds, and streams to paddle, please write to AMC Books at amcbooks@outdoors.org. Perhaps you'll see them in a future edition.

What each paddler looks for on any given day is different. Some days it's a relaxing jaunt; other days it's a longer, more rigorous excursion. If you are out for the quietest paddling, select sites that offer only boating and fishing, and possibly camping. Swimming, picnicking, and recreational facilities tend to draw large crowds, particularly in July and August. If the whole family is out for the day and you are the only one who paddles, you will want to choose a place that provides additional activities for the family to enjoy. The at-a-glance trip planner will help guide you to the sites that meet your needs.

SAFETY

The single most important piece of safety equipment is the PFD, also called a life jacket, a life vest, or a personal floatation device. Always wear a PFD, because even the most experienced paddlers can find themselves on the wrong side of the waterline or in a difficult situation. Attach a waterproof whistle so you can get attention if it becomes necessary to call for help. Make sure your PFD fits properly, and tighten the straps enough that you cannot slip out of it. PFDs also protect the covered areas from sun exposure and add a bit of warmth on chilly days.

Kids should always, without exception, wear properly fitting PFDs; you can set a good example by wearing your own. And don't forget to caution small children riding in a canoe or in the front compartment of a tandem (two-person) kayak not to lean over the vessel's side, stand up, or move about suddenly.

As for considerations outside of your own small craft, motorboats can be unsettling to novice paddlers as they zip by, throwing large wakes. If caught unexpectedly, turn the bow of your canoe or kayak into the motorized boat's wake as quickly as possible to prevent swamping. Most waters listed in this book permit only slow-moving electric motorboats, and a few allow only manually powered boats. Some that permit limited (usually 20 horsepower) or unlimited motorboats have paddler-friendly no-wake zones.

Fishing is very popular at many of the destinations in this book. As you are paddling, be aware that you may encounter fishing lines extending out from the shoreline or from fishing boats, and many monofilament lines are difficult to see. Be considerate of others and keep your distance from the lines.

Some bodies of water are within or adjacent to prime hunting areas. Check with park officials or state fish and game offices for specific hunting seasons, particularly in spring and fall.

WHAT TO BRING

Always bring the following items with you and know how to use them:

- PFD: If you plan to kayak regularly, invest in a comfortable PFD with pockets. These come in handy and give you easy access to essential items.
- Hat: A hat with a brim not only shields your eyes and face from the damaging effects of the sun. It also helps retain body heat when the air is chilly and offers a degree of protection from overheating when the sun is hot.
- Proper footwear: Wear closed-toe water shoes to protect against sharp rocks, glass, and shells.
- Water and food: Make sure you have enough fluids and some food, such as protein bars, to reenergize. One quart of fluid is sufficient for a short trip; carry two or more quarts for longer trips.
- Sunblock: The sun is always stronger on the water. Wear a high-SPF sunblock and remember to reapply as necessary.
- First-aid kit: At a minimum, have a few bandages, first-aid ointment, gauze pads, tape, and, in season, insect repellent.
- Map (compass and GPS unit optional): And make sure to store it in a waterproof case.
- Whistle: This should be attached to your PFD. A shout for help is extremely difficult to hear, especially if it's windy, whereas a whistle sound carries a long way.
- Dry bag: Pack all of the above, and any other essentials, such as extra dry clothes, in a roll-top, seam-sealed, waterproof bag.
- Rope throw bag: A throw bag is a valuable rescue device that you can toss to a swimmer in trouble or use to tow another boat to shore. You can also use it to tie your craft to a dock or a tree if you stop for lunch on a windy day.

PADDLING AT NIGHT

Full-moon paddles are becoming increasingly popular, but paddling at night requires extra equipment and safety precautions. Do not paddle a site at night before becoming familiar with it during daylight. Even if you paddle with people who are very familiar with the location, there is a risk of becoming separated. Plan your route in advance, take a cell phone, and make note of compass directions. Log the launch coordinates into your GPS as a waypoint. If possible, paddle with others. Always let someone know where you will be, when you plan to start out, and when you plan to call and let the person know you've returned.

Equipment for night paddling, in addition to the previously listed items, should include:

- Map of the body of water: The map should have a north indicator, as well as GPS coordinates noted for the launch and any other notable landmarks. Make sure it is in a waterproof map case; sealable plastic bags don't always keep things dry and readable.
- Compass or GPS: These will be your best tools to assure good navigation. Carry additional charged batteries in a waterproof container.
- Cell phone: Cell service can be unreliable, so download the local map to your navigation app ahead of time.
- Waterproof flashlight or headlamp: Headlamps with different light intensity levels are best. A low level allows you to read your map without blinding yourself or those around you. A high level is useful for spotting logs or other obstructions when you're coming close to land or to your launch.
- Extra clothes: Temperatures can change unexpectedly as the sun goes down. Be prepared.

To improve your visibility to others on the water, attach reflective tape to your hat, PFD (front and back), the backside of your paddle, and even along both sides of your bow. Additional equipment, such as a VHF radio, could be useful on some waters; much depends on the type of water you'll be paddling on. If possible, go with someone who's experienced at night paddling to become familiar with the risks involved.

HYPOTHERMIA

Hypothermia (a lowering of the body's core temperature) is most often caused by exposure to cold weather or immersion in cold water. You can usually prevent hypothermia by being prepared. Prime conditions for hypothermia exist in spring and early summer, when water temperatures are cold, but warm air lulls us into wearing less-than-adequate clothing. The first noticeable sign of hypothermia is shivering. As soon as you or someone in your group is shivering and feeling cold, take steps to prevent hypothermia by stopping and warming up. Change into warm, dry clothes, including a hat, as soon as practical and drink warm liquids. Other symptoms of hypothermia include slurred or scrambled speech, and stumbling and loss of dexterity, evidenced by difficulty paddling. Be sure to respond quickly if you suspect the onset of hypothermia. Consider taking a Wilderness First Aid class through the Appalachian Mountain Club (AMC) or another organization to learn more; find upcoming offerings at outdoors.org/activities.

EQUIPMENT

There are as many types of kayaks, canoes, and paddles as there are types of bodies of water. Styles are available for whitewater, rodeo, sea, surf, touring, and racing, which can set even the most experienced paddler's head spinning when reviewing models on the market. Don't let the options overwhelm you. For paddling quiet water, you'll want a boat that is stable and tracks well. Your best bet is to rent a craft a few times until you get the feel of paddling and are comfortable. Renting a different model each time also allows you to experience different designs and find the best fit for you.

Recreational kayaks come in two basic styles: sit-in and sit-on-top. Both are available as singles or doubles (called tandems) and as hard shells or inflatables. The biggest difference between the two types is that sit-ins are enclosed and have a cockpit rim to which you can attach a spray skirt to keep water out. The best sit-in kayaks will also have a built-in backrest, creating a much more comfortable experience. Sit-ins shelter your lower body from the wind, which makes them warmer. Sit-on-tops are lighter weight, a little easier to get in and out of, and generally less expensive than sit-ins.

Materials also vary. Roto-molded plastic is the least expensive and a good choice for beginners because it can take quite a bit of abuse, but these models are on the heavier end of the spectrum. Fiberglass increases the cost tremendously, and although the craft move faster than their plastic counterparts, they are more susceptible to damage from rocks or gravelly bottoms. Kevlar added to the fiberglass increases durability but also cost. Boats made with carbon fiber are the lightest and most expensive but also more susceptible to damage.

Since your paddle is essentially your motor, picking the right one is critical. Paddles come in different sizes and materials. For recreational paddles, blades are typically plastic, and shafts are generally aluminum, fiberglass, or carbon fiber. The paddle should feel light, strong, and comfortable. If you will be paddling in cold weather, a fiberglass or carbon fiber shaft will be significantly warmer than aluminum. If you regularly paddle for more than two hours, a lighter-weight carbon fiber paddle will save your strength, giving you more endurance. As for paddle length, a general guide is that when you hold your paddle horizontally in front of you with your arms bent at a 90-degree angle, your hands should be about two-thirds of the way between the center of the shaft and the inside edge of the blade. Most paddle manufacturers provide size recommendations on their websites based on your height, paddling style, and boat width.

Outfitters and paddle shops gladly recommend canoe or kayak models and paddles they feel best suit your needs and your physical characteristics, such as height and weight. When you're ready to buy, find a craft that handles well for your current skill level. Dealers located near a lake usually let you test models for free or for a small fee. Paddle festivals held from late spring through early fall offer opportunities to try out a number of boats and different types of paddles. Some rental operations offer end-of-season sales on used equipment—an inexpensive way to pick up a kayak. Most of all, make sure you're comfortable in the boat.

If you plan to visit sites where you'll have to carry your boat any distance, wheeled carts and canoe yokes are available. Carts are compact and can be folded up and stored in the bottom of your boat or can be lashed on the rear deck.

For a list of books and websites with more information on paddling equipment, see Appendix B.

TECHNIQUE

Unlike whitewater kayaking, quietwater paddling requires few special skills. Knowing how to execute the basic forward, backward, sideways (draw), and turning strokes, however, will make for a more enjoyable experience and lessen the risk of injury. It's always better to learn correct technique initially than to correct sloppy habits later.

If you can, find the time to take a lesson. Most outfitters offer basic instruction, and your local AMC chapter likely offers paddling workshops; learn more at outdoors.org/activities. Beginners should stay on smaller ponds before tackling larger lakes, where wind and waves can present challenges beyond your current capabilities. Lakes are often glasslike and easier to paddle in the early-morning hours, and windy and more difficult midday. Winds tend to die down in late afternoon or early evening. Early morning and late afternoon are also prime times to observe wildlife.

Learn brace strokes to recover if you have lost your balance as well as self-rescue techniques before venturing into the middle of a large lake or reservoir. Take a few minutes to review these skills at the beginning of, and periodically throughout, your paddling season. Improving your skills will not only make you more comfortable in your craft but also will instill confidence when less-than-ideal conditions arise—and they eventually will.

Basic navigation skills come in handy on larger lakes, where rainstorms or fog can suddenly obscure the shoreline. (Fog, most prevalent in early morning and late afternoon during spring and fall, is caused by a marked difference between land and air temperatures.) Always bring a waterproof compass on large bodies of water and know how to use it properly. A GPS is a wonderful tool, but if your batteries die, a regular compass is an excellent backup.

For a list of books and websites with much more information on paddling techniques, see Appendix B.

PADDLING WITH KIDS

One of the best things about kayaking is that it's a healthy and fun activity to share with your whole family. Kids can join in as passengers even before they can paddle, but there are some important considerations. In addition to wearing PFDs, children must understand the importance of proper etiquette while in a boat, such as moving slowly, not suddenly; sitting and staying low; and knowing the correct procedures for entering and exiting the boat. It's always a good idea for children to take swimming lessons and learn to swim the length of a pool so they'll be comfortable and competent in open water.

Plan on short trips initially. Most children are so excited to be going out in a canoe or kayak, they'll sit quietly and absorb the sights and sounds. Try to include them in the adventure. Play games that involve spotting birds or turtles. Ask their opinions on which way to go or what they think about the scenery in a particular cove. Inexpensive binoculars will help engage them in observing nature.

Be sure to bring water and snacks for the trip. Pack an extra sweater or jacket for kids, even in summer, as a light breeze over cool mountain waters or in dense shade near shore can be chilly for those not paddling. Keeping a change of clothes in the car will be handy if they accidentally trip and fall into the water getting in or out of the boat.

Kids typically want to start paddling themselves—rather than simply riding as passengers—between the ages of 8 and 10. The age that kids are ready to paddle their own kayak varies, depending on their skills and on water and weather conditions. To check their readiness, start with a short excursion on a nice day. A sit-on-top kayak is a good way to go once kids are big enough to start paddling. Child-sized canoe and kayak paddles are available. In a canoe or tandem kayak, always have the strongest paddler sit in the rear, where the real work of steering happens. Above all, enjoy the experience of sharing this wonderful world with children.

WILDLIFE

Kayaking can be a great way to view wildlife, both above and below the water. Once you're out on the water, sit still. If you drift slowly toward animals, you have a better chance of closer observation for longer periods of time than if you startle them. Dawn and dusk are the best times to spot birds, deer, raccoons, otters, and other mammals that come to drink water. When observing, keep a distance of at least 25 yards from most animals. Birds are particularly sensitive during nesting periods, typically March through July. Use binoculars for close viewing. Check your destination's website for wildlife-viewing restrictions before leaving home.

Remember that we share nature with raccoons, bears, skunks, foxes, and coyotes, particularly in the mountainous northern regions. Do not feed these or other wildlife, and never attempt to touch or approach wild animals. Raccoons and bears have been known to open coolers and rummage through food containers, and any wild animal can harbor diseases, such as rabies. In addition, never get between a wild animal and its young. If you accidentally find yourself in this situation, lower your eyes and back away slowly. If you are ever bitten or scratched, seek medical attention immediately. Keep food tightly packed and stored in your vehicle or away from the campsite, never in your tent, and clean all cooking implements immediately after use.

And then there are smaller creatures. Mid-Atlantic states are home to the deer tick, which carries the bacteria responsible for Lyme disease. This tick typically crawls around on the body for three or more hours before settling on a spot. It takes another hour or two before burrowing deep into the skin. While you have plenty of time before a tick can do damage, it is wise to check yourself often if you brush past foliage while loading or unloading your canoe or kayak. Always do a thorough tick check at the end of the day.

CAMPING

There's nothing like paddling to a campsite and spending a night or several in the great outdoors. In addition to tent sites, many of the state parks in the Mid-Atlantic region have cabins that you can rent during the warmer months of the year. Be respectful of these public places and always leave your site as clean as (or cleaner than) you found it. Keep noise to a minimum and observe the rules for quiet hours. If you want to bring a dog, make sure the campground accepts pets before leaving home, and always pick up after it. The trips in this book include information on campsites near the given paddles. You can find a list of all the campgrounds in Appendix A.

Kayak or canoe camping is an exciting adventure but requires planning. Always test to make sure everything you intend to bring fits in dry bags and that the dry bags fit in your boat. Pack the essentials first then add personal amenities and extras, as room permits. A boat loaded with camping equipment will handle differently than when empty, and weight distribution becomes important. If you stash all of your heavy items in the bow, the boat's nose will dive when you encounter waves. If all of your heavy items are in the stern, the bow will ride high in the water, and steering can become an issue. It's worth the time and effort to do a test paddle with all your equipment on a nice day and redistribute equipment, if necessary, before your first paddle-in camping trip. The best paddle-in campsites fill up quickly, so call well ahead of time for reservations. Find a list of campgrounds in Appendix A.

Your local AMC chapter and other paddling groups are wonderful resources, and some even offer demos day to go over the essentials of paddle-in camping. A list of area paddling groups can be found in Appendix C.

FISHING, CRABBING, AND PERMITS

Catching your own dinner, whether you plan to eat it over your camp stove or upon returning home, is a rewarding experience. If you're camping, bring along some backup food—just in case the fish aren't biting that day. Break-apart rods that come in two or three sections are relatively inexpensive and stow easily in even the smallest boat. Rod holders are available for canoes and kayaks.

In most states, anyone between the ages of 16 and 69 must display a valid license to fish in fresh waters. Licenses may be obtained from county or municipal offices, online or in person, or from agents, such as sporting goods stores and bait shops.

Blue crabs can be found in brackish coastal regions from late June through September, peaking in August. Crabbing with handlines requires no license, but crabbing and fishing laws and restrictions vary by state. In Maryland and Virginia, you are limited to two dozen male hard-shell crabs per day.

WATER TRAILS

Water trails are becoming more and more popular. These recreational routes provide opportunities to learn about the value of local water resources and cultural heritage. State governments, through partnerships with local governments, citizen associations, and nonprofit organizations, have designated water trails with maps and access routes to promote recreation along the rivers, streams, and lakes in their region. The trail systems vary from state to state: New Jersey has only one, an interstate trail, while Maryland has more than two dozen.

New Jersey: delawareriverwatertrail.org
Pennsylvania: pfbc.pa.gov/watertrail.htm
Maryland: dnr.maryland.gov/boating/pages/mdwatertrails_state.aspx
Washington, D.C.: anacostiaws.org/anacostia-water-trail
Virginia: dcr.virginia.gov/recreational-planning/wal-wtrails

The National Water Trails System was established in early 2012. To date, only a small number of water trails have been given a national designation, none of which are in the Mid-Atlantic region.

WHAT TO EXPECT IN THE MID-ATLANTIC REGION

While the Mid-Atlantic region is one of the most densely populated parts of the country, with sprawling cities and suburbs, it has thousands of great destinations for quietwater paddling. With mountains to the west and the coastal lowlands to the east, New Jersey, Pennsylvania, Delaware, Maryland, the District of Columbia, and Virginia share many common flora and fauna. The ponds, lakes, and rivers of this region are home to a diverse population of animal life that includes more than 240 species of birds. Some of the most regularly seen in the wetlands are bald eagles, great egrets, great blue herons, cormorants, Canada geese, vultures, and a variety of ducks and seagulls. You will likely see many frogs, as well as turtles, snakes, and other reptiles. Keep in mind that the wildlife you see is determined by time of day, weather, and other factors.

The Mid-Atlantic is also home to thriving populations of foxes, hares, squirrels, bats, groundhogs, and chipmunks. You may not see them, but there are owls, beavers, mice, muskrats, opossums, otters, raccoons, skunks, and weasels living in the wild, as well. As for plants, there are more than 1,000 species found in the Mid-Atlantic, including flowering and nonflowering varieties. Deciduous trees are most common in local forests, although there are multiple kinds of evergreens and conifers, too. There are also dozens of invasive aquatic plants that threaten the health of quietwater ecosystems. To the untrained eye, invasive plants are difficult to distinguish from native plants. Contact your state natural resource agency or native plant society for more information about aggressive aquatic plant species.

How to Use This Book

Each trip in this book includes a description of the relevant body of water and the surrounding area; driving directions to the parking area, with GPS coordinates; a map of the body of water, including parking, launch site/s, and natural features, such as islands and inlet streams; estimated time and distance of the paddle; notes on natural features you can expect to see; and information on other relevant maps and local hikes. Although information is provided about nearby hiking trails, you should procure a detailed trail map from the land manager or another source. Some trip descriptions also include suggestions of nearby attractions that are worth a visit if time allows.

The GPS coordinates provided are usually for the launch, but there are a few instances where the unimproved road to the launch is not well marked or is easily passed. In those situations, when the GPS coordinates given are for the entry road rather than the launch site itself, simply follow the road to the launch. GPS units are wonderful tools, but they can strand you in the middle of a big green blotch when it comes to unimproved roads.

Backcountry roads also have a habit of changing names, further confusing matters. A topographic atlas not only shows topographic features but also many unimproved roads not included on county maps. (DeLorme, the Mid-Atlantic and Northeast's best-known publisher of road atlases was bought by Garmin, the Swiss GPS firm, in 2016, but the latter has indicated it will continue to produce the venerable map books.) Topographic maps of individual quadrangles are the best for exploring remote areas. They show almost all unimproved roads and trails, one of which may provide the only way to a new pond. U.S. Geological Survey maps are available from outdoor shops or directly from USGS: usgs.gov or 888-ASK-USGS. Index maps showing the available USGS quads in any state and the informative pamphlet Topographic Maps are available from USGS and are free by request.

Estimated times are based on the average paddler traveling at a casual pace, pausing to observe wildlife, along the route described—usually around 2.5 MPH. If you're a newcomer, don't let high times deter you. You don't have to paddle the whole lake in one outing. For a few of the larger lakes and longer rivers, you'll find the trip descriptions broken into suggested sections, sometimes using different launch sites, to provide several days of pleasant paddling.

In the "Take Note" section of each trip, you'll find information on the type of motorized traffic allowed on the body of water, whether any special permits are required, and any potentially dangerous conditions, such as unmarked dams or the potential for high winds. The majority of sites allow only electric motorboats, and a few allow only manually powered boats, but some permit higher horsepower. Fortunately, most of those sites have paddler-friendly no-wake zones, which are noted on the maps.

Various state parks, particularly those with recreational facilities, charge an entrance fee, often from Memorial Day through Labor Day. A few of these charge a separate fee to use the boat launch. You also can buy an annual permit from any state park office that offers unlimited access to that state's parks. Pennsylvania state parks are free, except for some with a swimming pool that charge a small fee.

Keep in mind that land ownership around lakes and ponds can change hands, voiding or allowing public access. New housing developments and roads that spring up may render a site less desirable or change accessibility.

Stewardship and Conservation

The more often you get out to enjoy the water, the more you will appreciate our precious ecosystems and the need to help protect them. Numerous community organizations, including AMC chapters, college clubs, and paddling clubs, host cleanups of various waterways—a great way for paddlers to meet other paddlers. On an individual level, my friends and I often carry a trash bag with us to remove discarded refuse. It may be a small effort, but it makes the water cleaner for everyone and safer for wildlife. It's a good idea to carry a trash bag or two in your vehicle, as many sites lack refuse containers, instead following a carry-in, carry-out policy.

AMC CONSERVATION EFFORTS IN THE MID-ATLANTIC

The Appalachian Mountain Club (AMC) has a long history of water conservation in the Mid-Atlantic. In the New Jersey and Pennsylvania highlands, AMC supported the 2006 federal designation of the Musconetcong River as a National Wild and Scenic River (a national program that celebrates its 50th anniversary in 2018). Also in the Pennsylvania Highlands, AMC was an active supporter of Buffers 100, a campaign to create a corridor of at least 100 feet on either side of every stream in the commonwealth, protecting communities and waterways from erosion, pollution, flooding, and drought.

But the site of AMC's longest-standing engagement in Mid-Atlantic conservation is the Delaware River. In the 1950s, AMC and like-minded advocates successfully blocked the federal government's proposed Tocks Island Dam, which would have interrupted the river's flow and impounded the adjacent communities. In place of a dam, the Delaware Water Gap National Recreation Area was born: a 70,000-acre parcel of public land managed by the National Park Service. In the decades since, AMC has remained actively involved in water conservation, as a member of the Coalition for the Delaware River Watershed and a supporter of the Delaware River Basin Conservation Act, as well as other public policy initiatives focused on improving access to the river.

This interest in conservation isn't purely philanthropic. It's also pragmatic: More than 15 million people, including the populations of New York City and Philadelphia, rely on the Delaware River basin as their source of drinking water. At 330 miles, the Delaware is the longest undammed river in the United States east of the Mississippi, providing exceptional habitat for animal and plant species. Its health directly affects the health of the entire ecosystem around it.

The Delaware River watershed is also home to AMC's Mohican Outdoor Center. A 90-minute drive from New York City, Mohican offers front-porch access to the Delaware Water Gap, with self-service cabins, comfortable bunkrooms, a fully stocked kitchen, and the river, wetlands, and Appalachian Trail a stroll away. To learn more about AMC's conservation efforts throughout the Mid-Atlantic and Northeast, and to find out how you can get involved, visit outdoors.org/conservation. To learn more about AMC's work in the Delaware River watershed, visit outdoors.org/conservation/land-water. To find volunteer opportunities and trips in the region, search outdoors.org/activities, and to request a reservation at Mohican Outdoor Center, visit outdoors.org/mohican.

LEAVE NO TRACE

AMC is a national educational partner of the Leave No Trace Center for Outdoor Ethics, an international nonprofit organization dedicated to responsible enjoyment and active stewardship of the outdoors by  all people worldwide. The organization teaches children and adults vital skills to minimize their impacts when they are outdoors and is the most widely accepted outdoor ethics program used today on public lands across the nation. Leave No Trace unites five federal land management agencies—the U.S. Forest Service, the National Park Service, the Bureau of Land Management, the U.S. Army Corps of Engineers, and the U.S. Fish and Wildlife Service—with manufacturers, outdoor retailers, user groups, educators, organizations such as AMC, and individuals.

Seven principles guide the Leave No Trace ethic:

Plan ahead and prepare. Know the terrain of the area you're planning to visit and any applicable regulations, and be prepared for extreme weather or other emergencies. This will enhance your enjoyment and ensure that you've chosen an appropriate destination. Small groups have less impact on resources and the experience of other backcountry visitors.

Travel and camp on durable surfaces. Travel and camp on established trails and campsites, rock, gravel, dry grasses, or snow. Good campsites are found, not made. Camp at least 200 feet from lakes and streams, and focus activities on areas where vegetation is absent. In pristine areas, disperse use to prevent the creation of campsites and trails.

Dispose of waste properly. Pack it in, pack it out. Inspect your camp for trash or food scraps. Deposit solid human waste in catholes dug 6 to 8 inches deep, at least 200 feet from water, camp, and trails. Pack out toilet paper and hygiene products. To wash yourself or your dishes, carry water 200 feet away from streams or lakes and use small amounts of biodegradable soap. Scatter strained dishwater.

Leave what you find. Cultural or historic artifacts, as well as natural objects such as plants or rocks, should be left as found.

Minimize campfire impacts. Cook on a stove. Use established fire rings, fire pans, or mound fires. If you build a campfire, keep it small and use dead sticks found on the ground.

Respect wildlife. Observe wildlife from a distance. Feeding wildlife alters their natural behavior. Protect wildlife from your food by storing rations and trash securely.

Be considerate of other visitors. Be courteous, respect the quality of other visitors' backcountry experience, and let nature's sounds prevail.

AMC is a national provider of the Leave No Trace Master Educator course, designed for outdoor guides and land managers. AMC offers this five-day course, as well as the two-day Leave No Trace Trainer course, at locations throughout the Northeast. To register for a course near you, visit outdoors.org /activities. For Leave No Trace information and materials, contact the Leave No Trace Center for Outdoor Ethics at 800-332-4100, or visit lnt.org.

1 | NEW JERSEY

New Jersey is a geographically diverse region that lies in the highly populated northeast corridor of the United States between two major cities: Philadelphia and New York City. According to the New Jersey Division of Fish and Wildlife, the state is home to more than 4,100 freshwater lakes, ponds, impoundments, and reservoirs that cover 1 or more acres each. While most of these are privately controlled, there is no shortage of locations where you can rent a kayak or canoe or launch your own craft.

New Jersey has a wealth of geological features, ranging from billion-year-old rocks formed during continental collision to recent sediments deposited along the shoreline. Most of the largest lakes are in the northwestern quadrant of the state, tucked in valleys between the mountains that compose part of the Appalachian Ridge and Valley and the Piedmont Plateau. The Atlantic Coastal Plain is flat and inundated with tidal marshes, back bays, and barrier islands. Creeks and streams along the western edge of New Jersey drain into the Delaware River. From the central and eastern parts of the state, these waterways flow into the Hudson River and the Atlantic Ocean.

Facing page: A paddler navigates the narrow Mullica River. Photo by George Schnakenberg Jr., Creative Commons on Flickr.

The Appalachian Trail traverses the crest of the Kittatinny Ridge in the northwest corner of New Jersey. This area contains some of the oldest rocks in the state: Martinsburg shale, which was created during the Ordovician period. Paddling in this area offers dramatic scenery and wonderful opportunities for hiking, biking, fishing, hunting, and bird-watching.

Running along the state's border is the the Delaware River, and the corresponding Delaware River Water Trail, with numerous kayak and canoe launches. The river is divided into three sections: Upper, Middle, and Lower. The river's lower section is the longest and runs nearly 76 miles, from just below the Delaware Water Gap to Trenton, New Jersey, and Morrisville, Pennsylvania. Geologic and scenic vistas include the glorious red shale Nockamixon Cliffs and Milford Bluffs. The terrain and paddling conditions vary along the river as it cuts through the Great Valley, Highlands, and Piedmont regions. AMC is an active member of the Coalition for the Delaware River Watershed, supporting initiatives to protect the watershed. Since 1993, AMC has operated Mohican Outdoor Center within the Delaware Water Gap National Recreation Area, which hosts more than 10,000 visitors every year.

The Pine Barrens is a heavily forested area that stretches across more than seven low-lying coastal counties of southern New Jersey. It is known for its rare pygmy pitch pines and sandy, nutrient-poor soil. Despite rapid urbanization of surrounding areas, the Pine Barrens remains largely rural, and its streams and rivers are typically slow-moving and shallow. Lakes and large ponds are associated with agricultural activities such as cranberry and blueberry farming.

While New Jersey does not have as many remote areas per square mile as other parts of the country, it has some beautiful bodies of water that are quite isolated. Some lakes and ponds within highly populated towns offer pleasant oases, thanks to dense woods surrounding some or all of the water and private houses set well back from the banks. A number of sites in the state have tidal saltwater and brackish marshes, which contain extensive wildlife and are among some of the best places to paddle.

1 | Lake Nummy and East Creek Pond: Belleplain State Forest

Belleplain State Forest offers raptors galore, magnificent bird-watching, 40 miles of hiking trails, pine and oak forest with white cedars, and a remote setting.

Location: Woodbine, NJ
Maps: State of New Jersey, Department of Environmental Protection: state.nj.us
Area: Lake Nummy: 26 acres; East Creek Pond: 62 acres
Time: Lake Nummy: less than 1 hour; East Creek: 1 to 1.5 hours
Average Depth: 6 feet in both
Development: Rural
Access: Park entrance fee; no fee to launch at East Creek
Information: Belleplain State Forest, County Route 550, P.O. Box 450, Woodbine, NJ 08270, 609-861-2404, state.nj.us
Camping: Three large camping areas surround Lake Nummy, with a lakefront group cabin located at East Creek Pond; for reservations call the park office or visit state.nj.us
Take Note: Electric motorboats only. The best seasons are spring and fall during bird migration.

GETTING THERE
To the park office: From NJ 47 on the south side of Woodbine, drive north 3.1 miles on County Route 557, turn left onto CR 550, and drive 1.4 miles (cumulative: 4.5 miles) to the park entrance on the left. The visitor center will be on the right, 100 feet inside the park. (39° 14.907′ N, 74° 50.550′ W)

   To Lake Nummy: Continue past the visitor center 0.35 mile (cumulative: 4.85 miles), turn right onto Meisle Road, and drive 0.4 mile (5.25 miles) to the dock at Lake Nummy. (39° 147.731′ N, 74° 51.446′ W)

   To East Creek Pond: From CR 557, drive north 0.7 mile on NJ 47. The road forks here, so take the right fork onto NJ 347 and drive 2 miles (cumulative: 2.7 miles). Turn into the boat ramp area on the right at the end of the guardrail. From inside the park at Lake Nummy, turn onto Savage Bridge Road directly across from the dock and drive 0.8 mile (3.5 miles) to the T intersection. Turn right onto Sunset Road and drive 1.7 miles (5.2 miles) to Hands Mill Road. Turn

TRIP 1: LAKE NUMMY AND EAST CREEK POND: BELLEPLAIN STATE FOREST

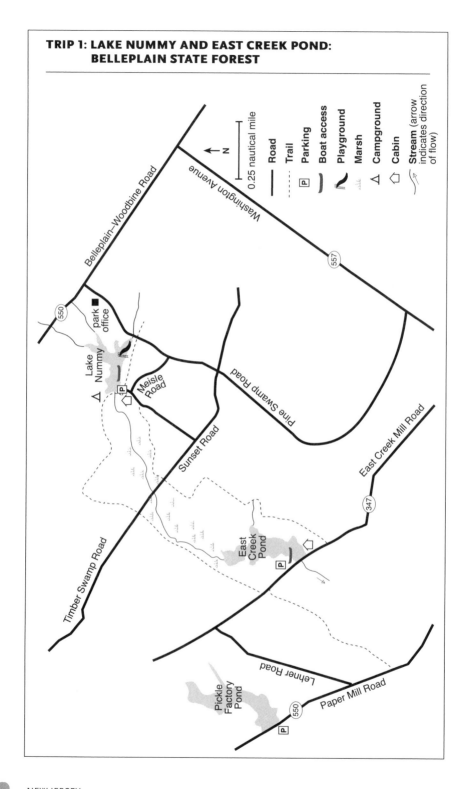

left and drive 0.8 mile (6 miles) to NJ 347. Turn left onto NJ 347 and drive 1.5 miles (7.5 miles) to the launch site on the left. (39° 13.347′ N, 74° 53.138′ W)

WHAT YOU'LL SEE

Belleplain State Forest is an ideal destination for outdoor recreation. More than 20,000 acres of upland oak and pine forests, white cedar swamps, and bogs offer 42 miles of hiking and multiuse trails. Situated on the outskirts of the Pine Barrens, the soil here has better conditions than in the Pine Barrens and allows for a wider variety of trees and shrubs, including hickory, beech, and ash. You can literally spend several camping weekends paddling the lakes and hiking all the trails. The crisp, clean, pine-scented air will grab your attention as you drive into the park on a road lined with tall trees bordering dense woods.

Two bodies of water, East Creek Pond and Lake Nummy, lie completely within the park's boundaries. The northwest shore of Lake Nummy, the smaller of the two lakes, is in the center of the park's campground, swimming beach, and recreational area and can become quite crowded in summer. The lake was named after the last Lenni-Lenape chief in Cape May County, where Belleplain is located. He lived during the mid-to-late 1600s. A third body of water, Pickle Factory Pond, also called Paper Mill Pond, only has its northeast portion within the park's boundary.

Lake Nummy

After launching from the floating dock, paddle right along the southern shoreline to a marshy, narrow cove where you will likely find turtles, ducks, and wading birds. Continue along the shoreline and pass under the footbridge in the northwest corner. In summer, large numbers of tanagers, warblers, finches, and songbirds can be seen flitting about the trees.

Belleplain attracts numerous species of birds because it is just north of the Cape May Peninsula, part of a major migratory route known as the Atlantic Flyway. The diverse habitats within the park enhance its desirability as both a stopover during spring and fall migrations and a home for summertime residents that nest and reproduce. Sit quietly and observe. Let the wildlife come to you. Although this lake is small, it offers a peaceful setting and makes an ideal paddle for novices or for parents taking their children out for the first time.

East Creek Pond

East Creek Pond's launch area can be a little noisy with road traffic, particularly on summer weekends, but once you start paddling north, the noise seems to disappear. Numerous coves and inlets house large populations of painted

Look for ospreys on Pickle Factory Pond. Photo by Kathy Kenley.

and bog turtles that bask in the sun on picturesque logs and cedar stumps set against a background of dense forest. In summer, sweet pepperbush develops thin, elongated clusters of white flowers, which fill the air with a pleasant aroma detectable for more than 50 feet. For a natural snack in July and August, look for blueberry bushes that peek out along the edge of the lake. Arrowweed, picker-elweed, and waterlily along the shallower shores provide a protective environ-ment for young pickerel, smallmouth bass, catfish, sunfish, and crappie. Eagles and hawks abound here throughout the year: it's rare not to spot at least one.

As you paddle along, you will see two northern coves that become a little marshy. Here you're likely to encounter green and blue herons perching on branches just above the water looking for a meal. You're also out of sight of any roads, giving you a better wilderness experience. Listen to the different sounds of various wildlife and the breeze rustling through the trees, and look for an eagle or osprey soaring overhead, scouting for dinner. In fall, the dark evergreen foliage of pines, cedars, and mountain laurels creates a stunning contrast to the bright colors of deciduous trees and bushes. A group cabin sits on the opposite shoreline of the lake along NJ 347. This would be a great place to rent with a bunch of friends in late spring or early fall when bird migrations are at a peak.

Round out your stay with an invigorating hike on one or more of Belleplain State Forest's 42 miles of trails. East Creek Trail is one of the more popular options, taking hikers through hardwood forests and past white cedar swamps and tall pine stands.

2 | Lake Lenape and Great Egg Harbor River

Look for eagles, hawks, wading birds, ospreys, and other waterfowl around the more secluded islands, coves, and marshes.

Location: Mays Landing, NJ
Maps: DeLorme *New Jersey Atlas & Gazetteer,* Map 70; USGS Mays Landing
Area: 350 acres
Time: Lake Lenape: 2.5 to 3.5 hours; Great Egg Harbor River: 1.5 to 2 hours
Average Depth: Lake Lenape: 12 feet; Great Egg Harbor River: 4 feet
Development: Lake Lenape: suburban; Great Egg Harbor River: remote
Access: Park entrance fee
Information: Atlantic County, NJ: atlantic-county.org; Lake Lenape Park Reservation Office: 6303 Old Harding Highway, Mays Landing, NJ 08330, 609-625-8219
Camping: The park has eighteen tent-only sites at the lake, which can be reserved by calling the reservation office; Pleasant Valley Family Campground is 10 minutes south (see Appendix A)
Take Note: Motorboats are limited to 10 horsepower

GETTING THERE

From US 322 (Black Horse Pike), drive south 1.8 miles on NJ 50. Turn right onto US 40 and drive 0.3 mile (cumulative: 2.1 miles) to a T junction. Turn left onto NJ 50 (Mill Street) and drive for 0.1 mile (2.2 miles), and then turn right onto CR 559 (Old Harding Highway). Continue for 0.2 mile (2.4 miles) to the park entrance on your right. Follow the park road for 0.3 mile (2.7 miles) to the recreation center. A concrete boat ramp is on the north side of the building. You must sign in (provide your name and an emergency contact name) at the boathouse prior to launching and sign out once you're off the water. Access to Great Egg Harbor River is from the north end of the lake. (39° 27.404′ N, 74° 44.313′ W)

WHAT YOU'LL SEE

Lake Lenape

On its way to the Atlantic Ocean, the scenic Great Egg Harbor River was dammed to create Lake Lenape, most of which lies within the confines of the county-owned Lake Lenape Park. The 1,900-acre park protects the lake and major portions of the river. Private property and the park's recreational facilities

TRIP 2: LAKE LENAPE AND GREAT EGG HARBOR RIVER

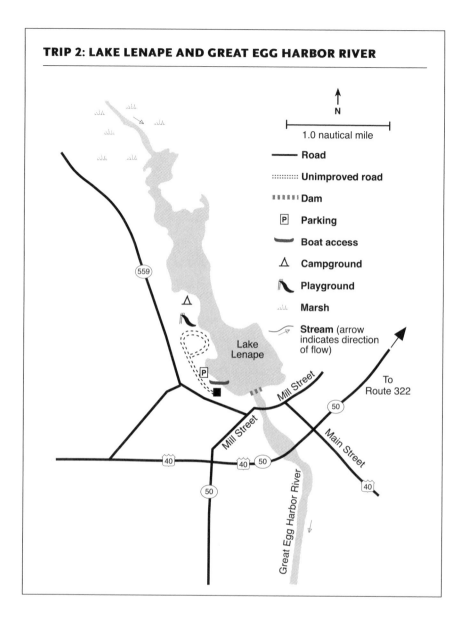

(swimming beach and playground) rim the southern end of the lake, but escape to wilder waters is an easy paddle away. An extra bonus is that this park is home to one of the few tent-only campgrounds in New Jersey. In addition to the concrete boat launch, there is a large sandy beach that many people use to launch their boats, even though it is a small portage down a grassy slope from the nearby gravel parking lot.

Lake Lenape's distinctive tower is a great place to watch rowers. Photo by Ken Marshall, Creative Commons on Flickr.

This is one of the best locations in southern New Jersey to observe eagles. Try the northern half of the lake, where it becomes wider and the houses on the east shore thin dramatically. From the boat ramp, turn left and paddle up the heavily tree-lined west side, where you'll find big and little coves and fingers galore providing long, narrow stretches of glacial water to explore. Deep-green cedar trees line the shores in front of mixed oak and pine forests. Blueberry, sheep laurel, and mulberry bushes fill the understory, while stands of phragmites and cattails grow in open shallows. After a somewhat narrow central portion, the lake opens wide and beautiful. Plenty of islands dot the far northern end and are a delight to paddle around. Lots of small sweet gum trees add a spectacular array of colors in fall.

Birds and waterfowl are abundant, especially around islands, coves, marshes, and small inlets that provide good nesting and feeding environments. Keep your eyes open for otters; they have been spotted in the area. Colorful painted and red-bellied turtles abound on swollen cedar logs jutting from swampy shallows. Hawks, falcons, vultures, ospreys, and eagles are common in the skies, while kingfishers, blue jays, crows, and songbirds flit about the shoreline. In shallow areas and marshy shorelines, you'll find blue herons, egrets, gulls, and abundant waterfowl.

After the paddle, cool off in the water. A large public beach with lifeguards on duty in season is on the opposite side of the lake from the launch.

The lake also offers a 2-mile hiking and biking trail that skirts lakefront properties and wildlife observation points. A number of local bird-watchers walk the sand road that leads to the camping area and the campground launch for a rewarding experience.

Great Egg Harbor River

The Great Egg Harbor River enters Lake Lenape in the northwest corner. In 1614, Cornelius Jacobsen Mey, a Dutch explorer, named it *Eyren Haven*, which translates to "Egg Harbor," when he came into the inlet of the river and saw the meadows covered with shorebird and waterfowl eggs. In 1992, Congress designated the river and its tributaries as a recreation site and part of the National Wild and Scenic River system.

You can paddle upstream 2 to 3 miles, depending on the water level and flow rate, before the oncoming current becomes too difficult. You will pass only a few modest riverside residences along the way—the rest is pristine wilderness. As you depart the lake and enter the river, numerous islands and wetland marshes invite you to bask in the wide variety of wetland shrubs and flowers. This is a bird-watcher's heaven and botanist's delight. Numerous fingers and small inlets in the first 1.5 miles will keep you busy. You will hear and see blue jays, pine warblers, blackbirds, vireos, and other woodland birds along the way. Waterfowl and wading birds are common in the more open marsh areas and larger inlets. In early summer, wild blue iris can be found at the edge of low marshes and the white blossoms of swamp magnolia lightly scent the air. By late summer, joe-pye weed develops large mauve flower heads, and the vibrant red cardinal flower comes into bloom.

Atlantic white cedar, oak, and pine dominate. River birch, white birch, red maple, and white gum are sprinkled along the river's edge, with sumac, huckleberry, and sheep laurel filling in the understory. Fallen and overhanging trees create interest, and sometimes a challenge, as you meander along the sinuous river.

Along some sections, bluffs rise 3 to 5 feet high. Kingfishers make their nests here, 2 to 3 feet above the surface of the water. Pure sand bluffs are too soft for them, but where the bluffs are a darker sandy loam, listen and watch for these crested birds and look for their nests. Enjoy this beautiful river as far up as you can paddle.

3 | Union Lake

You'll find large islands, waterfowl, and raptors at Union Lake.

Location: Millville, NJ
Maps: DeLorme *New Jersey Atlas & Gazetteer,* Map 68; USGS Millville
Area: 898 acres
Time: 3 to 4 hours
Average Depth: 14 feet
Development: Urban, but mostly surrounded by a large and quiet wildlife management area
Access: No fees
Information: New Jersey Division of Fish and Wildlife, Southern Region (Winslow Wildlife Management Area), 220 Blue Anchor Road, Sicklerville, NJ 08081, 856-629-0090
Camping: Parvin State Park, 25 minutes north; Lazy River Campground, 25 minutes east (see Appendix A)
Take Note: 10 horsepower motor limit; there is a large dam on the lake

GETTING THERE

From NJ 55 near Millville, take Exit 29 to Sherman Avenue and turn west onto Sherman Avenue. Drive 2.5 miles, turn left onto CR 608 (Carmel Road), and drive 3.4 miles (cumulative: 5.9 miles) to Union Lake Wildlife Management Area on the left. Drive 0.2 mile (6.1 miles) to the parking area and concrete ramp. (39° 24.484′ N, 75° 04.036′ W)

From NJ 49 (Main Street), Carmel Avenue veers off NJ 49 about 1.2 miles west of NJ 47. Drive 2 miles (cumulative: 3.2 miles) west on Carmel Avenue to the lake entrance on the right. (39° 24.484′ N, 75° 04.036′ W)

WHAT YOU'LL SEE

Located in the southeast corner of Cumberland County, this 898-acre body of water was created by the damming of the Maurice and Mill rivers. The oblong lake is 4 miles long and 1.2 miles wide. The state acquired the lake and surrounding property in the early 1990s, and it is now a 5,000-acre fish and wildlife management area. As at many other waterways in New Jersey, people have found American Indian artifacts here. The Vineland Historical and Antiquarian Society, at Seventh and Elmer streets in Vineland, displays many of the items

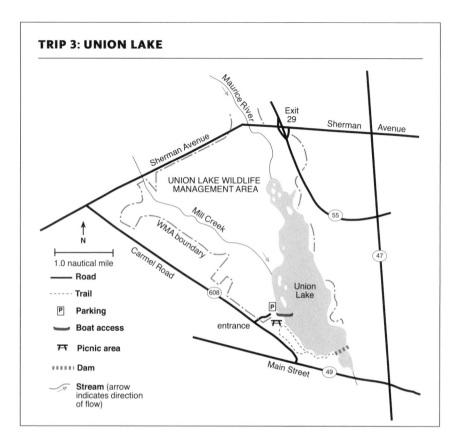

TRIP 3: UNION LAKE

Maurice River
Exit 29
Sherman Avenue
Sherman Avenue
UNION LAKE WILDLIFE MANAGEMENT AREA
Mill Creek
WMA boundary
Carmel Road
55
47
608
Union Lake
entrance
P
Main Street
49

N
1.0 nautical mile
— Road
----- Trail
P Parking
Boat access
Picnic area
Dam
Stream (arrow indicates direction of flow)

uncovered over the years. If you do find an artifact while at the lake, take notes on its location and notify the historical society. Don't move or remove it, since archaeologists reconstruct the history of an area based on the exact location of various artifacts. Because this is state-owned property, keeping artifacts is illegal.

Pollution in the form of various chemical by-products from a now-defunct paint production company in North Vineland once plagued this waterway all the way to Delaware Bay. Dumping stopped in the early 1980s, largely due to pressure from surrounding communities and local environmental groups. With the rivers and lake cleaned up, you'll find not only some of the best fishing in southeastern New Jersey but also some of the cleanest and clearest water for swimming and paddling.

A line of buoys warns of danger 70 feet in front of the dam. Be very careful, especially after a heavy rain when water flow increases. The drop over the dam is 45 feet.

Most coves along the shore have shallow margins that are only 2 to 4 feet deep, which is perfect for a refreshing swim. Along the shoreline you'll also

A young kayaker explores the large islands in Union Lake. Photo by Kathy Kenley.

find red maple, birch, swamp magnolia, cedar, and mountain laurel. In late spring and early summer, dainty, pale-pink mountain laurel and white sheep laurel blossoms sprinkle the landscape like pixie dust against a background of dark-green cedar and evergreen laurel leaves.

Three islands are within a mile of the put-in's southwest shore, each with one or two landing sites with small clearings for a picnic lunch and short walking trails to stretch your legs. The largest of the three is Rattlesnake Island, named for the reptile once found in abundance there. Never fear—rattlesnakes have not been seen on the island for more than ten years.

Local anglers catch largemouth bass, colorful sunfish, catfish, pickerel, and yellow perch under the watchful eye of ospreys, which nest along Union Lake's western shore. The lake is also stocked with a hybrid fish, a cross between a striped bass and largemouth bass. Numerous species of ducks and geese frequent the area. Look to the skies for a bald eagle scouting the clear water. In the fall, watch carefully and you might spot wood ducks or hooded mergansers, particularly in the coves. At dawn, you're likely to see white-tailed deer and raccoons sauntering along the shore. Short cliffs, about 0.75 mile down from the landing, host a few kingfisher nest holes. Look for the cavities about 2 feet above the waterline.

Miles of unmarked sand roads and hiking trails meander along the western and northern lakeshores and through the interior of the wildlife management area. One unmarked trail from the top of the launch ramp leads south along the shoreline. Another trail leads off from the north corner of the parking lot and follows the lake for about a half-mile before turning west away from the water.

While outboards are permitted, there is a 10-horsepower limit. Most outboard traffic is on the deeper, southeastern end of the lake close to the dam. The best and least-crowded paddling is along the western and northern shores, where you can meander around islands and quiet coves enjoying the scenery and looking for wildlife.

4 | Mullica River

You'll find bogs; waterfowl; beavers; turtles; eagles; ospreys; wild irises; and pine, oak, and white cedar woods on this Pine Barrens river.

Location: Pleasant Mills, NJ
Maps: DeLorme *New Jersey Atlas & Gazetteer,* Map 64; USGS Batsto
Length: Up to 7.5 miles round-trip
Time: 3 to 4 hours
Average Depth: 6 feet
Development: Rural
Access: Park entrance fee
Information: Wharton State Forest office at Batsto Village, 4110 Nesco Road, Hammonton, NJ 08037, 609-561-0024, state.nj.us
Camping: Bodine Field primitive campground, 25 minutes east; Turtle Run Campground, 20 minutes east (see Appendix A)
Take Note: Stay clear of powerboats

GETTING THERE
To the canoe- and kayak-friendly launch: From US 30, drive 8.5 miles on CR 542 East. At that point the Mullica River will be directly in front of you. There is a large sand parking area and an informal sand beach launch. You will pass Batsto Village and the entrance to Batsto Lake along the way. (39° 37.590′ N, 74° 37.553′ W)

To Crowley's Landing launch: Crowley's Landing, an additional 0.4 mile (cumulative: 8.9 miles) east on CR 542, is another option, but it's a concrete ramp that is heavily used by personal watercraft and motorboats and thus can be very crowded on summer weekends. Restrooms located here are open seasonally. (39° 37.587′ N, 74° 37.160′ W)

TRIP 4: MULLICA RIVER

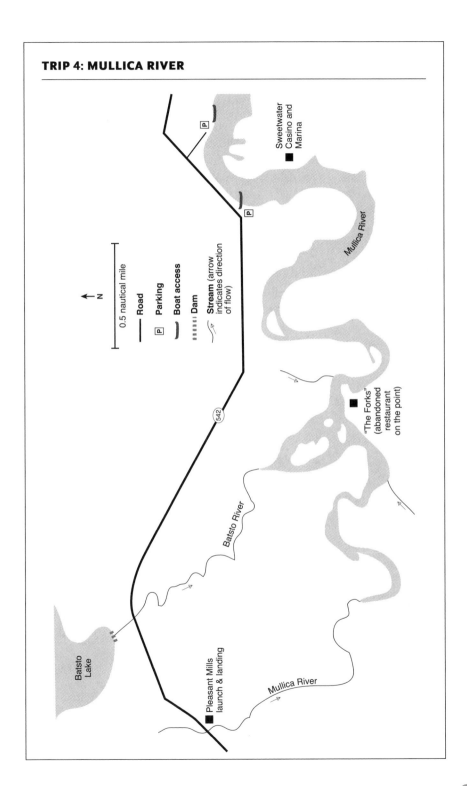

Sweetwater Casino and Marina

Mullica River

"The Forks" (abandoned restaurant on the point)

Batsto River

Batsto Lake

Pleasant Mills launch & landing

Mullica River

542

N

0.5 nautical mile

— Road
P Parking
) Boat access
░░░ Dam
Stream (arrow indicates direction of flow)

WHAT YOU'LL SEE

This stretch of the pristine upper Mullica River is a favorite with paddlers from central and southern New Jersey as well as southeastern Pennsylvania. When paddlers talk about heading to "the Pines" to paddle a river, they're referring to the Pine Barrens of southern New Jersey, and most likely the Mullica River.

The headwaters start in Berlin, New Jersey, 19.5 miles northwest of the launch. On the river's way here, a number of smaller watersheds drain into it, including the Batsto River, Atsion River, Sleeper Branch, Nescochague Creek, and Hammonton Creek. A number of other waters drain into the river downstream, the largest of which are Wading River, Bass River, and Nacote Creek.

Posts planted in the river with either a green square or a red triangle are channel markers, which denote the deepest water. You'll want to stay close to the channel, but not within it, in case a small motorboat goes up or down the river. In some areas, the water becomes shallow quickly once outside the marked channel, but it is deep enough for canoes and kayaks. Although this portion of the river is still tidal for half of the trip upstream, the flow is minimal and suitable for novices.

Paddling right (upstream) from the launch, you'll notice a large marina and restaurant a quarter-mile ahead, the Sweetwater Marina and Riverdeck. Beyond that point you may encounter a few small powerboats. Across from the marina is a large marsh area. Give it a 20-foot berth because it quickly becomes shallow and has numerous cedar stumps close to the surface at low tide. Marsh birds, ducks,

Kayakers explore coves along the gentle waters of Mullica River. Photo by Kathy Kenley.

and geese are common here, and you might spot a muskrat in the water around the denser grass stands. Around the first bend, thick stands of white cedar trees interspersed with oak and pine woods give the air a nice, clean smell. Around the second bend there will be a marshy area on the right where egrets and herons are commonly seen. It's technically an island, but the channel between it and the mainland is too shallow and narrow to allow passage even at high tide.

At the third bend, you will come to an abandoned restaurant and long storage barn that sit on a peninsula-like tip of land. The restaurant was called The Forks because this is where the Batsto River forks off to the right from the Mullica River. The entrance to the Batsto River is wide, with a large island in the middle. You can circumnavigate the island before continuing upstream on the Mullica River, or you can paddle past the island and take the Batsto River to the dam at the bottom of Batsto Lake. There's a small landing on the east side of the island where you can stop for lunch, but a better location is a sand beach less than a quarter-mile past the island, with much more room and a few logs to sit on.

This is a beautiful, pristine area with abundant birdlife and colorful swamp and bog flowers. Keep an eye on the sky for eagles and ospreys, a number of which are known to have nests nearby. The Batsto River is an important spawning ground for herring and hickory shad, which turn a few of the small feeder streams white with frenzied spawning activity in spring.

As you continue upstream on the Mullica River, only the left shore has houses, and they quickly become few and far between. Downed trees and thick limbs jutting out of the water are prime spots for basking turtles. River otters are uncommon, but they appear at least a couple of times each year. The river becomes quite twisty, with numerous downfalls and overhanging trees to paddle under or around.

A good turnaround point for the trip is the boat launch at Pleasant Mills, about 200 feet south of the CR 542 bridge. It becomes tougher to paddle upstream much farther because of swifter moving water and low overhangs. If you haven't stopped for lunch yet, eat at this landing before heading back downstream.

A trip up the Mullica River from the launch near Crowley's Landing to the launch at Pleasant Mills is 3.6 miles one-way. If you circumnavigate the island at the mouth of the Batsto River, add another 0.6 mile. A paddle up the Batsto River from the Mullica River is about 1.3 miles. There's so much wildlife and beautiful scenery here that it will take a few trips to see it all.

Hiking trails are available at Batsto Lake, five minutes northwest. After your paddle, you might also visit Batsto Village, the site of a nineteenth-century bog iron and glassmaking industrial center that currently consists of 33 historical buildings, including a gristmill, general store, and Batsto Mansion.

PINE BARRENS TREE FROG

Appearing nowhere else in New Jersey outside of the Pine Barrens, the Pine Barrens tree frog fills the air with its chorus on late-spring evenings during breeding season. These amphibians inhabit shallow pools in sphagnum bogs, cranberry bogs, backwater and slow-moving streams, and cedar swamps. Requiring acidic environments, the tree frog is susceptible to any human infringement on its habitat that raises the level of pH or decreases the water table. Listed as a threatened species, the frog's survival depends on the preservation of its specific wetland habitat. Only a few disjoined populations have been found elsewhere, in the acidic bogs of the Carolinas, Georgia, and western Florida.

These 1.5-inch beauties are characterized by lavender to plum stripes bordered in white, creating a striking contrast against their rich, emerald-green bodies, with bright yellow to orange coloring on the concealed surfaces of their legs. As with other tree frogs, their long-webbed toes end in adhesive discs that enable them to cling to twigs and bark. Their diet consists primarily of insects and other invertebrates found in moist environments. Males produce the nasal *quonk-quonk-quonk* sound through vocal sacs that inflate like balloons.

Although heard in vast numbers, these frogs are difficult to find unless you patiently, and very quietly, follow the call to its source. Breeding and egg-laying take place during May and June, with the larvae metamorphosing into adults by July and early August. Due to the tree frogs' secretive lives, little is known about their behavior outside of the breeding season.

5 | Cooper River Lake and Newton Lake

Look for waterfowl, turtles, and abundant birdlife.

Location: Collingswood, NJ
Maps: DeLorme *New Jersey Atlas & Gazetteer,* Map 54; USGS Camden
Area: Cooper River Lake: 150 acres; Newton Lake: 40 acres
Time: Cooper River Lake: 2 to 2.5 hours; Newton Lake: 1.5 to 2 hours
Average Depth: 5 feet in both

TRIP 5: COOPER RIVER LAKE AND NEWTON LAKE

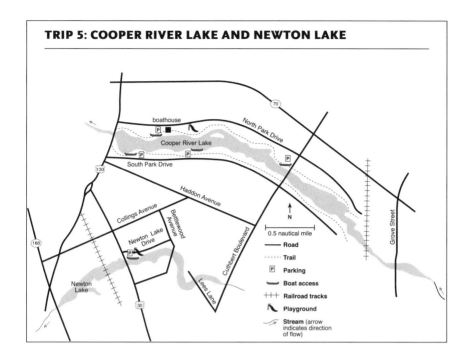

Development: Both: urban with greenway

Access: No fees

Information: Camden County Parks Department, 1301 Park Boulevard, Cherry Hill, NJ 08002, 856-216-2117; camdencounty.com

Take Note: Electric motorboats only

Outfitter: Cooper River Lake: Cowboy Mike's Canoe Rental, 510 Park Boulevard, Cherry Hill, NJ 08002, 609-332-5065, cowboymikescanoerental .com

GETTING THERE

To Cooper River Lake north shore boathouse and northeast launch: From the US 130/30 circle, drive north 0.6 mile on US 130. Turn right onto North Park Drive immediately after crossing the lake and drive 0.55 mile (cumulative: 1.15 miles) to the north shore boathouse parking lot on the right. (39° 55.597′ N, 75° 04.424′ W) For the northeast launch, drive an additional 1 mile (2.15 miles) to the dirt entrance on the right. (39° 55.555′ N, 75° 03.371′ W)

   To Cooper River Lake south shore launch: From the US 130/30 circle, drive north 0.4 mile on US 130, turn right onto South Park Drive, and continue 0.7 mile (cumulative: 1.1 miles) to the boat launch parking area on the left. (39° 55.467′ N, 75° 04.271′ W)

To Newton Lake: From the US 130/30 circle, drive east 0.7 mile on US 30, turn left onto Newton Lake Drive, and make an immediate right into the boat launch parking lot and drive to the ramp. (39° 54.484′ N, 75° 04.896′ W)

WHAT YOU'LL SEE
Cooper River Lake

The city of Collingswood has cleaned up its waters and created a lovely riverside park. The 2.5-mile stretch of the Cooper River widens to a few hundred yards—enough to call it a lake, at least by the standards of southern New Jersey, which is not known for having extremely large bodies of water. For those who live in the densely populated Camden area and need a place to escape close to home, this section of the river, landscaped with trees, shrubs, small gardens, sculptures, a multiuse trail, and a playground, provides the perfect refuge.

The best paddling is on the eastern end, where the shores become more wooded and you're farther from bustling traffic. Carp, bass, sunfish, and catfish inhabit the lake, as do large populations of turtles and frogs. Herons, egrets, ducks, and geese make their homes here. Many paddlers who live along the Delaware River from Gloucester City to Riverside stop by after work or on weekends for a workout. The boathouse is primarily used by rowing teams and

Newton Lake's tranquil waters offer verdant scenery. Photo by Kathy Kenley.

may become crowded at times, but both the restrooms and launch facilities are open to the public. The large public floating docks usually have portable toilets.

If you feel adventurous, you can paddle from the far eastern end of the lake under the railroad bridge and into Cooper River. Depending on water levels, this will add a round-trip of 2 to 3 miles to your day. Within the first three-quarters of a mile, there are three islands to explore and a few open areas where you can see waterfowl. It's a very pleasant and quiet paddle with only a few houses and businesses along the route. As the river gets narrow, however, dead trees across the water may block your passage.

Biking and hiking trails snake along both shores of Cooper River Lake, and portable toilets are conveniently located all around the grounds. The total length of the trail system is 5 miles, but the loop from the boathouse parking lot east to East Cuthbert Boulevard and around to US 30 and back is only 3.8 miles. For the 5-mile trail walk, continue past East Cuthbert Boulevard on the north side of the lake for an additional 1.2-mile loop. The park is open from 6 A.M. until midnight, leaving plenty of time for a moonlight paddle.

Newton Lake

Long and narrow, attractive Newton Lake sits amid a highly populated area. A rim of the 104-acre municipal park of the same name surrounds about 60 percent of the 40-acre lake. Many improvements and amenities have been added to the park since the early 2000s, one of which is a nice boat launch with plentiful parking. The main recreation space next to the ramp features a small playground, a restroom, picnic spots, and a landscaped lakeside sitting area with benches. Camden County has started several ongoing programs that will one day connect multiuse trails throughout the county.

The lake's serpentine shape provides a long, relaxing paddle, with patches of yellow pond lilies, purple pickerelweed, and yellow-and-white-stalked hornwort. In shallow, marshy shoreline areas, you'll probably find egrets and herons fishing, stretching their long necks as they focus on the task at hand. Don't just paddle past. Sit and observe these graceful birds for a while. Turtles bask on a few limbs that stick out of the water and are most common on the northeast area of the lake, where you're also likely to find ducks, geese, and swans. The four bridges that cross over the lake add an element of interest as you wonder what the next section will bring. Anglers love to cast from shore for carp, bass, sunfish, and catfish.

If you'd like to stretch your legs after a paddle, walking paths weave around trees along the landscaped swath of land and are dotted with lakeside benches and small gardens. The total length is 2.4 miles, but you can cross over the Lees Lane bridge to shorten your walk.

6 | Rancocas Creek

Turtles everywhere, pretty scenery, frogs, beavers, raptors, ducks, and other birds are common sights on this quiet waterway.

Location: Pemberton, NJ
Maps: DeLorme *New Jersey Atlas & Gazetteer,* Map 47; USGS Mount Holly; Burlington County: co.burlington.nj.us
Length: 6.6 miles round-trip
Time: 2.5 hours
Average Depth: 5 feet
Development: Suburban/rural, woodland surrounded by small farms and county lands
Access: No fees
Information: Burlington County Division of Parks, 601 Pemberton Browns Mills Road, Pemberton, NJ 08068, 609-265-5858
Take Note: No horsepower limit specified, but you won't encounter anything except a very rare electric motorboat
Outfitter: Clark's Canoe Rental: 201 Hanover Street, Pemberton, NJ 08068, 609-894-4448, clarkscanoe.com

GETTING THERE

To Pemberton launch: From the junction of US 206 and NJ 38/CR 530, drive 2.7 miles on CR 530 East (NJ 38 on the west side of US 206). The road becomes Hampton Street in the town of Pemberton. Turn left onto Hanover Street and drive 0.15 mile (cumulative: 2.85 miles) to the access road on your left immediately before crossing the bridge. Clark's Canoe Rental is on Hanover Street at the corner of the access road. (39° 58.210′ N, 74° 41.137′ W)

   To Burlington County College launch: From the junction of US 206 and NJ 38/CR 530, drive 2.7 miles on CR 530 East (NJ 38 on the west side of US 206). At the junction with Hanover Street, continue straight onto Pemberton Bypass and drive 2.1 miles (cumulative: 4.8 miles) to a T intersection. Turn right and drive 0.7 mile (5.5 miles), then turn right onto Rancocas Road and drive 0.3 mile (5.8 miles) to the access road on your left. It's a 50-yard carry to the water. Portable toilets are available in the parking lot. (39° 57.718′ N, 74° 38.460′ W)

TRIP 6: RANCOCAS CREEK

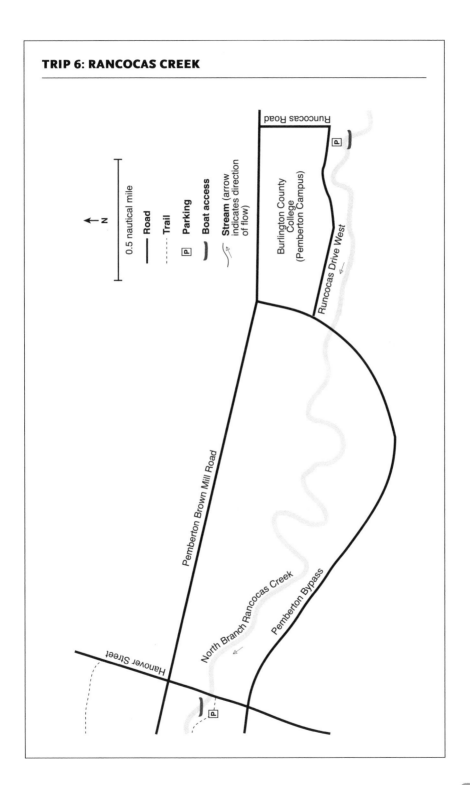

Runcocas Road

Burlington County College (Pemberton Campus)

Runcocas Drive West

0.5 nautical mile

N

Road
Trail
Parking
Boat access
Stream (arrow indicates direction of flow)

Pemberton Brown Mill Road

North Branch Rancocas Creek

Pemberton Bypass

Hanover Street

A canopy of trees envelops paddlers on scenic Rancocas Creek. Photo by Kathy Kenley.

WHAT YOU'LL SEE

The Rancocas Watershed drains 350 square miles in south-central New Jersey. It comprises the Rancocas Creek Main Stem, North Branch Rancocas Creek, and the South/Southwest Branch Rancocas Creek. Although a large part of the watershed lies within the New Jersey Pinelands, it is the only Pinelands waterway that drains into the Delaware River instead of the Atlantic Ocean.

The Rancocas Creek Canoe Trail along the North Branch Rancocas Creek is 14 miles long, beginning at Burlington County College in Pemberton and ending at Mill Dam Park in Mount Holly. A 200-yard portage is involved to bypass two dams at Smithville, and the section between Birmingham and Pemberton can only be paddled downstream because of its shallow and swift water. The prettiest section, described here, is the slow-moving water between Pemberton and Burlington County College. It's also the least populated, with only about ten quaint riverside homes along the whole route. While you can put in at either end, the easiest is Pemberton. The launch parking lot is located next to the Hanover Street Bridge. You can launch into the downstream side that goes into Birmingham, but it's shallow and rocky, and the current is swift enough that it is impossible to paddle back upstream to the launch. Use the dirt launch on the upstream side of the dam and paddle upstream, where current is minimal.

The creek attracts many turtles: red-eared sliders rest on logs side by side with yellow-bellied and painted turtles—some as big as dinner plates. Where leaf litter catches on snags close to shore, look for frogs. The trail takes you through a variety of habitats, from lowland woods to reed clumps to swampy side channels. Bends in the creek tend to be gradual, with only a few sharp turns. Most of your adventure will be skirting downed limbs and ducking under overhanging branches along this scenic waterway.

Dirt banks, 2 to 3 feet steep, line most of the creek, but there are some spots with gradual slopes that lead to shallow side inlets and tiny coves. Many of those areas have very small, almost hidden, passageways into the creek. Inside you can often find egrets, mallards, and pintails seeking a more secluded environment blanketed with pond lilies and duckweed. Along mossy embankments, look for the tiny dark-green leaves of wild cranberry, which has fruits smaller and more tart than their cultivated cousins. In the understory, you'll find wild blueberry, mulberry, mountain laurel, and sheep laurel. In a few places, wild grapevines twist around trees and bushes. Birdlife includes vireos, orioles, thrushes, kingfishers, tanagers, woodpeckers, and blue jays. Because of the many small farms close to the woodland edges, you'll see hawks, falcons, and vultures in the sky.

You might spot muskrat in areas of reeds or other dense aquatic grasses. Birch trees with the bark freshly gnawed off in a 2-foot area near the ground are a telltale sign of recent beaver activity. Small, narrow paths leading to the water's edge are usually deer trails, but you might also see a fox or raccoon.

The public ramp at Burlington County College is a perfect place to stop for lunch and stretch your legs. There's a portable toilet at the top of the ramp in the parking lot. From the college, you can paddle another 1.5 miles upstream to the next dam. Since upstream from the college is not part of the water trail, the county doesn't maintain passageways for canoes and kayaks, and trees might impair your ability to cross farther along the creek. The entire trail requires two portages, the longer of which is 200 yards at Smithville. The other, about 55 yards, is at the dam in Pemberton. Because it is impossible to paddle upstream from Birmingham to Pemberton, you need to set up a shuttle with another paddler if you choose to do the entire route.

Hikers can enjoy a well-marked trail that leads off from the west end of the parking lot and travels 1.25 miles into the town of Binghamton. A fork off to the right 0.9 mile into the hike heads back to Pemberton, crossing the creek along the way, and ends at the restored old Pemberton train station for a 1.9-mile hike. From there, you can either return along the same route or turn right onto Hanover Street and walk 0.5 mile to the launch access road.

7 | Lakes Carasaljo and Shenandoah

Look for waterfowl, wading birds, and freshwater marshes.

Location: Lakewood, NJ
Maps: DeLorme *New Jersey Atlas & Gazetteer,* Map 50; USGS Lakewood;
Ocean County Department of Parks and Recreation: co.ocean.nj.us
Area: Lake Carasaljo: 67 acres; Lake Shenandoah: 50 acres
Time: 2 hours for each lake
Average Depth: 8 feet in both
Development: Urban/suburban
Access: No fees
Information: Carasaljo Municipal Park: Lakewood Township Parks
Department, Municipal Building, 231 Third Street, Lakewood, NJ 08701,
732-367-6737; Lake Shenandoah County Park: Ocean County Department
of Parks and Recreation, 700 NJ 88, Lakewood, NJ 08701, 732-506-9090,
oceancountyparks.org
Camping: Allaire State Park, 20 minutes northeast (see Appendix A)
Take Note: Electric motorboats only

GETTING THERE
To Lake Carasaljo: From the junction of NJ 70 and US 9, drive north 2.7 miles,
turn left onto Central Avenue and drive 100 feet, then turn right onto South
Lake Drive. Drive 0.8 mile (cumulative: 3.5 miles) to the parking lot and ramp
on the right. (40° 05.575′ N, 74° 13.695′ W)

    To Lake Shenandoah public launch: From the junction of NJ 70 and US
9, drive north 3 miles and turn right (east) onto NJ 88. Drive 0.85 mile (cumulative: 3.85 miles), then turn right onto Clover Street and drive 0.15 mile (4
miles) to the parking lot and launch on the left. (40° 05.311′ N, 74° 11.968′ W)

    To Lake Shenandoah boat rental: From the junction of US 9 and NJ 88,
drive east 1.5 miles on NJ 88 and turn right into the park. There will be a large
brown sign on the road. You cannot launch private boats here, but there are
canoes and rowboats for rent on a first-come, first-served basis. (40° 05.301′
N, 74° 11.342′ W)

TRIP 7: LAKES CARASALJO AND SHENANDOAH

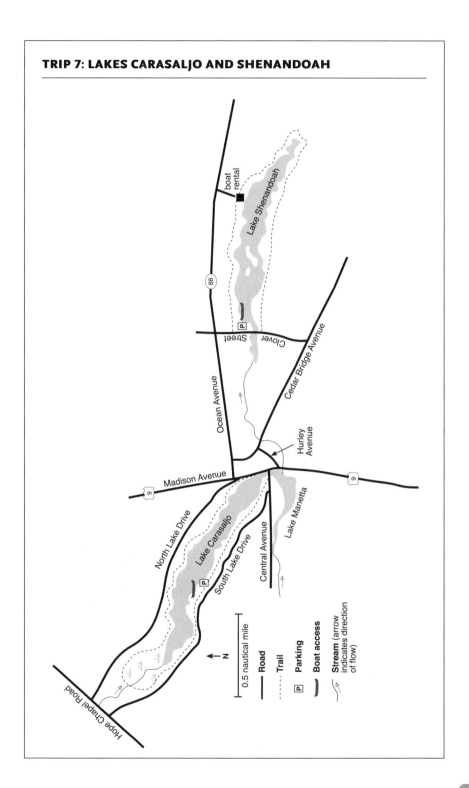

WHAT YOU'LL SEE

The South Branch Metedeconk River feeds both lakes. Lake Carasaljo is located within the 176-acre municipal park of the same name. Carasaljo derives from the names of the daughters of Joseph W. Brick, a businessman who lived on the property in the late 1800s: Caroline, Sara, and Josephine. The smaller "lake" attached to Lake Carasaljo is named after Brick's wife, Manetta. Lake Manetta is not actually a lake, but an arm of Lake Carasljo. It cannot be launched into, but paddling is allowed.

Lake Carasaljo

In this congested urban/suburban area, a narrow tree-lined swath of the park surrounds Lake Carasaljo. The far eastern end borders busy US 9, which creates quite a bit of road noise in that section. The eastern half of the lake has the most population, but the houses are separated from the lake by a road and a border of trees. There is a nice section of calm and quiet waters awaiting you at the southeastern tip of the lake.

Paddle south along the US 9 embankment and under a footbridge that's part of the circular hiking trail around the lake. Continue paddling under the Central Avenue bridge and enter the 18-acre Lake Manetta. No outboards of any kind are allowed. The south shore borders a wide area of dense woods, and you can usually find a spot or two of sandy beach to land your boat and take a

Watch for waterfowl on Lake Carasaljo's wide banks. Photo by Kathy Kenley.

break under the shade of overhanging trees. Watch for kingfishers darting along the tree edge. You'll often find ducks and geese back here too.

Head back out to Lake Carasaljo and up to the western end. Here the lake borders a wide area of woodland and freshwater marsh. Herons, egrets, and waterfowl like this place and find feeding an easy task. Depending on water levels, you may be able to paddle up the South Branch Metedeconk River for a half-mile or more. The entrance to the river is a little left of center and should be easy to locate if you look for signs of a small current.

Bikers, joggers, and walkers make their way along a 5-mile trail that circles the lake and meanders through three sections where footpaths and footbridges traverse wetlands, including the bridge you paddled beneath if you went into Lake Manetta. You can take an interesting short hike starting from the parking lot off South Lake Drive just west of Lake Park Drive. This end of the park is woods, wetlands, and swamp, so you'll find a number of footbridges along the trails, the first of which you'll cross as you enter the trail from the parking lot. *GPS coordinates for this parking lot:* (40° 05.892′ N, 74° 14.339′ W)

Lake Shenandoah

Lake Shenandoah County Park was once part of John D. Rockefeller's vacation estate, to which hemlock and unique specimens of other trees were imported from all over the country. The 140-acre park offers recreation trails, a small picnic area, fishing piers, a bait and tackle shop, canoe and rowboat rentals, a coffee shop, and restrooms. Although smaller than Lake Carasaljo, Lake Shenandoah has far fewer houses and businesses nearby, making it more of a getaway.

Wide and dense woods of pine and oak surround the lake on almost all sides. Part of the north side has a narrow swath of trees between the lake and a sand access road. On the northwest side, tall grasses and dense shrubs provide a perfect habitat for box turtles, painted turtles, and black snakes. The most exciting part of the paddle is the two islands, which have a few small, sandy beaches where you can land and take a break. This lake is also known for its good fishing, particularly for herring when they're running in May. Besides herring, you'll find pike, largemouth bass, perch, catfish, pickerel, bluegill (sunfish), eel, and many more species.

A 2-mile loop trail goes around the lake. The trail on the south side is the most interesting because it winds through the woods and has short feeder paths leading to the lake, where you might see a lone angler or spot an egret or heron fishing in the shallow water.

8 | Lake Mercer

The county park in which Lake Mercer is located is home to waterfowl, wading birds, raptors, and turtles.

Location: West Windsor, NJ
Maps: DeLorme *New Jersey Atlas & Gazetteer,* Map 42; USGS Princeton
Area: 275 acres
Time: 2.5 to 3 hours
Average Depth: 15 feet
Development: Urban/suburban
Access: No fees
Information: Park ranger office, 609-443-8956; Mercer County Park Commission, 197 Blackwell Road, Pennington, NJ 08534, 609-303-0700, mercercountyparks.org
Take Note: Electric motorboats only. There are two launch sites for canoes and kayaks, on the north and south sides of the lake.
Outfitter: On-site, 609-448-4004, closed on Mondays

GETTING THERE

To the main marina and park office on the south side: From CR 571, drive south 3.8 miles on CR 535 (Old Trenton Road). Turn right (west) onto Paxson Avenue into the park entrance and drive 1.1 miles (cumulative: 4.9 miles) to the marina entrance on the right. The park ranger office is to the left if you want to stop in for a park brochure. Stay to the right when you drive into the marina entrance. The lower-level parking lot is for big boats that need to be hauled by a trailer. After unloading your kayak or canoe, drive back up and around to the upper-level parking lot. From NJ 33, drive north 3.8 miles on CR 535. Turn left onto CR 602 (South Post Road) and continue as above. (40° 15.933´ N, 74° 38.503´ W)

To the more scenic north launch: From CR 571, drive south 1.9 miles on CR 535 (Old Trenton Road). Turn right onto Village Road East and drive 2.1 miles (cumulative: 4 miles), then turn left onto Village Road West and drive 0.2 mile (4.2 miles). At the T junction, turn left (south) to continue on Village Drive West and drive 0.5 mile (4.7 miles). Turn left onto South Post Road and drive 0.9 mile (5.6 miles) to the launch. (40° 16.174´ N, 74° 38.484´ W)

TRIP 8: LAKE MERCER

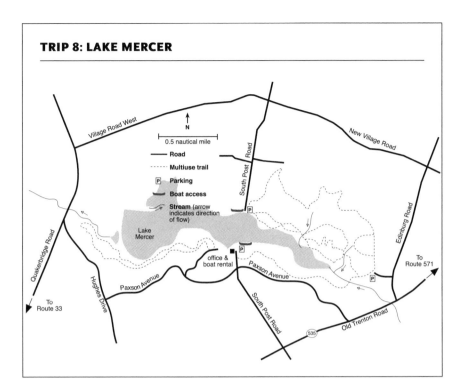

From NJ 33 in Nottingham, drive north on Whitehorse Mercerville Road 0.2 mile and continue straight onto Quakerbridge Road for 3.1 miles (cumulative: 3.3 miles). Turn right onto Village Road West and drive 1.8 miles (5.1 miles), then turn right onto South Post Road and drive 0.9 mile (6 miles) to the launch. (40° 16.174′ N, 74° 38.484′ W)

WHAT YOU'LL SEE

Mercer County Park is a major recreational area located in the densely populated region midway between Princeton and Trenton, New Jersey. With more than 2,500 acres and the 275-acre Lake Mercer, the park offers something for everyone, including golf, soccer, tennis, and, of course, boating.

Most of the amenities, including a marina, kayak and pedal boat rentals, food concessions, and a nature center, are located on the south side of the lake. Thus, this side gets extremely busy on summer weekends. There is a specially designated sand beach launch for kayaks and canoes to the right of the concrete boat ramp. However, most kayakers launch from the ramp on the north side of the lake. Not only is it prettier than the launch at the main office, but parking is a lot more convenient. No park activities are located on this side either, except for the rowing center.

A kayaker has some company on Lake Mercer. Photo by slgckgc, Creative Commons on Flickr.

Small sailboats tend to use the more open and usually windier western area of the lake. A large portion of that area is lined with thick woods and provides a nice paddle. Ducks, Canada geese, and swans are everywhere. The only things that detract from the scenery are the tall power-line towers. Water close to the shore can become quite shallow quickly, and some areas have a lot of sunken logs and limbs—good for providing a protective environment for young fish, not so good on gelcoats.

More scenic and tranquil paddling conditions can be found on the far eastern end, where thick woods line the shores and you are beyond the rental use zone. Turtles become more plentiful. Assunpink Creek flows into the lake at the densely wooded narrow tip of the eastern end. Water levels are usually good enough to paddle upstream for a quarter-mile or so, providing a brief shaded respite on a hot summer's day.

A wide variety of trees, including shagbark hickory, maple, sycamore, various oaks, tulip, and sweet gum, create a magnificent array of colors in fall. Blue jays squawk and cardinals make their *tink, tink* sound throughout the woods. You may even see a pheasant. The diverse flora hosts numerous bird species in their specific habitats of upland woods, moist lowlands, or marshes. Mammals such as deer, opossums, skunks, and red foxes all reside in the park. Muskies, shad, and largemouth bass are the primary fish species.

The park holds bass-fishing tournaments each year. University and high school sculling crews practice from the boathouse next to the north launch. The lake is closed to boat traffic when there's a rowing regatta. One or more roads into the park are closed, in part or in whole, for a few special events like marathon bike races and walkathons. If you go on a weekend, check the park schedule first.

There are a few trails, mostly multiuse; be careful on the multiuse trails, which are heavily used by very energetic mountain bikers. The bicycle path and the short nature trail northwest of the tennis center are marked on the park map. A walking trail starts from the kayak launch at the marina and links into the nature trail.

MUSKRAT

The muskrat, a semi-aquatic rodent, lives in and around lakes, ponds, fresh- and saltwater marshes, and slow-moving streams throughout North America. Its common name is derived from the animal's musk glands, located beneath the skin of the male's lower abdomen, which produce a strong scent. Averaging 2 feet in length, these critters' dark gray to brown fur fools many people into thinking they've spotted a beaver.

Adaptations supporting the muskrat's swimming skills include partially webbed hind feet (which act as paddles) and a long, scaly, hairless tail, flattened sideways (which acts as a rudder). Muskrat are mostly nocturnal, which means your best bets to spot them are dawn and dusk, when they leave their burrows to feed on aquatic plants. Primarily vegetarians preferring cattails, arrowheads, pond weeds, bulbs, and tubers, they will occasionally dine on snails, crayfish, frogs, and carrion when plants are scarce. Like otters, muskrat clean and wash all their food before they eat.

In marshlands, muskrat build dome-shaped houses as large as 6 to 8 feet across and 2 feet high using reeds and mud. Check channel corners as you paddle by for chewed-off reeds: the telltale sign a muskrat lives nearby, probably within 150 feet. Muskrat locate their houses near the water, with reeds and grasses lining the main room and an extensive tunnel system leading to several underwater entrances. In tidal waters, lakes, and slow-moving streams with steep banks, they will sometimes make their home by burrowing into the bank, building only a small dome as a surface entrance. Muskrat will build special huts, not unlike root cellars, near the main hut to store vegetative roots and grasses for food while nursing or in bad weather.

Muskrat are prolific breeders producing an average of four litters of five to seven young per litter each year. Breeding takes place from late March through July. Although muskrat do not mate for life, they are thought to have only one mate during rearing seasons. The gestation period lasts about a month, and the young are weaned by two months of age. As self-regulating animals, population density, habitat quality, and food availability reflect the number and size of litters in a given year. While muskrat are solitary animals except when mating, they often share a communal den during winter. Muskrat are prey to foxes, hawks, raccoons, coyotes, and owls.

A dense population of muskrat can be deleterious to aquatic vegetation necessary for other wildlife, and their burrowing activities can weaken dikes and earthen dams. On a commercial scale, muskrat are valued for their fur, often referred to as "river mink."

9 | Farrington Lake

Enjoy a scenic paddle and wildlife and bird viewing close to the densely populated towns of New Brunswick and East Brunswick.

Location: New Brunswick, NJ
Maps: DeLorme *New Jersey Atlas & Gazetteer,* Map 37; USGS New Brunswick
Area: 290 acres
Time: 2.5 to 3.5 hours
Average Depth: 6 feet
Development: Suburban with wide areas of wooded shoreline
Access: No fees
Information: New Jersey Division of Fish and Wildlife, Central Region (Assunpink WMA), 1 Eldridge Road, Robbinsville, NJ 08691, 609-259-2132
Take Note: Electric motorboats only

TRIP 9: FARRINGTON LAKE

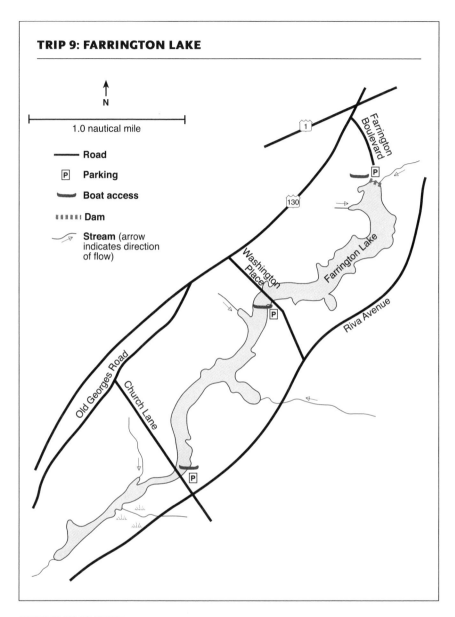

Road

P **Parking**

Boat access

⋕⋕⋕⋕⋕ **Dam**

⤳ **Stream** (arrow indicates direction of flow)

1.0 nautical mile

N

Farrington Boulevard

1

130

Farrington Lake

Washington Place

Riva Avenue

Old Georges Road

Church Lane

GETTING THERE

To Washington Place launch: From the junction of US 1 and US 130, drive 1.7 miles on US 130 South. Turn left onto Washington Place and drive 0.4 mile (cumulative: 2.1 miles) to the parking area and gravel launch on the right immediately after crossing the bridge. (40° 26.344′ N, 74° 27.986′ W)

   To Church Lane launch: From the junction of US 1 and US 130, drive 1.8 miles on US 130 South. Turn left onto Old Georges Road and drive 0.8 mile (cumulative: 2.6 miles), then turn left onto Church Lane and drive 0.8 mile (3.4 miles). Turn left onto Riva Avenue, and the parking area and dirt launch will be on the left. (40° 25.466′ N, 74° 28.608′ W)

WHAT YOU'LL SEE

Created by damming Lawrence Brook, this long, narrow lake is bordered on both sides by large sections of county and township parklands. Located in a suburban neighborhood on the south side of the bustling college town of New Brunswick, Farrington Lake offers a serene getaway and pleasant respite from traffic, crowds, and industry.

Wildlife is abundant all along the lake. Deer, raccoons, and even wild turkeys have been spotted in areas bordered by wide swaths of woods. Goldfinches, cardinals, wrens, warblers, blue jays, and other songbirds take refuge among the trees. The lake is stocked with trout and bass. Other fish commonly found here include sunfish, pike, pickerel, perch, and catfish. Electric outboards are permitted, but most fishing is done from shore or bridges.

The widest section of the lake is north of the Washington Place bridge. A paddle around that section yields a trip of about 3 miles. Some houses are located here, but they are set back from the water and have a border of trees. Immediately north of the bridge are two narrow strips of land jutting into

Farrington Lake is a long, narrow waterway providing a calm escape from a heavily populated area. Photo by Kathy Kenley.

the lake that are part of a submerged abandoned railroad. Some underwater pilings are close to land, but they are easily avoided. The south shoreline is wooded for a half-mile above the bridge, where most of the land is part of Bicentennial Park. A large cove in the park is reachable through a 50-foot opening from the lake.

North of the park is a small section of modest residential properties followed by a quarter-mile of wooded shoreline. Exercise caution at the north end, by the dam. You'll hear the sound of rushing water if lake levels are high. Two low concrete structures on either side of the lake signal the position of the dam, and there are white warning signs near the structures. Do not paddle past the warning markers as you cross over to the other side of the lake.

Paddling south on the west side from the dam area, you'll pass a three-quarter-mile stretch of North Brunswick Township Park. Here is a good opportunity for viewing birds and wildlife. Sit in your boat and simply enjoy the serenity. If you want to stop for a stretch, there are a few small spots to land a couple of boats.

A shoreline paddle between the Washington Place bridge south to the Church Lane bridge and back yields a trip of a little more than 3 miles. A cove next to a small farm on the west side, bordered by a wide swath of woods, is excellent for bird-watching. Look for towhees, kingbirds, chickadees, and finches. Halfway between the bridges on the east side is a large cove that is excellent for viewing waterfowl and birdlife, particularly on the northern edge of the cove, where there's a large stand of conifers rimmed by hardwood trees.

South of the Church Lane bridge, Farrington Lake narrows and becomes shallower. Lawrence Brook enters the lake at the far southern end. A paddle along the shoreline from that bridge and up Lawrence Brook a little past the Davidson Mill Road bridge and back yields a trip of 3 miles. There are few houses along the way, and the surrounding landscape is more wooded and wild. Two small streams enter the lake on the west side and are worth paddling into for a few hundred feet if water levels are high enough. While much smaller than the other two sections of the lake, this part is no less rewarding as far as wildlife is concerned—and it's more remote. You can see plenty of turtles, dragonflies, egrets, and herons among the lily pads. Beyond the Davidson Mill Road bridge, the water becomes very shallow, but you can paddle upstream for about a quarter-mile before you need to turn around.

10 | Spruce Run Reservoir

Explore dozens of coves and enjoy observing a wide range of wildlife along this huge body of water.

Location: Clinton, NJ
Maps: DeLorme *New Jersey Atlas & Gazetteer,* Map 29; USGS High Bridge; New Jersey Department of Environmental Protection: state.nj.us
Area: 1,300 acres
Time: 5 to 5.5 hours
Average Depth: 26 feet
Development: Rural
Access: Park entrance fee
Information: Spruce Run State Park, One Van Syckles Corner Road, Clinton, NJ 08809, 908-638-8572, state.nj.us
Camping: On-site; reservations can be made through reserveamerica.com or by calling 855-607-3075
Outfitters: Kayak East, Columbia, NJ 07832, 866-529-2532, kayakeast.com; Yellow Dog Paddle, Van Syckles Road, Clinton, NJ 08809, 908-310-3742, yellowdogpaddle.com
Take Note: Motorboats up to 10 horsepower are allowed

GETTING THERE

From the east: Take Exit 17 off I-78 for NJ 31/Clinton/Flemington. Drive 3.1 miles on NJ 31 North, turn left onto Van Syckles Corner Road, and drive 1.5 miles (cumulative: 4.6 miles) to the park entrance on the left.

From the west: Take Exit 12 off I-78 for NJ 173/Norton. Turn left onto CR 635 (Mechlin Corner Road) and drive 1.1 miles, then turn right onto Van Syckles Corner Road and drive 1.9 miles (cumulative: 3 miles) to the park entrance on the right.

The park office is behind the entrance booth. The road to the boat launch is the first left after the entrance booth. Turn left and drive 1.2 miles (5.8 miles; 4.2 miles respectively) to the boat launch area. There will be signs for the sand cartop launch on the west side of the parking lot. (40° 39.646′ N, 74° 55.493′ W)

TRIP 10: SPRUCE RUN RESERVOIR

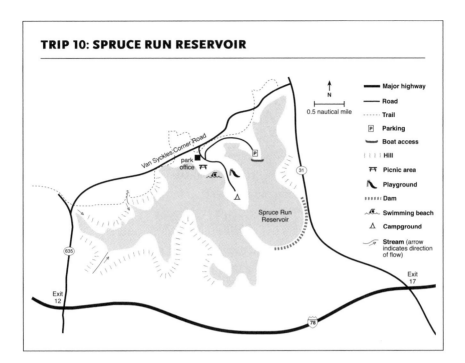

WHAT YOU'LL SEE

Spruce Run Reservoir is mostly surrounded by a section of the Clinton Wildlife Management Area and Spruce Run State Park, offering thousands of acres of forest and protected habitat, which provides ideal conditions for wildlife viewing and paddling. Built in 1965 for the Elizabethtown Water Company, this massive reservoir has a variety of recreational facilities, including boat rentals, a swimming beach, ball fields, and concession stands. Campsites are available, inviting you to spend a few rewarding days. Make reservations ahead of time to ensure a spot.

With 15 miles of shoreline, you could spend a few afternoons paddling in and out of all the little coves, nooks, and crannies. The most scenic section is to the south and southwest, where coves are abundant and give you a better chance for a quiet paddle on crowded summer weekends. Spruce Run has a tower that flashes red when winds increase to warn boaters to get off the water.

Because of the vast habitat provided by the adjacent wildlife management area, the reservoir has an enormous diversity of birdlife and small mammals. Eagles, hawks, harriers, vultures, and ospreys fly overhead, and it's fairly common to see an osprey plunge for prey if you're on the water for a few hours. Along tree-and-shrub-lined banks you'll find bobolinks, warblers, pewees, towhees, scarlet tanagers, and a variety of songbirds flitting about the branches overhanging the water and in and around stands of phragmites and cattails. Willows thrive along some shores, adding a softness to the landscape at the slightest breeze.

The big attractions at Spruce Run for the paddler are its size and convoluted shape. At any one place on the water, you can see only about one-quarter to one-third of the reservoir. It's the adventurous element of what's around the next corner that will keep you exploring happily for hours; every turn brings something new into view. The combination of natural features, from long sandy beaches and open grasslands to shrublands and wooded hillsides, is responsible for the diversity of wildlife visible from your boat.

Turn left after leaving the launch and head around into the northeastern arm of the lake. It's a pretty arm to explore, far away from the recreational and open areas that the sailors prefer. Then paddle along the eastern edge until you're near the dam, and head over to the peninsula on the west side of the dam. A large cove to the south has numerous smaller crannies to investigate before you continue along the southern shoreline.

One of the best places for a peaceful paddle is in the western quarter of the lake. Since it is farthest from the boat launch and sailing center and the water is shallow, it gets the least boat traffic. A few small streams enter the reservoir at the far western corner, and you can paddle upstream for a short way if water levels are high.

Numerous sandy beaches invite you to stop for a break or lunch. Look for beaver lodges all along the shores here; a number have been seen over the years. Head back toward the launch along the northern shoreline, past wooded shores

On a quiet day, you might have Spruce Run to yourself. Photo by Kathy Kenley.

interspersed with small grass or scrub-shrub environments. Past the swimming beach to the south is the campground peninsula. Perhaps you'll see a waterfront site to reserve for your next visit. Round the peninsula and explore the last cove, where the cartop launch is located.

For the hiker, the 2.6-mile Highlands Millennium Trail begins with a 0.9-mile one-way segment within the park boundaries and then extends immediately outside the park boundaries and takes you through the Union Furnace Nature Area and on to restored furnace buildings. To shorten the hike and see the most interesting part of the trail, exit Spruce Run State Park and turn right on Van Syckles Corner Road. Drive 0.9 mile to the parking area on your right. The furnace building sits directly across the road. The nature area is an additional 0.45 mile west, with a large parking lot on your right and the marked entrance directly across the road.

11 | Splitrock Reservoir

Maine-like geographic features, eagles, hawks, beavers, deer, islands galore, and clear water will entice you to return time and again.

Location: Rockaway, NJ
Maps: DeLorme *New Jersey Atlas & Gazetteer,* Map 25; USGS Boonton; New Jersey Division of Fish and Wildlife: state.nj.us
Area: 625 acres
Time: 4 to 5 hours
Average Depth: 20-plus feet
Development: Remote/rural
Access: No fees
Information: New Jersey Division of Fish and Wildlife, Bureau of Land Management, P.O. Box 402, Trenton, NJ 08625, 609-984-0547
Camping: Mahlon Dickerson Reservation, 30 minutes west (see Appendix A)
Take Note: Electric motorboats only

GETTING THERE
From I-80 east, take Exit 37 for CR 513. Turn left onto CR 513 North (Green Pond Road) and drive 6.4 miles. Turn right onto Upper Hibernia Road and drive 0.3 mile (cumulative: 6.7 miles) to a T intersection, then turn right to

TRIP 11: SPLITROCK RESERVOIR

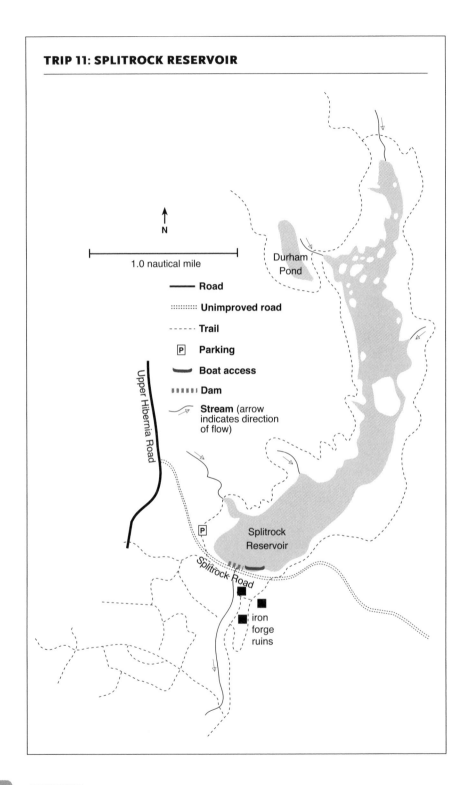

N

1.0 nautical mile

—— Road

:::::::: Unimproved road

----- Trail

P Parking

Boat access

IIIIII Dam

Stream (arrow indicates direction of flow)

Durham Pond

Upper Hibernia Road

Splitrock Reservoir

Splitrock Road

iron forge ruins

stay on Upper Hibernia Road and drive 0.7 mile (7.4 miles). Turn left onto Split Rock Road and drive 1.2 miles (8.6 miles) to the parking lot on your left, shortly after crossing over the dam. You will need to carry your kayak approximately 60 yards from the parking lot down a hill, which is steep for the last 10 yards. The path is wide and covered with wood chips. (40° 57.764′ N, 74° 27.443′ W)

From I-80 west, take Exit 37 for Rockaway/CR 513 and turn left onto Hibernia Avenue. After crossing under I-80, Hibernia Avenue becomes Green Pond Road. Continue as above, turning right onto Upper Hibernia Road.

(*Note:* Park only in the designated lot. The only other legal parking is 0.4 mile east of the dam and is for hikers to use when they enter the Four Birds Trail. Do not park anywhere else, or you may be ticketed.)

WHAT YOU'LL SEE

Splitrock Reservoir is one of the most beautiful sites to paddle in New Jersey. To the east, Farny State Park has two tracts of land that come close to the reservoir. Another 1,500 acres of land around the water are owned by Jersey City but protected by the Division of Fish and Wildlife under the Green Acres Program.

Be aware the launch is down a rather steep, 60-yard, wood-chipped path with large rocks at the entry. A small area on the left side has a gravel bottom about 10 inches below the surface, but you'll get wet up to midcalf or knee unless you're adept at launching from rocks, which can wreak havoc on all but

A prominent rock face dominates the shore opposite the launch. Photo by Kathy Kenley.

plastic boats. Wear a dry suit, wetsuit, or tall waterproof paddling boots when the water is cold so you don't risk a chill or hypothermia.

A landscape of huge boulders along the shores and a wonderland of rock islands in the north end make the scene look more like Maine than New Jersey. Wildlife abounds here. Ospreys, eagles, and hawks fly high over the water, blue herons are common, blue jays fill the air with their raucous calls, cormorants stick their thin necks and heads above the surface, kingfishers dart back and forth along some banks, deer come to the water's edge to drink, and beavers are active. Add to that a diversity of woodland, songbirds, wildflowers, and land mammals for a spectacular wildlife adventure. During spring and fall migrations, the lake provides an excellent stopover for food and rest for loons, wood ducks, mergansers, and other waterfowl. Anglers come here seeking large- and smallmouth bass, catfish, crappie, pickerel, and sunfish.

The lake is a little more than 3 miles long and averages 0.2 mile across. In the middle, it's bent slightly and has a very large island, so you can't see the whole lake at any one point. The southern half, below the island, has many picturesque, rugged boulder faces and numerous inlets to explore. Around every corner, something different sparks your interest, some new birds are spotted, and the lakeshore changes. Paddle to the north end of the lake along the western shoreline and you'll find a number of pretty coves. Great blue herons seem to be everywhere. If you see one and have a camera, paddle quietly toward it and then just drift to get as close as possible.

After passing the large island along the eastern shore, you'll see numerous rock islands ahead. Some are tiny, with only tufts of grass in the cracks; others are large enough that saplings and shrubs have been able to take root, creating mini-habitats. Paddling up the narrow northwest arm, look for beaver activity. Tree stumps with conical ends are telltale signs that beavers downed them.

Heading back to the launch along the eastern shore, enjoy paddling through the passage between the island and the mainland. Here you'll find the greatest abundance of turtles basking on the many limbs sticking out of the water. As elsewhere on the reservoir, look into the clear water to see fish swimming around.

Hiking opportunities abound. A 13.8-mile loop trail around the lake connects Split Rock Loop North on the east side of the water with part of Four Birds Trail on the west side. You might see deer, wild turkeys, and black bears along the woodland route, as well as a plethora of songbirds. Trails are moderate but rocky. Bring appropriate footwear.

12 | Appalachian Mountain Club's Mohican Outdoor Center: Catfish Pond

Just steps from the Appalachian Trail in the Kittatinny Mountains, this rugged and scenic lake hosts abundant wildlife.

Location: Millbrook, NJ
Maps: DeLorme *New Jersey Atlas & Gazetteer,* Map 23; USGS Bushkill
Area: 31 acres
Time: 1 hour
Average Depth: 10-plus feet
Development: Remote
Access: No fees
Information: AMC Mohican Outdoor Center, 50 Camp Mohican Road, Blairstown, NJ 07825, 908-362-5670, outdoors.org
Camping: On-site; call the office for reservations, 908-362-5670, 9 A.M. to 5 P.M.
Take Note: Manually propelled boats only
Outfitter: On-site boat rentals

GETTING THERE

From I-80, take Exit 4C if coming from the west or 4-A-B-C if coming from the east. Merge onto NJ 94 toward Blairstown and drive 7.9 miles, then turn left onto Mohican Road and drive 3.2 miles (cumulative: 11.1 miles). Turn left onto Gaisler Road and drive 0.5 mile (11.6 miles), then turn right onto Camp Road and drive 0.6 mile (12.2 miles). Continue straight on Camp Mohican Road for 0.6 mile (12.8 miles) to the public parking lot on the left. Stop at the center on the left 0.1 mile (12.8 miles) before the parking lot if you wish to procure a camping site. Once at the parking lot, continue straight past the "Authorized Vehicles Only" sign, and drive 300 yards (0.15 mile) to the unloading area and launch on the left. (41° 02.211′ N, 74° 59.838′ W)

The single-lane road to the launch is very narrow. Only one car at a time can enter the road beyond the sign. Unload your equipment, drive back to the parking lot, and then return on foot to the launch. Allow plenty of extra time to get on the water if there is more than one car, because of the long walk from the parking lot.

TRIP 12: APPALACHIAN MOUNTAIN CLUB'S MOHICAN OUTDOOR CENTER: CATFISH POND

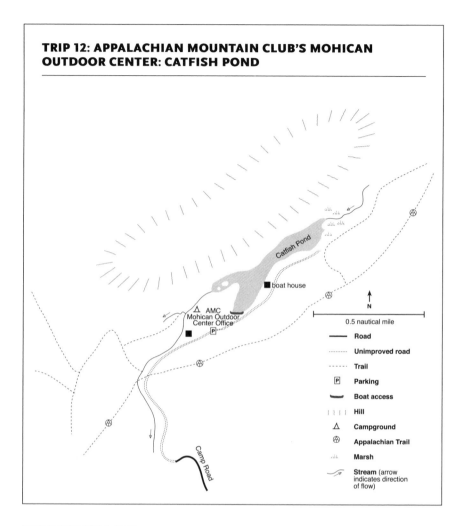

WHAT YOU'LL SEE

Catfish Pond sits atop the Kittatinny Mountain ridge within the 15,000-acre Delaware Water Gap National Recreation Area at AMC's Mohican Outdoor Center. Camping, hiking, and boating are offered at the center in this rugged and pristine environment, as well as boat rentals and lodging. Across from the launch, the mountains rise 120 to 150 feet above the pond and quite sharply at the eastern end. Rock faces and cliffs peek here and there between the trees, adding texture to the landscape. The forest is primarily hardwoods, with conifers along the shore and in small pockets on the mountain. At the northeast end of the pond, where the mountains rise quite steeply, coniferous trees are more prevalent.

Catfish Pond provides a quick dip for AT thru-hikers. Photo by Kathy Kenley.

Paddle left from the launch to explore the end of the cove where ducks forage among waterlilies and shallow grasses. Continue around the shoreline counterclockwise, dipping your paddle quietly as you near the tip of the peninsula, where you might spot a great blue heron. Around the peninsula is a narrower cove with three small islands just off the southern shore. Paddle softly between the islands and the shore to get a glimpse of birds and land mammals seeking refuge in this more secluded location. As you travel along the north side, look up to find raptors flying overhead while you enjoy the scenic mountains and shoreline.

Saplings interspersed with scrub-shrub mark the point where a small creek enters the pond at the northern end. You can't paddle up the creek any distance, but nudge the nose of your boat into a few places to get close-up views of the different vegetation and wildflowers growing in that marshy area. Paddling back along the south shore, perhaps just sit, look, and listen for a minute to the sounds and sights that surround you. Around the bend you'll find a small swimming beach, which might make a refreshing stop on a hot day. About a tenth of a mile beyond is the center's boat rental concession. Past that is one of the center's rustic lodges, with a picturesque deck overlooking the water. Enjoy paddling the rest of the way to the launch.

Hikers will be thrilled with the number and diversity of trails here, the most notable of which is the Appalachian Trail. Options range from 2.4 to 7.5 miles, and most are rated moderate. Trails traverse over footbridges and past small waterfalls, old mines, and swamp areas. On many of the trails, visitors see spectacular views of Catfish Pond, Lower Yards Creek Reservoir, and mountains. The terrain is rugged and can be wet in swamp areas, so bring appropriate footwear. Stop at the center for detailed trail maps and to check out the activities and workshops offered.

13 | Wawayanda Lake

Enjoy islands and beautiful scenery while exploring the interesting, highly irregular shoreline of this mountain lake.

Location: Vernon Township, NJ
Maps: DeLorme *New Jersey Atlas & Gazetteer,* Map 20; USGS Wawayanda; New Jersey Department of Environmental Protection: state.nj.us
Area: 255 acres
Time: 2.5 to 3 hours
Average Depth: 30 feet
Development: Remote
Access: Park admission fee
Information: Wawayanda State Park, 885 Warwick Turnpike, Hewitt, NJ 07421, 973-853-4462, state.nj.us
Camping: On-site group camping is available for seven to fifteen people; call the park office for reservations (see Appendix A)
Take Note: Electric motorboats only
Outfitter: On-site canoes, rowboats, and paddleboats are available to rent; call 973-853-4462

GETTING THERE
To the visitor center: Drive south 0.2 mile on NJ 23 from NJ 171 to the Clinton Road exit. Drive north on Clinton Road about 7 miles (cumulative: 7.2 miles) until you come to the T junction at CR 513 (Warwick Turnpike). Turn left onto

TRIP 13: WAWAYANDA LAKE

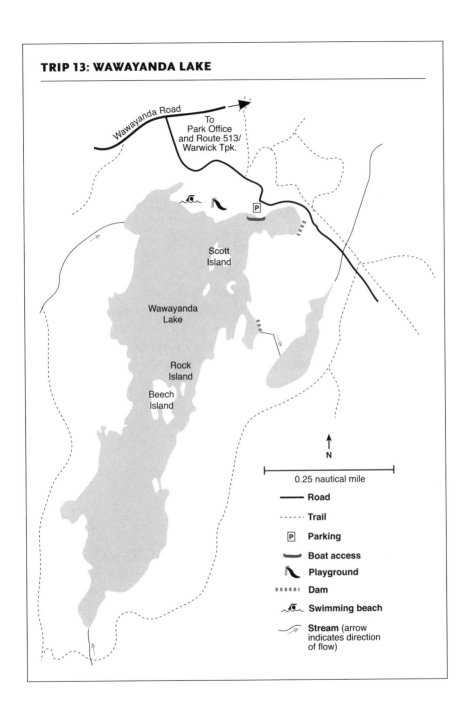

CR 513 and drive 2.3 miles (9.5 miles) to the park entrance on the left. Stop at the visitor center to pick up a map and other useful pamphlets. (41° 11.870′ N, 74° 23.845′ W)

To the boat launch: From the visitor center, continue 1.9 miles (11.4 miles) to the turnoff for the recreation area. The road to the boat launch will be on the left. There's a nice launch for cartop boats only. (41° 11.289′ N, 74° 25.573′ W)

WHAT YOU'LL SEE

Nestled in the vast mountains of Wawayanda State Park, this large lake offers hours of exciting paddling. Picnic grounds, a sandy bathing beach, and a playground are located at the park's recreation area on the north end of Wawayanda Lake. Boat rentals and launches are also on the north end of the lake, but they're separated from the recreation area.

Numerous deep coves and half a dozen islands provide plenty of adventurous exploring and opportunities for observing wildlife. The two largest islands have a few spots to land for lunch or a break. There are other scattered places to stop, mostly on the eastern shoreline. Many boaters do not venture past the large island in the middle of the lake, making the southern end a more peaceful experience.

A paddler heads out on a quiet afternoon to explore the lake. Photo by Kathy Kenley.

Wawayanda Lake is a good place to try your luck at fishing. Depths range from just a few feet close to shore to about 90 feet in the center of the northern half. Trout, largemouth bass, catfish, yellow perch, and large sunfish swim beneath the surface, and any of them would taste delicious cooked over a campfire at day's end. Bowfins can also be found here. Along with gars and sturgeons, these uncommon fish are among the few freshwater fish that existed at the same time as the dinosaurs.

Around the lake, wood and bog turtles inhabit swampy areas and sun themselves on logs at the water's edge. Raccoons, opossums, deer, rabbits, black bears, and skunks might be seen close to the water, along with coyotes and foxes. Throughout the park, birdlife is bountiful. Look for red-shouldered hawks, great blue herons, vultures, eagles, warblers, orioles, and various songbirds. Start out early in the morning or late in the afternoon for the most peaceful paddling. Those are also the best times to enjoy bird activity and look for other wildlife. Examine the long, shallow inlets, and you might be lucky enough to see a river otter.

Paddle left after leaving the launch to explore the first cove. Tall stands of wetland grasses on the east end support a variety of wrens. Return to the lake and start exploring, perhaps circling around those islands right in front of you. Continue paddling down the east shoreline, venturing in and out of coves and inlets until you reach Beech Island, which is the largest island in the middle of the lake. The smaller island off the northeast tip has plenty of passage room.

Head into the southern half of the lake and drink in the views while looking for river otters, kingfishers, hawks, and other wildlife. Hemlocks, pines, and diverse hardwood species create magnificent foliage displays in fall. On your return trip up the western shoreline, notice the many areas that rise sharply to a height of 15 to 20 feet, creating a different topography than the eastern shoreline. Birdlife is abundant around the stream inlet in the northwest corner of the lake, your last stop before returning to the launch.

Hiking and biking trails meander for more than 40 miles throughout 12,000 acres of Atlantic white cedar swamps and hardwood forests, not including a 19.6-mile stretch of the Appalachian Trail that runs along the western boundary of the park. Twenty marked trails, some designated hiking only, range from 0.4 to 6 miles in length, and from easy to difficult.

2 | PENNSYLVANIA

The Appalachian Highlands encompasses a wide swath of land that extends from Maine through Louisiana. It covers most of Pennsylvania, except for a narrow sliver of the Atlantic Coastal Plain along the southeast edge and a slice of the Central Lowlands along the northwest edge. It is further separated into three provinces: The Piedmont, or the rolling foothills of the Appalachian Mountains, borders the coastal plain in the southeast; the Ridge and Valley, with its steep-sided ridges and narrow valleys, lies west of the Piedmont, starting roughly from Chambersburg and continuing in an arc to Stroudsburg; and the Appalachian Plateau, where the topography starts to flatten, includes western and north-central Pennsylvania.

With such differences in geography, Pennsylvania offers a wide variety of scenic paddling. Bodies of water found in the lowland rolling hills, in wetlands, and tucked in the mountains provide a rich diversity of habitats and wildlife. The Appalachian Mountain Club plays an active role in protecting and promoting the Pennsylvania Highlands, including supporting the Highlands Conservation Act, created to protect the highest-valued conservation areas in the Mid-Atlantic Highlands of Pennsylvania, New Jersey, New York, and Connecticut. The act was passed in 2004, with funding for land conservation projects made available through the Federal Land and Water Conservation Fund. In 2014, Congress failed to reauthorize the Highlands Conservation Act. AMC supports legislation to reauthorize the program through 2021, and continues to raise awareness and support for its funding as well as funding for the Land and Water Conservation Fund more broadly.

The most densely populated part of eastern Pennsylvania falls along the Delaware River, around Philadelphia and northeast to Morrisville. Some mid-size to large cities, such as Harrisburg, Reading, and Allentown, are found along the major waterways of the Susquehanna and Schuylkill rivers. You don't have to travel far outside these areas to find lakes in rural and remote environments, due in part to the rugged landscape created by the Appalachian Mountains. Most Pennsylvania lakes and ponds have been dammed to some degree, increasing their holding capacity and acreage for recreational use, irrigation, or water storage to augment local reservoirs.

Within the rolling hills of the Piedmont, which occupies the land approximately east of I-81 south of Harrisburg and south of I-78 from Harrisburg to Easton, you will find numerous bodies of water, such as the Octoraro Reservoir and Hopewell Lake, tucked into valleys surrounded by rich farmlands, small suburban towns, or dense forests. In the Appalachian Highlands and Ridge and Valley provinces to the west and north of the Piedmont, the landscape grows more exaggerated, with higher mountains and zigzagging roads leading to lakes in remote places such as Beltzville State Park.

14 | Beltzville Lake

Enjoy steeply wooded cliffs, rock faces, crystal clear water, a hike to a waterfall, and abundant wildlife at this lake.

Location: Lehighton, PA
Maps: Pennsylvania Department of Conservation and Natural Resources: dcnr.state.pa.us
Area: 949 acres
Time: 4 to 4.5 hours
Average Depth: 40 feet
Development: Rural
Access: No fees

TRIP 14: BELTZVILLE LAKE

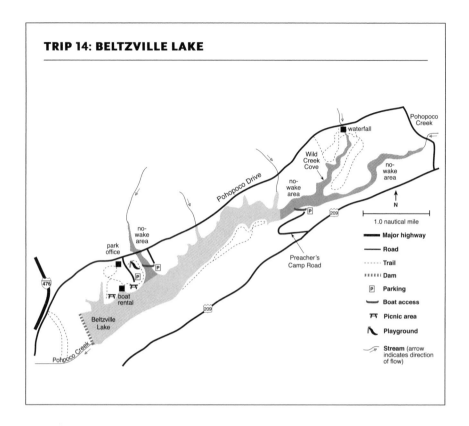

Information: Beltzville State Park, 2950 Pohopoco Drive, Lehighton, PA 18235, 610-377-0045, dcnr.state.pa.us

Camping: Mauch Chunk State Park, 20 minutes west; Don Laine Family Campground, 10 minutes east (see Appendix A)

Take Note: There are two no-wake zones, and no limit to the horsepower of motorboats, although they can only go up to 45 miles per hour. Be wary of winds. Pennsylvania boating regulations apply (see Appendix D).

Outfitter: On-site rentals include kayaks, paddleboats, rowboats, and small motorboats; call 610-377-1108

GETTING THERE

To the park office: From the intersection of US 209 and Harrity Road (the Pennsylvania Turnpike Northeast Extension overpass is next to and nearly above this intersection), drive north on Harrity Road for 0.1 mile. Turn right onto Pohopoco Drive and go 2.1 miles (cumulative: 2.2 miles) to the entrance road and park office on the right. (40° 51.832′ N, 75° 37.630′ W)

To Preacher's Camp boat ramp: From the intersection of US 209 and the Pennsylvania Turnpike Northeast Extension, drive 5.7 miles north on US 209 to Preacher's Camp Road. Make a very sharp left onto Preacher's Camp Road and drive 1 mile (cumulative: 6.7 miles) to the launch entrance on the left. (40° 52.371′ N, 75° 34.439′ W)

WHAT YOU'LL SEE

This long, narrow 949-acre lake sits within a 3,000-acre state park and offers a perfect setting for paddling. Motorboats are limited to a maximum speed of 45 MPH, which can produce quite a wake, but about 12 of the nearly 20 miles of shoreline lie within a strictly enforced "no-wake zone."

From the quiet boat launch at the end of Preacher's Camp Road within the no-wake zone, you can paddle left (west) for 0.5 mile before the zone ends at the beginning of the first long and narrow cove on the north side. Many paddlers simply head northeast across the water to enter Wild Creek Cove, the long arm of the lake. The cove is only a mile long, but it takes some time to paddle to the northeast tip as you look at wildlife, investigate the thinly layered rocks and numerous rock faces, and make *wow* sounds around every corner at the beautiful steep, wooded cliffs. Along the journey, particularly in the upper reaches, peer into the water at the huge boulders, some of which come within 2 to 3 feet of the surface. The water is so clear that you can sometimes see 20 feet down.

The best treat is the waterfall at the end. At the very tip of the arm, look for gravel bars on your right where Wild Creek enters the lake. You'll see a wooden bridge ahead where Falls Trail crosses the creek about 50 feet north of the gravel bars. The size of the bars will depend on water levels, but there's always room for at least six to eight boats. A bonus: because there are shallow gravel areas and sunken tree trunks along the last 100 feet or so, even small motorboats don't make it up this far—only canoes and kayaks. Exit your boat, grab your lunch, and look for a small trail that leads to the east side of the bridge and continues

A paddler beaches at Wild Creek Cove for a short hike. Photo by Kathy Kenley.

to the waterfall about 150 feet farther north. The path meanders through a primarily pine and hemlock forest with a needle-strewn understory and lots of mountain laurel. A huge boulder on the side of the waterfall offers a terrific spot to have lunch to the music of water cascading over rocks. It's not a large waterfall, perhaps only about 10 feet high, but the setting is gorgeous, and the walk through the shady forest is a welcome respite on a hot day.

After lunch, head out of Wild Creek Cove and turn left to enter Pohopoco Creek Cove on the southeast side of the lake. This cove is 2 miles long from its entrance to the Trachsville Hill bridge. Picturesque rock faces along the steep sides of the lake present numerous photo opportunities. If you have a fishing rod, cast your line for striped bass, large- and smallmouth bass, muskellunge, trout, walleye, perch, and panfish. Beyond the bridge, the right side of the creek hosts a patch of cattails, pickerelweed, and waterlilies where you'll likely find Canada geese and assorted ducks. If water levels are low, a gravel bar may extend too far across the surface to allow easy passage farther upstream into Pohopoco Creek.

Seven trails, ranging from 0.4 to 2.5 miles in length for a total of 15 miles, are located around the lake. Fossil hunters can search for Devonian period brachiopods, clams, bryozoans, crinoids, coral, cephalopods, snails, and trilobites, which have all been found in the park. There is also a historical covered bridge that was built in 1841 by local craftsman Jacob Buck. It was first used by horse and buggy traffic and later became a single-lane road. Today, it is for pedestrians only.

15 | Lake Nockamixon

Look for ospreys and other waterfowl as you enjoy views of the mountains and a natural rock waterfall from this beautiful lake.

Location: Quakertown, PA
Maps: DeLorme Atlas & Gazetteer *Pennsylvania*, Map 82; Pennsylvania Department of Conservation and Natural Resources: dcnr.state.pa.us
Area: 1,450 acres
Time: 4 to 4.5 hours
Average Depth: 40 feet
Development: Rural

TRIP 15: LAKE NOCKAMIXON

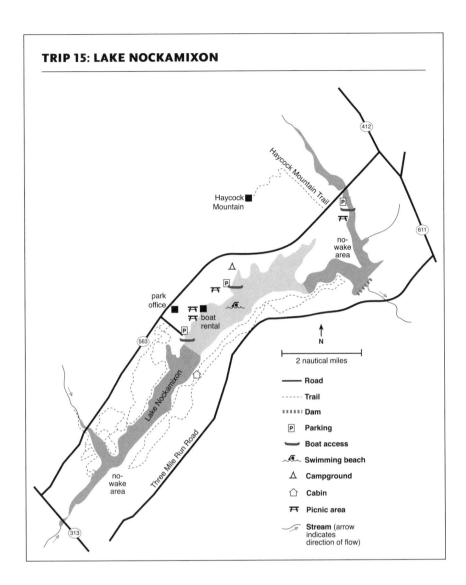

Access: No fees

Information: Nockamixon State Park, 1542 Mountain View Drive, Quakertown, PA 18951, 215-529-7300, dcnr.state.pa.us

Camping: Ten cabins are available on-site. To make a reservation, call the park office or go to visitPAparks.com. Colonial Woods Family Camping Resort is 10 minutes north, and Tohickon Family Campground is 10 minutes west (see Appendix A).

Take Note: Motorboats 20 horsepower except in the no-wake zones. Be aware of winds. Pennsylvania boating regulations apply (see Appendix D).

Outfitter: On-site rentals include motorboats, pontoons, kayaks, stand-up paddleboards, pedal boats, and rowboats; call 215-538-1340 or go to nockamixonboatrental.com

GETTING THERE

To the park office: From the intersection of PA 563 (Mountain View Drive) and PA 313 (Dublin Pike), take PA 563 north. Drive 3.5 miles to the park office on the right. (40° 27.787′ N, 75° 14.526′ W)

To the fishing pier launch: From the intersection of PA 563 (Mountain View Drive) and PA 313 (Dublin Pike), take PA 563 north. Drive 3.3 miles to Deerwood Lane on the right, turn right, and drive 0.5 mile (cumulative: 3.8 miles) to the parking lot at the fishing pier. (40° 27.391′ N, 75° 14.224′ W)

To Haycock Boat Ramp: Follow the directions to the park office. Pass the office and continue driving 3.3 miles to the entrance for Haycock Boat Ramp on the right. (40° 29.368′ N, 75° 11.640′ W)

WHAT YOU'LL SEE

Set in the beautiful rolling hills and farmland of northern Bucks County, the 15,283-acre Nockamixon State Park houses a 1,450-acre lake fed by three major streams and a number of smaller streams. A 2-mile swath of largely uninhabited forested hills borders the north side of the park, including Maycock and Haycock mountains on the northwest corner and Rock Hill off the southwestern tip, all of which also rise more than 400 feet above the lake's surface. The name Nockamixon comes from the Native American phrase *nocha-miska-ing,* which means "at the place of soft soil."

Of the lake's approximately 24 miles of shoreline, about 13.5 miles lie within no-wake zones. Off-season and during the week, the rest of the lake is quiet enough that you can explore it peacefully. The park's recreational day-use area, centrally located on the north side, is set back from the lake behind a thick cover of trees, away from the no-wake zones. It sports a large swimming pool and most of the designated picnic sites. A large marina sits on the eastern edge.

Haycock Boat Ramp is within the lake's northeast no-wake zone. Lakeside picnic tables under cool pine trees offer a lovely dining setting. From the launch, paddle left and head under the PA 563 bridge. You'll have road noise for a while but will soon be beyond it. Explore the nooks, crannies, and shallow coves on both sides of the lake. It gets shallow, with gravel bars and areas of lily pads, as you near where Haycock Creek enters, but most of the time there's a water path to the creek's entrance. You can't paddle up far at all, but it's nice to see one of

Lake Nockamixon's 24 miles of shoreline provide ample exploring. Photo by Kathy Kenley.

the input streams. Turn around, paddle back underneath the bridge, and head down the east (left) side where there are two large, narrow coves, the first of which has a small feeder stream at its tip. After exploring the coves, paddle out of the second one and head southwest along the shore and rock dam. Haycock Mountain dominates the landscape to the north.

On the far side of the dam, a solid line of white buoys slightly above the surface warns of the spillway 170 feet beyond. Look for ospreys here, hunting for fish both in the lake and at the small pond at the bottom of the spillway. If water levels are high, you will hear the magnificent rush of water cascading over the natural stone steps of the 300-foot-wide spillway. You can canvass the spillway from a viewing area off South Park Road after your paddle. You may see many anglers fishing on the water and from the shore; the lake is highly noted for its largemouth bass population. On the far end of the spillway buoys, there's a bit of a beach and then another about 0.15 mile farther where you can land and take a break to enjoy the scenery, watching ospreys, hawks, and vultures fly and fish jump. Deer and rabbits are often spotted along the shores, as well as kingfishers, warblers, and a variety of other songbirds.

Continue paddling and round the point, where you'll have another 0.8 mile before the no-wake zone ends at the tip of the peninsula to your right. You'll be able to see the park's marina a mile ahead of you. If boat traffic is low, consider rounding the peninsula and paddling into the half-mile-long stretch of the lake. The shallow area at the end is usually filled with waterfowl, frogs, butterflies, darners, and possibly some water snakes. On windy days, the center of the lake can whip up quite a chop. Take heed of the wind direction before you decide to venture out.

To launch into the other no-wake zone, drive to the fishing pier on Deerwood Lane, south of the main recreation area. Turn right just before the road heads to the pier, and there will be a grass-and-dirt launch immediately to your left. This is the other place where a lot of paddlers launch. You'll have 2 miles of paddling south, not counting all the coves, before reaching the end of the no-wake zone. A beautiful large cove, a little more than a quarter-mile long, will be on your right, 0.3 mile south of the launch on the same side. This is where another small feeder stream enters the lake. You might see raccoons, skunks, rabbits, and deer along this quieter section of the lake.

Once you come to a short peninsula where the lake narrows and you see a large inn a few hundred yards across the water, you're at the end of the no-wake zone. If conditions and boat traffic permit, paddle around the peninsula and into the long cove where Tohickon Creek enters the lake.

Hiking trails are between 1.2 and 5.6 miles and range from easy to more difficult. There is a paved 2-mile bicycle trail, as well as 10 miles of mountain-bike trails for the more adventurous. The park offers guided walks, environmental education, and interpretive programs.

SNOWY EGRET

"Oh, dem golden slippers": Part of the unofficial theme song of the Philadelphia's Mummers Parade, these words are heard each New Year's Day by those living in the Philadelphia area, but they also describe one of the most conspicuous features of the snowy egret, its bright yellow toes. Casual onlookers sometimes confuse the snowy egret with the great egret, another member of the family *Ardeidae* with stark white feathers, black legs, and a long, slender neck. But you call tell them apart by the great egret's yellow beak and black toes; the snowy egret has a black beak and yellow toes. Just remember the "golden slippers."

Snowy egrets typically frequent wetland environments, such as salt and brackish marshes, ponds, and swamps within the Coastal Plain. While it's not unusual to spot a solitary egret, they are more often found in small colonies, foraging for food. They will sometimes claim separate feeding territories, particularly during mating season. If you hear a lot of low croaking and see some feathers rustling, chances are an egret felt its territory infringed upon.

It's not all competition, all the time: Commensal feeding, in which one species gives an advantage to another, is prevalent between snowy egrets and ibis or herons. Most egrets and herons forage in a "stalk and strike" method, but snowy egrets also shuffle their feet in water to stir up aquatic invertebrates, a favorite meal. In the process, small creatures are sent scurrying, available to be picked up by other birds foraging within a few feet. Secondary food sources include small fish, reptiles, and insects.

Avid birders refer to snowy egrets as "snegs" and great egrets as "gregs," in a sort of shorthand. Members of *Ardeidae* have several things in common: long necks that fold into an "S" shape in flight, spear-like bills, and legs that trail when flying. Adult snowy egrets have shaggy plumes on their heads, necks, and backs, more clearly visible when not in flight—almost like they forgot to comb their hair.

Those head plumes, which develop during breeding season, led to a population plunge during the late nineteenth and early twentieth centuries. Large colonies of snowy, red, and great egrets were killed for the ornamental breeding feathers, which were popular decoration in America and Europe for women's hats. The feathers were also highly sought for East Asian ceremonial dress. In 1901, the National Audubon Society sponsored a U.S. law prohibiting the killing of any bird except game birds, but in the Florida Everglades, home to large breeding colonies of egrets, a labyrinth of narrow channels filled with mosquitoes and alligators made the law difficult to enforce. As a result, egret hunters continued to make money, and species counts dwindled. In 1903, plumes sold for $32 an ounce, slightly more than the price of gold at the time.

Snowy egret populations have rebounded in recent years, and the birds are no longer on the endangered watch list. They can be found throughout the United States in salt marshes, estuaries, and shallow bays.

16 | Blue Marsh Lake

Enjoy hours of paddling along wooded hillsides with scenic views and abundant opportunities for wildlife watching.

Location: Leesport, PA
Maps: DeLorme Atlas & Gazetteer *Pennsylvania*, Map 80; USGS Bernville; U.S. Army Corps of Engineers: www.nap.usace.army.mil
Area: 1,147 acres
Time: 2 hours or more
Average Depth: 25 feet
Development: Rural
Access: No fees
Information: Blue Marsh Lake, 1268 Palisades Drive, Leesport, PA 19533, 610-376-6337, www.nap.usace.army.mil
Camping: Eagle's Peak RV Park & Campground is 20 minutes southwest, and Appalachian RV Resort is 25 minutes northwest (see Appendix A)
Outfitters: Blue Marsh Rentals, 5097 Bernville Road, Bernville, PA 19506, 610-488-5540, bluemarshoutdoors.com
Take Note: There is no limit on motorboat horsepower except in the no-wake zones; both Sheidy and Pleasant Valley boat launches are within the no-wake zones. Pennsylvania boating regulations apply (see Appendix D).

GETTING THERE

To the visitor center: From PA 222, take the exit for Spring Ridge Drive. Turn left onto Spring Ridge and drive 0.1 mile, then turn right onto Papermill Road and drive 0.2 mile (cumulative: 0.3 mile). Turn right to stay on Papermill Road and drive 0.2 mile (0.5 mile), then turn left to stay on Papermill Road and drive 1.1 miles (1.6 miles). Turn right at Rebers Bridge Road and drive 0.6 mile (2.2 miles) to Palisades Drive, then turn left and drive 1.3 miles (3.5 miles) to the entrance to the visitor center on the left. (40° 22.852′ N, 76° 01.570′ W)

To Sheidy boat launch: From PA 222, take the exit for PA 183 (Bernville Road). Turn left on Bernville Road and drive 6.1 miles to the parking area and boat launch on the left. (40° 24.774′ N, 76° 05.128′ W)

To Pleasant Valley boat launch: From PA 222, take the exit for PA 183 (Bernville Road). Turn left on Bernville Road and drive 4.5 miles to the parking area and boat launch on the right. The turnoff for the launch is on the right

TRIP 16: BLUE MARSH LAKE

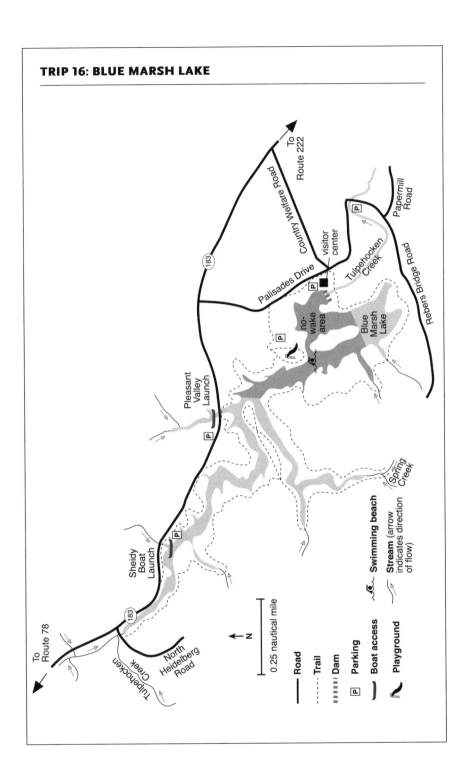

immediately after crossing a 150-foot bridge that spans one of the lake's small arms. (40° 24.152′ N, 76° 03.679′ W)

WHAT YOU'LL SEE

This 1,147-acre serpentine lake lies within 6,100 acres of Pennsylvania Fish & Boat Commission property and additional state game lands acreage. Facilities include the Dry Brooks Day Use Area with swimming beach, showers, food concession, and picnic areas. Of the 35 miles of shoreline, about 20 miles are within the northern no-wake zone, which fortunately is also the prettiest and most interesting part of the lake. If you want to fish, bring appropriate bait for trout, large- and smallmouth bass, striped bass hybrid, muskies, walleye, crappie, perch, catfish, carp, and sunfish.

Sheidy Launch and North

This leg is 4 miles round-trip to Robeson Road bridge and 7 miles round-trip if you paddle north of the bridge and into the left creek up to the old broken dam. From the launch, paddle north along the east (launch) side a short way to an

Paddlers head out to explore a narrow passage between the mainland (right) and the island (left). Photo by Kathy Kenley.

inlet, where you can paddle under two bridges to explore that little hideaway. Continuing north, you'll pass a point with a nice island at the tip; waterfowl usually hang out between the island and the point. From there, you will have varying amounts of road noise from PA 183 in summer, especially on weekends. Feast your eyes on the high wooded hills to your left to forget about the cars. Once at the tip, where Robesonia Road crosses the lake, PA 183 veers away. After you pass under the bridge, you can paddle up the right (east) fork, Little Northkill Creek, for about 0.3 mile until it gets too shallow and rocky.

Return and enter the left (west) fork, Tulpehocken Creek, where egrets and herons share the water with ducks and geese. Low shrubs and a few trees make this is a good habitat for the brilliant-blue indigo bunting. Depending on the water conditions, you can usually paddle upriver a half-mile or more. You'll find lots of wildlife here, including deer, rabbits, waterfowl, and songbirds. As you return along the densely wooded west shore to the launch area, watch for cardinals, wrens, kingfishers, flickers, woodpeckers, towhees, and kingbirds.

Sheidy Launch to Pleasant Valley

This leg is 6 miles round-trip and 7.5 miles round-trip if you include the arm across from the launch. Paddle south, investigating coves along the way and admiring the steep, wooded hillside on your right (west). On the other side of Old Church Road bridge, ramble around numerous coves and shallow inlets on the highly serpentine waterway. It's so squiggly, you may think you're in a garden maze—but on water. If you see a bird with a forked tail and boomerang-shaped wings that flies with quick, flicking actions, that's a swift. The next wide inlet leads off to your left (north) and passes under a bridge where Licking Creek enters the lake. Turn around here and paddle the other side of the lake back to the launch. Right before the launch, a half-mile arm is tucked between hills of forests and farmland where paddlers often see deer, rabbits, and groundhogs.

Pleasant Valley and South

This leg is 7 miles round-trip and 8.5 miles round-trip if you paddle up the Licking Creek arm. Paddle left from the launch to travel up the arm where Licking Creek enters. Lots of small coves and inlets provide ample opportunity to spot numerous species of birds, including waterfowl, hawks, and kestrels. When you pass under the bridge, stay left and paddle around the point until you see the inlet across the lake. Head directly for the inlet: the no-wake zone is somewhat nebulous in the center of the lake here, but the entire inlet is a no-wake zone. Enter the inlet, where the scenery and serenity are great. After about 1.5 miles, you'll come to a fork. The right side is a little less than 1 mile round-trip, with wooded hills on the north side and terraced farmland on the south. Watch for hawks and kestrels that fly over the farmland looking for small rodents. The left side is about 1.8 miles round-trip, mostly dense woodlands with some farmland. There are two small islands to play around that usually have waterfowl. Keep left as the route narrows to stay in the deeper channel and you can paddle up the creek about 250 yards if water levels are good. Then turn around and head back to the launch.

Trails include a 30-mile multiuse trail that circles the lake, and five additional trails totaling 7.5 miles in length. The Dry Brooks Day Use Area has a beach, numerous first-come-first-served picnic tables and grills, a concession stand, and public restrooms.

17 | Lake Luxembourg: Core Creek Park

Visit this popular lake, part of a dammed creek, on weekdays and off-hours to avoid the biggest crowds.

Location: Newtown, PA
Maps: DeLorme Atlas & Gazetteer *Pennsylvania*, Map 82; USGS Langhorne; Bucks County Department of Parks and Recreation: buckscounty.org
Area: 166 acres
Time: 2 to 3 hours
Average Depth: 10 feet
Development: Suburban
Access: Launch fee
Information: Core Creek Park, Bucks County Department of Parks and Recreation, 901 Bridgetown Pike, Langhorne, PA 19047, 215-757-0571, buckscounty.org
Take Note: Electric motorboats allowed. Bucks County boat permit required. Pennsylvania boating regulations apply (see Appendix D).
Outfitter: On-site rentals include rowboats, canoes, paddleboats, kayaks, and aquacycles; call 215-757-1225

TRIP 17: LAKE LUXEMBOURG: CORE CREEK PARK

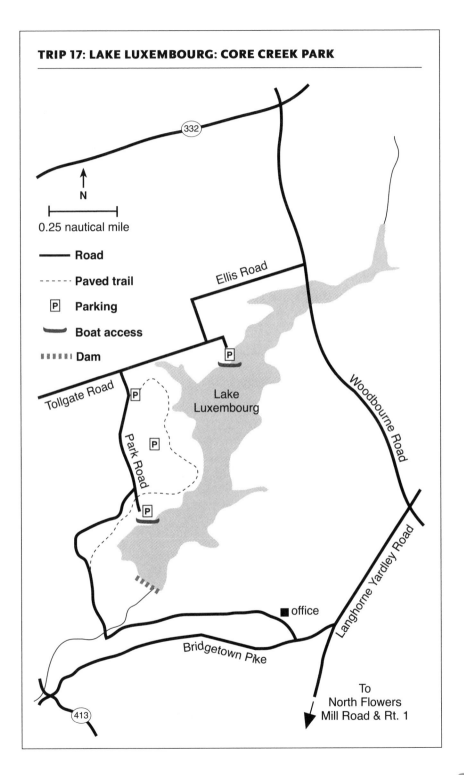

N

0.25 nautical mile

—— Road

----- Paved trail

P   Parking

⌣   Boat access

⫽⫽⫽⫽ Dam

332

Ellis Road

Tollgate Road

Park Road

Lake Luxembourg

Woodbourne Road

Langhorne Yardley Road

■ office

Bridgetown Pike

413

To
North Flowers
Mill Road & Rt. 1

GETTING THERE

To the park office and the south launch: From US 1 north in Langhorne, take Exit 213 south toward Langhorne. At the end of the ramp, continue straight on North Flowers Mill Road and drive 0.5 mile. Turn right on Winchester Avenue and drive 0.6 mile (cumulative: 1.1 miles). (*Note*: The road becomes Langhorne Yardley Road after the railroad tracks.) Turn left on Bridgetown Pike and drive 0.2 mile (1.3 miles) to Park Road on the right, the entrance to the park. Turn right on Park Road and drive 0.1 mile (1.4 miles) to the park office. If you do not stop at the park office, continue on Park Road 1.4 miles (2.8 miles), then turn right and drive to the boat launch straight ahead. (40° 11.997′ N, 74° 55.152′ W)

From US 1 South in Langhorne: Take Exit 213 south toward Langhorne and stay right to turn onto East Maple Avenue. Drive 0.1 mile and turn right on North Flowers Mill Road. Continue as above, turning right on Winchester Avenue.

To the quieter and more scenic north launch: From US 1 north or south in Langhorne, take Exit 213 south toward Langhorne. From the north, at the end of the exit ramp, continue straight on North Flowers Mill Road. From the south, stay right to turn onto East Maple Avenue and drive 0.1 mile

An angler prepares his kayak for a day of fishing on Core Creek. Photo by Kathy Kenley.

before turning right on North Flowers Mill Road. After 0.5 mile (cumulative: 0.6 mile), turn right on Winchester Avenue and drive 1.6 miles (2.2 miles). (*Note*: The road becomes Langhorne Yardley Road after you cross over the railroad tracks.) Turn left on Woodbourne Road and drive 1 mile (3.2 miles). Turn left on Ellis Road and drive 0.4 mile (3.6 miles), then turn left on Fulling Mill Road and drive 0.2 mile (3.8 miles) to the T intersection. Turn left onto an unimproved road, make an immediate right, and drive to the launch. (40° 12.538′ N, 74° 54.823′ W)

WHAT YOU'LL SEE

Lake Luxembourg is located in the 1,200-acre Core Creek Park, a county park within Bucks County, Pennsylvania. The 175-acre artificially constructed lake dams Core Creek, a tributary of Neshaminy Creek, which leads to the Delaware River. The park is the center of recreational activities for a large suburban area, so it can get crowded on weekends in summer. For a quiet paddle, arrive early or late in the day.

From the northwest launch, turn left and paddle northeast along the shore, which is lined with hardwood species such as maple, sycamore, oak, and willow. Continue under the Woodbourne Road bridge into the uppermost northeast corner of the lake. Shallow waters such as this usually attract waterfowl. Most of the lake's wildlife congregates here, including turtles, ducks, and geese. You can even paddle into Core Creek, which feeds into the lake, for more than a half-mile and enjoy the cool shade of the canopy. In times of drought, the creek can become quite shallow, so be careful you don't get stuck; otherwise your paddle may turn into a marathon. Return to the main part of the lake and venture down the eastern and southern shores lined with sugar maple, willow, beech, and oak. It is spectacular here in October when the trees are dressed in autumnal colors.

The southwest and western shorelines are open and have few trees. Here you'll find the main launch and a concrete boat ramp suitable for motorboats, plus open group picnic areas. Fishing is good here, so you may see many anglers along the banks, trying for bass, catfish, sunfish, and white perch. (A man fishing from a kayak told me that fishing is better in the center of the lake than along the edges.) You'll occasionally see members of Temple University's rowing team in their long, skinny boats, called shells, practicing on the lake. Don't get too close; the oars stick out quite far from the boats.

The park has a picnic area and miles of recreational trails for hiking, horseback riding, walking, and biking. Additional amenities include playgrounds, ball fields, tennis courts, a nature area, and an off-leash dog park.

18 | Marsh Creek Reservoir

Enjoy a paddle surrounded by hills and hardwood forests.

Location: Downingtown, PA
Maps: DeLorme Atlas & Gazetteer *Pennsylvania*, Map 81; USGS Downingtown
Area: 535 acres
Time: 3.5 to 4 hours
Average Depth: 15 feet
Development: Suburban
Access: No fees
Information: Marsh Creek State Park, 675 Park Road, Downingtown, PA 19335, 610-458-5119, dcnr.pa.gov
Camping: Brandywine Creek Campground, 10 minutes west (see Appendix A)
Outfitters: On-site rentals include rowboats, canoes, kayaks, paddleboards, and sailboats; call 610-458-5040
Take Note: Electric motorboats only. Be aware of winds. Pennsylvania boating regulations apply (see Appendix D).

GETTING THERE

To the park office and main (east) launch: Take Exit 312 off I-76 to PA 100 north toward Pottstown. Drive 2 miles and turn left onto Park Road (the road is Station Boulevard on your right), then drive 2 miles (cumulative: 4 miles) to the parking lot at the marina. The park office is on your left a few hundred feet before the parking lot. Parking is available for about 100 cars. (40° 03.980′ N, 75° 43.258′ W)

To the west launch: Take Exit 312 off I-76 to PA 100 north toward Pottstown. Drive 2 miles and turn left onto Park Road (the road is Station Boulevard on the right), then drive 0.1 mile (cumulative: 2.1 miles). Turn right on Little Conestoga Road and drive 2.6 miles (4.7 miles), then turn left to stay on Little Conestoga Road and drive 0.4 mile (5.1 miles). Continue straight on Marshall Road for 0.7 mile (5.8 miles), and then turn left on PA 282 (Creek Road) and drive 1.6 miles (7.4 miles). Turn left on Lyndell Road and drive 0.9 mile to the launch (8.3 miles). (40° 03.893′ N, 75° 43.762′ W)

TRIP 18: MARSH CREEK RESERVOIR

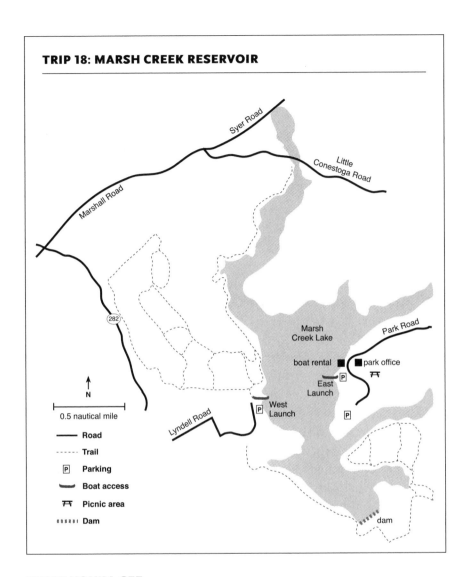

Marsh Creek Lake

boat rental ■ ■ park office

East Launch

West Launch

Park Road

Syer Road

Little Conestoga Road

Marshall Road

Lyndell Road

282

N

0.5 nautical mile

— Road

----- Trail

P Parking

⌣ Boat access

⛱ Picnic area

▮▮▮ Dam

dam

WHAT YOU'LL SEE

Marsh Creek State Park is composed of 1,705 acres of woods and fields and Marsh Creek Reservoir, a 535-acre lake frequented by paddlers throughout the year. In summer, it is also popular for windsurfing and sailing. The lake was created in the early 1970s when the small farming community of Milford Mills was vacated and a dam was built to flood the valley. Yes, under those deep waters are the remains of a town. On the southwest shoreline, you can still see remnants of an old road that went into the town. It may appear to be simply a dirt road leading to the water, but it actually continues beneath the surface.

Marsh Creek Lake is very popular with locals and visitors alike. Photo by Kathy Kenley.

From the main launch, head across the lake to the north arm and pass under the Little Conestoga Road bridge into the shallows adjacent to the Pennsylvania Turnpike. Amazingly enough, you won't hear as much road noise as you might think, especially if you focus on observing wildlife. Because much of this section has abundant aquatic vegetation, it's perfect for various ducks as well as wading birds and snapping turtles—huge ones big enough to chomp off half your paddle blade. Lots of sunken logs and water plants create an ideal environment for fish fry (young fish).

If water levels are high enough, paddle to the northwest corner, where you can go under the double-arched stone Styer Road bridge and enter Marsh Creek. The streambed gets rocky and you'll find some current. You can't travel far upstream, but it is a neat side venture in late spring and early summer while the waters are high. By mid-July, that corner may become so weed-choked that you can't paddle beyond the Little Conestoga Road bridge.

Return to the main lake and head south along the western shoreline, winding your way to the dam while scanning the skies for ospreys, which are frequent visitors here. Past the dam, the land rises more steeply. The first arm is short and usually chock-full of waterfowl and wading birds. Gaze into the water next to your boat and notice the good visibility. Continue on to the long, narrow eastern arm, populated by painted turtles and wading birds. By late summer that arm becomes overrun with weeds, but the wildlife is still present.

Continue to paddle north along the shoreline back to the launch, enjoying the views and wooded hillside. That last leg, less than a half-mile, can be tough if the winds come up. Before heading out for the day, check the local weather.

The weedy, shallow areas in a couple of lake arms serve as fish hatcheries. If you like to fish, cast your line for largemouth bass, crappie, walleye, tiger muskellunge, and channel catfish. (*Note*: The reservoir is a designated "big bass" lake, which means that only bass 15 inches and greater may be kept.)

Marsh Creek State Park boasts six miles of trails. Hikes are usually moderate due to the hilly landscape, but they are well worth the effort, particularly on the paths that overlook the lake. Most of the trailheads are in the west launch parking lot. The park offers a wide variety of hands-on activities, guided walks, and environmental and educational programs.

19 | Susquehanna River: Conowingo Reservoir and Lake Aldred

Paddle through a wonderland of rock islands, see petroglyphs, and view abundant birdlife, including eagles and ospreys.

Location: Slab and Pequea, PA
Maps: DeLorme Atlas & Gazetteer *Pennsylvania*, Map 83; USGS Holtwood and Conowingo Dam; Susquehanna Gateway Heritage Area: susquehannawatertrail.org
Area: Conowingo Reservoir: 15,875 acres, but only about 10,000 acres are in Pennsylvania; Lake Aldred: 2,400 acres
Time: Conowingo Reservoir: 3 to 5 hours; Lake Aldred: 3 to 4 hours
Average Depth: Conowingo Reservoir: 15 feet; Lake Aldred: 20 feet
Development: Rural
Access: No fees
Information: Susquehanna River Water Trail, susquehannawatertrail.org; Conowingo Reservoir (managed by Exelon Corporation), Exelon Generation Headquarters, 300 Exelon Way, Kennett Square, PA 19348, 800-483-3220; Lake Aldred (managed by Pennsylvania Power and Light), Holtwood Environmental Preserve, 9 New Village Road, Holtwood, PA 17532, 800-354-8383

TRIP 19: SUSQUEHANNA RIVER: CONOWINGO RESERVOIR

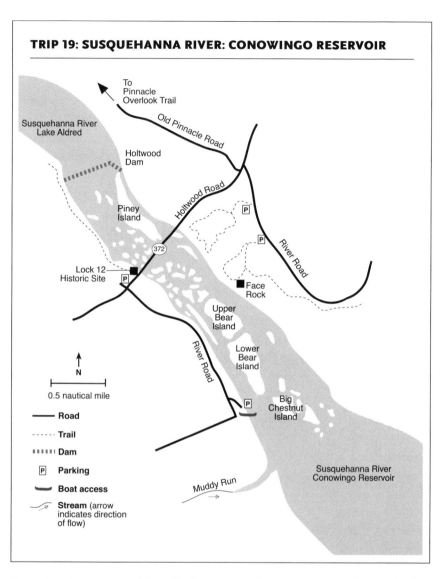

Camping: Tucquan Park Family Campground, 10 minutes southeast of Lake Aldred and 13 minutes north of Conowingo Reservoir (see Appendix A)

Take Note: There is no limit on motorboat horsepower. On Conowingo Reservoir, within the described trip, you'll only encounter motorboats for 0.5 mile, if that. Be aware of winds. The dam releases (with warning). Pennsylvania boating regulations apply (see Appendix D).

GETTING THERE

To Conowingo Reservoir: From PA 74, go north on East McKinley Road. After 2.5 miles, turn right onto Slab Road. Turn right onto River Road and drive 1.4 miles (cumulative: 3.9 miles) to the Muddy Creek boat launch entrance on the left. (39° 47.913′ N, 76° 18.362′ W)

To Lake Aldred: From US 30 just west of Lancaster, take the exit for PA 741 toward Rohrerstown/Millersville. Turn right onto PA 741 South (Rohrerstown Road) and drive 6.9 miles, then continue straight onto PA 324 (Marticville Road/Pequea Boulevard) and drive 8.3 miles (cumulative: 15.2 miles). Turn right onto PA 324 (Duck Hill Road) and drive 0.2 mile (15.4 miles), then turn left onto PA 324 (River Hill Road) and drive 0.5 mile (15.9 miles) to the parking lot on your right. (39° 53.282′ N, 76° 21.987′ W)

WHAT YOU'LL SEE

The Susquehanna River, at 464 miles, is the longest river on the East Coast. The Lower Section of the Susquehanna River Water Trail runs 53 miles in Pennsylvania, from Harrisburg through Lancaster and York counties. With 33 access points along this part of the river, there are endless opportunities to enjoy boating, fishing, birding, and hiking. Some of the boat routes require shuttle services to return you to your car. The two trips described here allow you to make a round-trip and paddle back to your launch site.

Conowingo Reservoir and Lake Aldred are dammed sections of the Susquehanna River. Lake Aldred is bordered by Safe Harbor Dam on the north and Holtwood Dam on the south; Conowingo Reservoir is bordered by Holtwood Dam on the north and Conowingo Dam on the south (in Maryland). These dammed sections are called "lakes" or "reservoirs" because they're generally quiet, except when there's been heavy rainfall that causes the waters to run fast—or if there's a dam release (rare).

Fishing is bountiful, with anglers commonly catching large- and smallmouth bass, northern pike, walleye, muskellunge and tiger muskellunge, pickerel, striped bass, shad, herring, sunfish, crappies, carp, catfish, and yellow perch. On the river, you can't help but stare in awe at the gorge the water has carved over millions of years. Cliffs rising 300 to 400 feet, too steep for residences, are covered with hardwood and conifer forests.

Conowingo Reservoir

Conowingo Reservoir's paradise of islands are fun to weave through and provide hours of exploration and wildlife observation pleasure. Where you'll

TRIP 19: SUSQUEHANNA RIVER: LAKE ALDRED

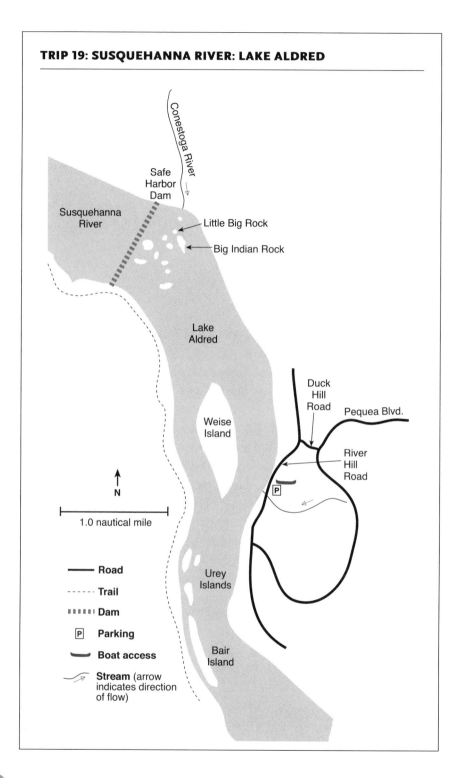

The striking rock formations make Conowingo Reservoir a wonderland. Photo by Kathy Kenley.

paddle, to the north of the launch, is so rock-strewn that you won't have to worry about motorboats.

From the launch, paddle across to nearby Lower Bear Island, and hug the shore as you travel north (upstream). A long line of barely underwater rocks leads out from the western shore about 400 feet north of the launch—you will want to avoid this. Continue north along Upper Bear Island. About halfway up the reservoir, numerous islands with narrow passageways are laid out in front of you to explore. Wind in and out, looking at the awesome formations.

One type of formation that will attract your attention: the perfectly cylindrical, sculpted holes carved into some of the rocks, a result of nature at work over thousands of years. When the Susquehanna River was engorged with glacial meltwaters, tons of abrasive sediment acted like hundreds of drills, swirling and sculpting the forms you see today.

Some small islands will have barely a tuft of grass on them, while larger ones have collected dirt, silt, and other debris over thousands of years and now support wildflowers, shrubs, and even large stands of trees. A few have cabins on plots of land leased from the state; remember, even though these are summer weekend getaway cabins, they are private property. You can spend hours here and not explore every nook, cranny, and passageway. Look for great blue herons, eagles, scarlet tanagers, kingfishers, great white egrets, and dozens of other species.

On calm days, return to the launch from the eastern edge of the islands, and perhaps explore a few immediately southeast of the launch. Travel through passageways in and among them, marveling at the wildlife and the geographic features. When you return to the launch, hug the islands as much as you can if there's motorboat traffic around in order to avoid wakes.

A word of warning: Do not paddle north of the PA 372 bridge. You are permitted to do it, but on the rare occasion of a dam release, things can become squirrelly while the water is running swiftly. Within the safe harbor of islands south of the bridge, even if there is a release, you're out of the main channel, which is river-left, and in a very protected area. The water might rise about a foot, and the current will increase some, but it's primarily a safe haven to wait until things return to normal.

Lake Aldred

The closest launch into Lake Aldred for access to Indian Rock Island is from the town of Pequea, 2.5 miles south of Safe Harbor Dam and 5 miles north of Holtwood Dam. This upper section of the lake is at most 20 feet deep. For that reason, most anglers and large pleasure boats will be in deeper areas to the south. From the launch, head upstream (north) for the 2.5-mile paddle to an area of small islands about 500 yards in front of Safe Harbor Dam. As you cruise by Weise Island, in the middle of the lake offshore from Pequea, look for bald eagles, usually seen flying over and around the island.

Indian Rock Island and the smaller island upstream, dubbed Little Indian Rock, both have petroglyphs, but it's best to either have a GPS or paddle with someone who knows where they are. Paddle north along the eastern shore toward the dam. When you're near Indian Rock Island, which is rounded with a few petroglyphs, 600 yards downstream from the dam, check your GPS. GPS coordinates for this island are 39° 54.966′ N, 76° 22.972′ W.

Little Indian Rock, about 80 yards upstream, has many more petroglyphs. Once you've located them, you'll be able to find them again easily. There are petroglyphs on other rocks directly out from the mouth of the Conestoga River, which feeds into Lake Aldred on the eastern shore right below the dam. (*Caution:* Always stay a few hundred yards from the dam. Boaters are warned to stay at least 100 yards downstream; paddlers should stay farther away.)

20 | Pinchot Lake: Gifford Pinchot State Park

Enjoy rocky shorelines and forested hillsides at this lake within Gifford Pinchot State Park.

Location: Lewisberry, PA
Maps: DeLorme Atlas & Gazetteer *Pennsylvania*, Map 78; USGS Dover; Pennsylvania Department of Conservation and Natural Resources: dcnr.state .pa.us
Area: 340 acres
Time: 4 to 4.5 hours
Average Depth: 10 feet
Development: Rural
Access: No fees
Information: Gifford Pinchot State Park, 2200 Rosstown Road, Lewisberry, PA 17339, 717-432-5011, dcnr.state.pa.us
Camping: On-site; for reservations call the park office or go to visitPAparks .com (see Appendix A).
Outfitters: On-site rentals include canoes, kayaks, paddleboats, rowboats, and electric motorboats
Take Note: Electric motorboats only. Pennsylvania boating regulations apply (see Appendix D).

GETTING THERE
To the park office: From I-83, take Exit 32 for PA 382 toward Newberrytown. Drive 3.7 miles on PA 382, then turn left onto PA 177 (Rosstown Road) and drive 3.7 miles (cumulative: 7.4 miles). Turn left onto Gifford Pinchot State Park Road, and you'll see the park office on the left. (40° 5.226′ N, 76° 53.303′ W)

To the first launch ramp: From the park office, continue south on PA 177 (Rosstown Road), without turning onto Gifford Pinchot State Park Road as above, and drive 1.6 miles to the boat launch, which will be on the right, immediately after the bridge. (40° 4.097′ N, 76° 54.512′ W)

To the second launch ramp: From the park office, continue south on Gifford Pinchot State Park Road for 0.4 mile to the boat launch on the right. (40° 4.994′ N, 76° 53.027′ W)

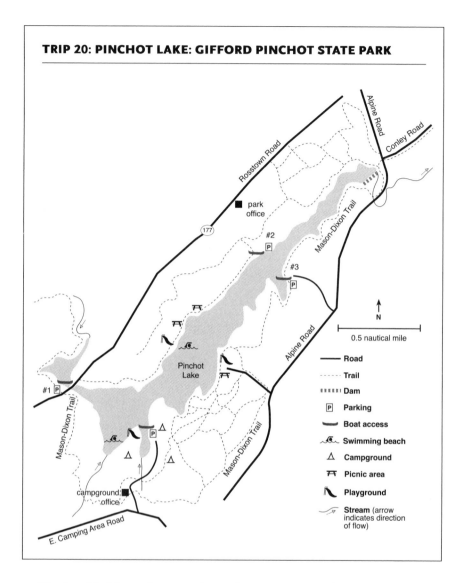

TRIP 20: PINCHOT LAKE: GIFFORD PINCHOT STATE PARK

Alpine Road

Conley Road

Rosstown Road

Mason-Dixon Trail

■ park office

177

#2 P

#3 P

N

0.5 nautical mile

—— Road

---- Trail

╏╏╏╏╏ Dam

P Parking

Boat access

Swimming beach

△ Campground

Picnic area

Playground

Stream (arrow indicates direction of flow)

Pinchot Lake

Alpine Road

#1 P

Mason-Dixon Trail

Mason-Dixon Trail

P △

△

△

campground; ■ office

E. Camping Area Road

To the third launch ramp: From the intersection of PA 177 and Alpine Road, drive south on Alpine Road 1.6 miles to the launch road entrance on the right. There will be a sign on Alpine Road. (40° 04.636′ N, 76° 52.512′ W)

WHAT YOU'LL SEE

Pinchot Lake sits within the 2,338-acre Gifford Pinchot State Park, named after the first chief of the U.S. Forest Service and former governor of Pennsylvania. Large, dark-colored diabase boulders can be found throughout the park, along the shoreline, and at Rock Creek in the northeast corner of the lake. Diabase is created when molten rock intrudes into sandstone and transforms it. One of the more picturesque spots where diabase is abundant is Boulder Point, the tip of the peninsula, directly across the lake from the second launch ramp. An interesting formation on the point is Balanced Rock, where environmental processes rounded the top and eroded the boulder around the base, leaving a gap between the boulder and the underlying rock. The result looks like a giant rock mushroom. It can be seen on Lake Side Trail, a short walk from the third launch ramp on the east side of the lake.

The second and third launch ramps are most recommended for your first trip here. They're both fairly close to the middle of the lake, giving you the option of a short or long paddle. The park's sailing club center operates from the south side of the second ramp. Sailboats are generally more active in the afternoon when the winds are up.

From either ramp, paddle to Boulder Point for a close look at the diabase rocks. Then head to the northeast end of the lake to explore the many coves, observe the wildlife, enjoy the solitude, and listen to the sounds of birds and frogs and the breezes rustling leaves. Mountains rise 120 feet on the north side and up to around 40 feet on the south side. The park is noted for having at least seven species of woodpeckers.

A couple heads toward Boulder Point, where they'll find diabase rock, formed by the cooling of molten lava. Photo by Kathy Kenley.

Spring and fall are the best seasons to observe migrating forest birds as they stop to rest here before flying on. The large size of Pinchot Lake invites thousands of waterfowl, such as mergansers, mallards, loons, teals, and geese. Spring also shows the beauty of redbud trees that burst into dusky pink and lavender flowers. Fall is a feast for the eyes, with deep-green pine and cedars popping out in contrast to the yellows, oranges, and reds of deciduous trees.

When you reach the tip of the lake, a row of red buoys warns of a spillway. The little cove in the northwest tip is where Rock Creek enters the lake. Paddle into the cove to study the natural rock steps of this ephemeral stream. Water levels are usually conducive to landing, so you can saunter up the steps for a closer inspection.

Paddle back toward Balance Point and continue toward the more open portion of the lake. Large scenic coves on the south side have shallow areas where you're likely to spot fish swimming beneath the surface. Anglers come here seeking largemouth bass, walleye, muskellunge, crappie, sunfish, carp, catfish, and hybrid striped bass.

The next lake section, which contains a large beach area on the north side and a day-use playground on the south side, might be a just-get-past-it paddle if there's heavy activity. It's the only downside of paddling this lake, but fortunately there are still a lot of quiet places. (*Note:* On days with strong northeast or southwest winds, this part of the lake can have short, choppy waves.) Activity areas on the south side are a little back from the shoreline, so this will be the quieter passage. Waterlilies carpet the far southeast tip by midsummer. Their bright-green leaves and yellow and white flowers provide a pretty change of scenery. Meander over and paddle under the bridge to the north where PA 177 crosses over a very narrow neck of the lake. Immediately to the left you'll see the first launch ramp, another access to the water you can try at a later date. This section is rather shallow, with waterlilies and aquatic grasses taking over the edges as summer wears on. Ducks, geese, egrets, and herons are common visitors here. On the right (northeast) side is the channel where Beaver Creek enters the lake.

More than 18 miles of marked trails are located within the park. Most trails interconnect to create longer or shorter hikes. They range from 0.4 to 8.5 miles in length and from easy to difficult. Additionally, 8.5 miles of the 193-mile Mason-Dixon Trail pass through the park.

3 | DELAWARE

Only 100 miles long and 30 miles wide, Delaware ranks among the smallest states. It is bordered on the north by Pennsylvania, on the south and west by Maryland, and on the east by the Atlantic Ocean. To the northeast, across the Delaware River and Delaware Bay, lies New Jersey. Despite its size, Delaware offers an abundance of scenic destinations for paddling, fishing, and wildlife viewing, from its inland bays to its state park millponds.

The state is divided into only three counties, from north to south: New Castle, Kent, and Sussex. New Castle County, the primary area surrounding Wilmington and Newark, is urban and industrialized, while the southern two counties are more rural, with a mix of farmland and outlying residential areas. Most of Delaware's land is very flat, averaging 58 feet above sea level. The only significant exception is the hilly terrain along the northern edges of the state border. A low-lying stretch of land adjacent to the Atlantic Ocean contains bays, creeks, and marshes, while the state's southernmost boundary is swampland.

Delaware's most popular tourist attraction is its expansive oceanfront, which extends from Fenwick Island at the Maryland border to Cape Henlopen, nearly 25 miles north at the mouth of Delaware Bay. Bethany Beach, near the southern end, and Rehoboth Beach, near the northern end, both offer miles of sandy shore and stay busy with vacationers throughout the summer months. Kayakers tend to head to Delaware Bay, where the terrain is marshy and the crowds are smaller. (*Note:* The mouths of some tributaries, such as the Murderkill and the St. Jones, are very shallow and often not navigable by boat.) Rehoboth and Indian River bays are popular for boating and fishing.

Paddling in Delaware's state parks offers the chance to view a wide range of wildlife, including horseshoe crabs, turtles, salamanders, frogs, otters, ospreys, and even dolphins. Distances range from an easy mile to more advanced paddles several miles in length. Beginners might opt to kayak in Delaware Bay at Cape Henlopen State Park or in ponds at Killens Pond and Lums Pond state parks.

The 14-mile Chesapeake and Delaware Canal, also called the C & D Canal, connects the Delaware River with Chesapeake Bay. A popular destination for kayaking and canoeing, the constructed waterway is accessible via a public launch at Fort DuPont State Park, the former home of a military base that operated from the Civil War through World War II. Throughout the state, paddlers can venture through marsh systems and tidal wetlands while viewing abundant wildlife and historic areas.

21 | Lums Pond

Enjoy a scenic paddle on the largest pond in Delaware.

Location: Bear, DE
Maps: Delaware State Parks: destateparks.com
Area: 200 acres
Time: 2 to 3 hours
Average Depth: 5 feet
Development: Rural
Access: Park entrance fee
Information: Delaware State Parks, 302-368-6989, destateparks.com
Camping: On-site yurts are available for rent year-round and offer an alternative to pitching a tent; features include bunk beds and a futon, electricity, and a deck with fresh water and a grill (see Appendix A)
Outfitter: On-site
Take Note: Electric motorboats only

TRIP 21: LUMS POND

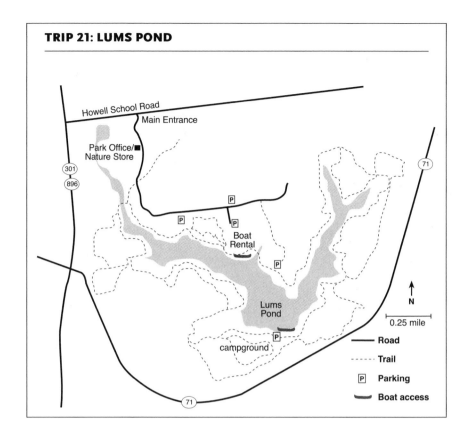

GETTING THERE

From I-95, take Exit 1A toward Middletown. Take DE 896 South and turn left on DE 71 (Red Lion Road). Pass the campground entrance. Turn left at the boat ramp entrance. The boat launch is located on the south side of the pond. The main entrance to the park and the boat rental area are located on the opposite side (north) from the boat ramp, at 1068 Howell School Road. You must carry your boat nearly 1,000 feet from the parking lot to launch on the north side of the pond. The launch on the south side is recommended. (39° 33.193′ N, 75° 42.782′ W)

WHAT YOU'LL SEE

Lums Pond is a prime place to kayak, with great scenery and easy access from I-95. It is nestled in an oak and poplar woodland and is the largest freshwater pond in Delaware, spanning 200 acres, so the technical distinction of it as a pond rather than a lake is misleading. The state park that surrounds the pond offers camping, fishing, hiking trails, and a zip line course. With such a wide

Great blue herons and many other birds make for rewarding wildlife viewing on Lums Pond.

variety of recreational opportunities, this is an ideal spot to spend the day or even a whole weekend.

Although the 1,790-acre state park wasn't established until 1963, these lands were used by the region's earliest settlers. Nearby St. Georges Creek was once the site of native people's hunting camps. The creek was dammed and the pond was formed to power a mill in the early 1800s when the C & D Canal was built. Lum's Mill House was built here in 1713 and still stands on the property. It was designated as a historic site in 1973.

Lums Pond is renowned for offering some of the best freshwater fishing in Delaware. Native fish include largemouth bass, catfish, carp, pickerel, and crappie. Hybrid striped bass are also plentiful, stocked by the Delaware Department of Natural Resources and Environmental Control's Division of Fish & Wildlife.

The boat launch is sandy and easy to use. You can paddle in either direction and see plenty of gorgeous scenery and wildlife. The surrounding trees and plants include sweet gum, red maple, sycamore, sassafras, and club moss, which looks like small pine trees growing along the ground. The waters are calm, and the scenery is so serene that you can easily relax and slowly explore the shores. It is one of those rare places where you will see a variety of birds, including great blue herons and white egrets, soaring overhead. You may also see black rat snakes and eastern painted turtles.

At the east end of the pond, there's a small section closed off as a dog training area. No boating or fishing is allowed. On the west end of the pond, you will pass boat rentals, picnic areas, and a nature center on the right side. The 6.4-mile Swamp Forest Trail loops around the edge of the pond through forested wetlands of black cherry, sweet gum, and maple. The campground is adjacent to the boat launch on the south side of the pond. South of the park lies the C & D Canal Wildlife Area, which consists of nearly 5,000 acres of land protected and managed by the Delaware Division of Fish & Wildlife for hunting, fishing, and recreation.

Lums Pond State Park has more than 10 miles of multipurpose trails. During the summer months, the Whale Wallow Nature Center hosts a variety of hands-on programs and events. Large groups can reserve picnic areas and pavilions. Rowboats, canoes, kayaks, and pedal boats are available for rent.

The historic C & D Canal, dating back to the early nineteenth century, is just south of the park and DE 71 (Red Lion Road). It is worth a visit and even a full day of exploration. You can kayak, hike, or bike along the 14-mile structure that carries barges and sailing vessels. It is the only major commercial canal in the United States still in use today.

22 | Prime Hook National Wildlife Refuge

Paddle along a quietwater trail and see a variety of habitats, waterfowl, and amphibians.

Location: Milton, DE
Maps: U.S. Fish and Wildlife Service: fws.gov
Length: 7 miles
Time: 3 hours or more
Average Depth: 2 to 3 feet
Development: Rural
Access: No fees
Information: U.S. Fish and Wildlife Service, fws.gov; Prime Hook National Wildlife Refuge, 11978 Turkle Pond Road, Milton, DE 19968, 302-684-8419

TRIP 22: PRIME HOOK NATIONAL WILDLIFE REFUGE

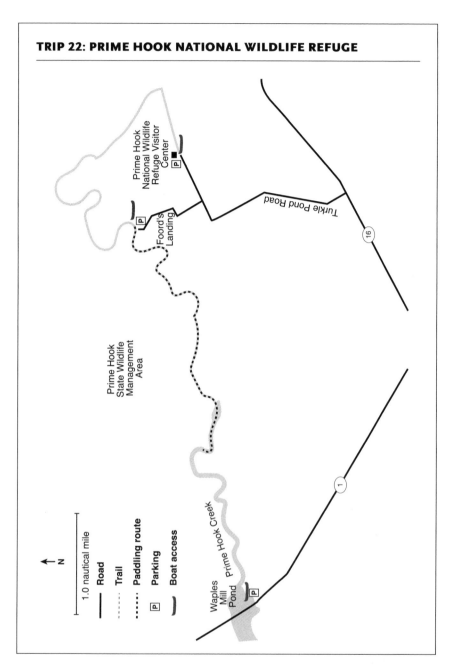

Camping: Cape Henlopen State Park, 15 miles southeast; Delaware Beaches Jellystone Park Camp, 10 miles northwest; Tall Pines Campground Resort, 9.5 miles south; Homestead Campground, 12 miles south; Big Oaks Campground, 13 miles southeast (see Appendix A)

Take Note: Motorboats are limited to 30 horsepower. The boat ramps at the refuge office and the Prime Hook State Wildlife Management Area are closed from the beginning of October to March 15. At the time of this writing, the online map and brochure (published in 2002) was outdated and did not show the access road to the Foord's Landing Boat Access Ramp.

GETTING THERE

To the refuge headquarters and visitor center: From DE 1, take DE 16 east for 1.1 miles toward Broadkill Beach; turn left onto Turkle Pond Road and travel 1.6 miles (cumulative: 2.7 miles) to the refuge office, visitor center, and Friends Store at Prime Hook. The boat ramp is on the east side of the building next to the Boardwalk Trail and the Pine Grove Trail. (38° 49.823′ N, 75° 14.891′ W)

To the Foord's Landing boat ramp: From DE 1, take DE 16 east for 1.1 miles toward Broadkill Beach; turn left onto Turkle Pond Road. Continue on Turkle Pond Road for 1.1 miles (cumulative: 2.2 miles). Turn left at the sign for Foord's Landing and follow it for about 0.5 mile to the boat ramp (2.7 miles). (38° 50.101′ N, 75° 15.478′ W)

To the Waples Mill Pond boat ramp: The ramp is just off of DE 1, approximately 2.5 miles north of DE 16. It is reachable only from the northbound lanes and is before the bridge, next to Coastal Wines & Spirits. (38° 49.382′ N, 75° 18.420′ W)

WHAT YOU'LL SEE

Prime Hook National Wildlife Refuge is a surprisingly quiet 10,144-acre expanse on the west shore of Delaware Bay just north of the coastal resort towns of Lewes and Rehoboth Beach. It is an easy place to escape the crowded beaches and enjoy a few hours or a whole day of peaceful paddling amid beautiful scenery. Visitors can paddle 14 miles or more along creeks, streams, and marshes and may have limited interaction with other humans along the way.

The area gets its name from Dutch settlers who discovered an abundance of purple beach plums there and called it *Prime Hoek,* meaning "Plum Point." The mix of wetlands, uplands, and forest provides a protected habitat for a wide variety of native species of birds, mammals, fish, reptiles, amphibians, insects, and plants.

The U.S. Fish and Wildlife Service has created a self-guided canoe trail that has three possible starting points. At the eastern end, you can launch from the boat ramp at the refuge office. At the western end, you can launch from the southeast bank of Waples Mill Pond near the intersection of DE 5 and DE 1.

A third boat ramp is in the middle of the waterway at Foord's Landing, part of the state-operated wildlife management area.

The refuge is an important stopover for migratory birds. Established in 1963, under the authority of the Migratory Bird Conservation Act, the wetlands protect these birds and provide a breeding habitat for threatened and endangered species. Thousands of ducks, geese, and shorebirds fly here each year. The habitat also attracts bald eagles and endangered Delmarva fox squirrels. Features include salt- and freshwater marshes, ponds and impoundments, wooded swamps, and upland grasslands and forest.

Launching from Foord's Landing offers the most ideal paddling conditions, as the waters are very shallow and easy to navigate. However, if you are with a group or even one companion, this section is so narrow—as small as 8 feet in some places—that you will have to paddle single file, and there is not much room to navigate around one another. Head west and continue paddling for about 3 miles through forested wetlands before they lead into an open marsh impoundment. Continue paddling another 1.5 miles to the west to reach Waples Mill Pond. Water levels along the trail are manipulated by the refuge to optimize food resources for migrating birds. Dead trees that are still standing after saltwater flooding from Hurricane Sandy provide an eerily beautiful background as you paddle along a long stretch near the Prime Hook State Wildlife Management Area.

The narrow waters of Prime Hook National Wildlife Refuge provide a peaceful trip.

At the Waples Mill Pond launch, the initial section is wide and moderately deep. If you begin there, head north for about 1,000 feet to the end of the forested area, where you will find the entrance to Prime Hook Creek. Turn right and follow the creek. It opens into a wide marsh that twists and turns for about 1.5 miles and then narrows as it continues for another 5.5 miles.

As you paddle along the water trail, notice the wide variety of colorful plants along the shoreline. Among the most common trees in this region are red maples and sweet bay magnolias, which are spectacular to see in their showy spring and fall colors. Other trees that line the banks of the creek include sweet gum, green ash, and a variety of evergreens.

As you travel east and make your way into the open marsh, you'll notice a change in the flora. In the freshwater areas, you will see plants such as cattail, wild rice, and Walter's millet. In salt marsh areas, salt grass and cordgrass are common. The marshy areas are quite shallow and good spots to look for frogs, snakes, and invertebrates. Shorebirds and other waterfowl are most often seen as they feed along the wetlands throughout the wildlife management area.

The wildlife refuge allows hunting and fishing and is a great place for wildlife viewing and photography. Self-guided hikes and ranger-led programs are available to help visitors learn more about the species that thrive here and their habitats. After your paddle, hike the 1.4-mile Blue Goose Trail and visit the wildlife observation areas. You could also check out the 0.8-mile Pine Grove Trail, which provides a different vantage point for viewing ponds and marsh.

NATIONAL WILDLIFE REFUGE SYSTEM

Wildlife refuges make wonderful paddling destinations, providing pristine scenery and the opportunity to observe a variety of birds, mammals, and other wildlife. There's nothing more awe-inspiring than paddling beneath a flock of migratory birds or beside a beaver dam.

The National Wildlife Refuge System, a division of the U.S. Fish and Wildlife Service within the Department of the Interior, was created to conserve and protect fish, wildlife, plants, and their habitats. President Theodore Roosevelt designated the first wildlife refuge, Florida's Pelican Island, in 1903 to help save egrets and pelicans, as well as other birds, from extinction. Since then, the system has grown to include more than 560 refuges, protecting more than 150 million acres of land and water across the United States and its territories.

There is at least one wildlife refuge within an hour's drive of most of the populated areas in the nation. In addition to providing habitat for land-based animals, refuges protect more than 1,000 species of fish and more than 280 threatened or endangered varieties of plants that you may never have heard of. Each year, migrating birds are attracted to these natural environments, stopping over as they fly thousands of miles between their seasonal homes and numbering in the tens of thousands during peak migration. Refuges are good for people, too, as these sites protect our ecosystem and provide us with clean air and water—not to mention restorative places to visit.

Each year, more than 45 million people participate in a wide variety of recreational activities and environmental education programs at wildlife refuges, including hiking, fishing, wildlife observation, and photography. (*Note*: Not all refuges are open to the public. Always call ahead.) Paddlers in the Mid-Atlantic can explore tidal marshes and brackish ponds for a close-up look at eagles, ospreys, herons, and muskrat. On land, nature trails, observation decks, and photo blinds provide vantage points for some of the best wildlife-viewing opportunities. Refuges also offer extensive calendars of educational programming for groups, families, and individuals, and many have visitor centers with interactive exhibits. Some offer cultural and historical sites with special programming—for example, the former Maroon communities at the Great Dismal Swamp National Wildlife Refuge in Virginia (see Trip 55).

Wildlife enthusiasts engage in conservation activities at the refuges through more than 200 nonprofit Friends organizations. To learn more or to get involved, visit fws.gov/refuges/friends.

Refuges in the Mid-Atlantic States

DELAWARE
- Bombay Hook National Wildlife Refuge, 2591 Whitehall Neck Road, Smyrna, DE 19977, 302-653-9345
- Prime Hook National Wildlife Refuge, 11978 Turkle Pond Road, Milton, DE 19968, 302-684-8419 (see Trip 22)

MARYLAND
- Blackwater National Wildlife Refuge, 2145 Key Wallace Drive, Cambridge, MD 21613, 410-228-2677 (see Trip 27)

- Eastern Neck National Wildlife Refuge, 1730 Eastern Neck Road, Rock Hall, MD 21661, 410-639-7056 (see Trip 38)
- Glenn Martin National Wildlife Refuge, Smith Island, MD 21824, 410-228-2692
- Patuxent Research Refuge, National Wildlife Visitor Center, 10901 Scarlet Tanager Loop, Laurel, MD 20708, 301-497-5760
- Susquehanna River National Wildlife Refuge, Battery Island, MD, 410-228-2692

NEW JERSEY
- Cape May National Wildlife Refuge, 24 Kimbles Beach Road, Cape May Court House, NJ 08210, 609-463-0994
- Edwin B. Forsythe National Wildlife Refuge, 800 Great Creek Road, Galloway, NJ 08205, 609-652-1665
- Great Swamp National Wildlife Refuge, 32 Pleasant Plains Road, Basking Ridge, NJ 07920, 973-425-1222
- Supawna National Wildlife Refuge, 199 Lighthouse Road, Pennsville, NJ 08070, 609-463-0994
- Wallkill River National Wildlife Refuge, 1547 County Route 565, Sussex, NJ 07461, 973-702-7266

PENNSYLVANIA
- Cherry Valley National Wildlife Refuge, Lower Cherry Valley Road, Saylorsburg, PA 18353, 973-702-7266
- Erie National Wildlife Refuge, 11296 Wood Duck Lane, Guys Mills, PA 16327, 814-789-3585
- John Heinz National Wildlife Refuge, 8601 Lindbergh Boulevard, Philadelphia, PA 19153, 215-365-3118

VIRGINIA
- Back Bay National Wildlife Refuge, 4005 Sandpiper Road, Virginia Beach, VA 23456, 757-301-7329 (see Trip 57)
- Chincoteague National Wildlife Refuge, 8231 Beach Road, Chincoteague Island, VA 23336, 757-336-6122 (see Trip 53)
- Eastern Shore of Virginia National Wildlife Refuge, 32205 Seaside Road, Cape Charles, VA 23310, 757-331-3425
- Elizabeth Hartwell Mason Neck National Wildlife Refuge, High Point Road, Lorton, VA 22079, 703-490-4979

- Featherstone National Wildlife Refuge, 12638 Darby Brooke Court, Woodbridge, VA 22192, 703-490-4979
- Fisherman Island National Wildlife Refuge, 5003 Hallett Circle, Cape Charles, VA 23310, 757-331-2760
- Great Dismal Swamp National Wildlife Refuge, 3100 Desert Road, Suffolk, VA 23434, 757-986-3705 (see Trip 55)
- James River National Wildlife Refuge, 4550 Flowerdew Hundred Road, Hopewell, VA 23860, 804-829-9020
- Nansemond National Wildlife Refuge, 3100 Desert Road, Suffolk, VA 23434, 757-986-3705
- Occoquan Bay National Wildlife Refuge, 13950 Dawson Beach Road, Woodbridge, VA 22191, 703-490-4979
- Plum Tree Island National Wildlife Refuge, Poquoson, VA 23662, 804-829-9020
- Presquile National Wildlife Refuge, 4700 Bermuda Hundred Road, Chester, VA 23836, 804-829-9020
- Rappahannock River Valley National Wildlife Refuge, 336 Wilna Road, Warsaw, VA 22572; Hutchinson Unit: 19180 Tidewater Trail, Tappahannock, VA 22560; Laurel Grove Unit: 736 Laurel Grove Road, Farnham, VA 22460; Port Royal Unit: Caroline Street, Port Royal, VA 22535; 804-333-1470
- Wallops Island National Wildlife Refuge, Wattsville, VA 23483, 978-465-5753

23 | Trap Pond

Paddle along a beautiful pond through an extensive stand of bald cypress trees and look for a variety of waterfowl and other wildlife.

Location: Laurel, DE
Maps: Delaware State Parks: destateparks.com
Area: 90 acres
Time: 2 hours
Average Depth: 3 to 5 feet
Development: Rural
Access: Park entrance fee
Information: Delaware State Parks: 302-875-5153, destateparks.com
Camping: On-site (see Appendix A)

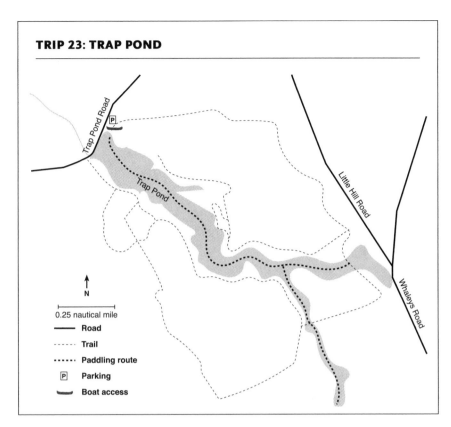

TRIP 23: TRAP POND

Trap Pond Road

Little Hill Road

Whaleys Road

P — Parking

Trap Pond

N

0.25 nautical mile

—— Road

----- Trail

••••• Paddling route

P Parking

Boat access

Outfitters: On-site

Take Note: Electric motorboats only. Check the water level gauge, located below the Pepper Pond Road spillway or at the Hitch Pond Road crossing, before launching.

GETTING THERE

From US 50 East, travel to MD 404 East. Follow MD 404 East for 31.8 miles to US 13 South. Turn right onto US 13 South and drive for 14.8 miles (cumulative: 46.6 miles). Head northeast on DE 24 East for 4.7 miles (51.3 miles), and then turn right on Trap Pond Road. Drive for 0.9 miles (52.2 miles). Turn left into the boat ramp parking lot. If you cross over the water and reach the main park entrance you have gone too far. (38° 31.517′ N, 75° 28.278′ W)

WHAT YOU'LL SEE

Trap Pond is a nature preserve, managed by Delaware State Parks, that features the northernmost natural stand of bald cypress trees on the East Coast. These lofty trees grow within the forested wetlands and create a unique paddling route that makes this park one of the most interesting places to explore in the Mid-Atlantic region. It is probably one of the best places for photography and videography.

The bald cypress tends to grow in standing water and is the classic tree of southern swamps. They are deciduous conifers that are green in summer and turn fiery orange and shed their needlelike leaves in fall. Their bark is dark in color with a stringy texture. Bald cypresses are most known for their unique and distinctive-looking "knees," which grow from their roots and protrude upward from the ground or in water. Since bald cypresses often grow in swampy conditions, it's thought that the knees provide air to roots underground.

You will often see frogs, toads, and salamanders near bald cypresses as the swampy conditions provide breeding grounds. Wood ducks nest in hollow trunks, bass spawn in submerged hollow logs, and ospreys nest in the treetops.

The 90-acre Trap Pond is a freshwater wetland and an unusual place to kayak. You can explore the swamp and paddle right through a grove of bald cypress trees. There is even one that is estimated to be more than 550 years old.

A kayaker paddles through the breathtaking bald cypress forest that sits in the center of Trap Pond.

The tree is 127 feet tall and almost 25 feet wide. The park is also the home of a very large American holly, which is Delaware's state tree.

The boat ramp is located at the west end of the pond and is the best place to launch. You can also put in anywhere along the shoreline of the park; however, you would have to carry your boat a distance from the parking lot.

Paddle to your left and you will pass several boat docks and campsites, including a few cabins and yurts. Stay to the left, and eventually you will reach a small cove filled with water lotuses and several bald cypress trees standing in the middle of the pond. You can paddle right between the trees and enjoy a beautiful panoramic view of most of the park. Continue along to the left, and you will encounter dozens of large trees in the center of the pond. Off to the left side, there are about 100 trees grouped together, and you can easily thread your way among them for a very cool experience.

Trap Pond was created in the late 1700s to power a sawmill during the harvest of large bald cypress from the area. During the 1930s, the U.S. government purchased the pond and surrounding farmland and the Civilian Conservation Corps, a federal public work relief program, began to develop the area for recreation. In 1951, the land surrounding the pond was transferred to state jurisdiction and the property became one of Delaware's first state parks.

Today the park is home to many native bird species such as great blue heron, owl, hummingbird, bald eagle, and the elusive pileated woodpecker. Fishing is popular here and anglers may get lucky and catch largemouth bass, pickerel, crappie, and bluegills.

In addition to exploring the 1.3-mile Trap Pond water trail, you can extend your excursion by exploring two other trails: Terrapin Branch water trail (0.4 mile) and Racoon Pond water trail (0.9 mile). These trails stretch southeastward on the pond into a low-lying forested area. Terrapin water trail narrows, forks to the left, and passes under a foot bridge while Raccoon water trail forks to the right and continues to Raccoon Pond Dam. You may have additional wildlife-viewing and birding opportunities here and see critters such as otter, water snakes, and warblers.

The park offers a variety of recreational activities including bicycling, boating, disc golf, fishing, horseshoes, volleyball, and picnicking. Rowboats, pedal boats, canoes, kayaks, and stand-up paddleboards can be rented onsite during the summer season. Narrated pontoon boat tours are available on weekends and holidays, from Memorial Day weekend through Labor Day. You may also enjoy views of the bald cypress trees along the 4.9-mile Boundary Trail that traverses the pond. The onsite nature center features a state-of-the-art exhibit gallery, education and recreation activities, and a conference facility.

24 | Brandywine Creek

Explore the shallow waters of Brandywine Creek and enjoy great wildlife viewing and birding opportunities.

Location: Wilmington, DE
Maps: DE State Parks: destateparks.com
Length: 6 to 7 miles
Time: 2 to 3 hours
Average Depth: 2 feet
Development: Rural
Access: Park entrance fee
Information: DE State Parks: destateparks.com; Friends of Brandywine Creek State Park: FriendsofBCSP.org, 302-577-3534 or 302-655-5740
Camping: Primitive camping on-site for youth groups only (see Appendix A)
Outfitters: Wilderness Canoe Trips: wildernesscanoetrips.com
Take Note: Launch at the Thompson Bridge day-use parking lot. Beware that low- or high-water levels may limit creek access. If paddling below Thompson Bridge parking area, use extreme caution at Rockland Dam and other downstream dams. An additional launch is available at Brandywine River Museum on US 1 in Chadds Ford, Pennsylvania.

GETTING THERE

Take Exit 8 off I-95 North to US 202 North (Concord Pike) toward West Chester. Use the middle lane to follow signs for DE 141 North/DE 261 North/Foulk Road North. Use the left lane to turn left onto DE 141 South/Foulk Road. Turn right onto Rockland Road and continue for 1.2 miles. Turn right on Adams Dam Road. Drive for 1 mile (cumulative: 2.2 miles), passing the first entrance to Brandywine Creek State Park, and turn right onto Thompson Bridge Road. Continue until you cross over the bridge; turn right at the park entrance. (39° 49.048′ N, 75° 34.150′ W)

WHAT YOU'LL SEE

Brandywine Creek, a tributary of the Christina River that runs from southeastern Pennsylvania to northern Delaware, was an important waterway throughout early American history. Algonquian tribes lived in the area before the European settlement. On March 29, 1638, the Swedish colonists landed on the

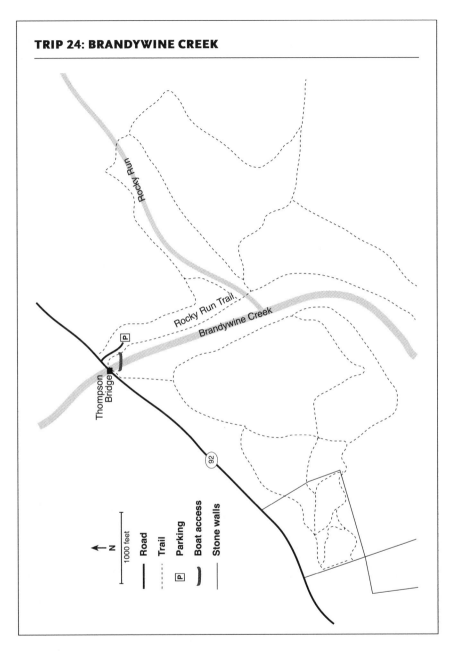

mouth of the Brandywine in Wilmington, and the area became known as the New Sweden colony. The creek was named for the 1777 Battle of Brandywine during the Revolutionary War. The British defeated the Americans along the creek near Chadds Ford, Pennsylvania, in what was the longest one-day battle of the war. Early flour and paper mills were located along the creek.

As you drive along the main roads before entering 933-acre Brandywine Creek State Park, you may notice that the site is divided by gray stone walls, which were built of local stone in the late 1800s. At that time, the property was a dairy farm owned by the du Pont family, one of the richest families in America. This historically significant area became a state park in 1965 and was one of the first in the nation to be purchased with Land and Water Conservation Funds. The park is beautiful and offers a wide range of natural scenery and outdoor recreational activities.

The kayak access area is located about 2 miles from the main park entrance on the north end of the park. The Thompson Bridge day-use parking lot over-looks Brandywine Creek and provides limited access for kayaks. This area has picnic tables and access to the 2.9-mile crushed-stone Brandywine Trail, which runs along the east bank of the creek. There is no boat launch here, but there is a low point directly across from the parking lot that leads to the water.

The Brandywine is a very slow, shallow, meandering river and is ideal for beginner paddling. The water level is always in direct relation to the amount of recent precipitation. As you enter the river, beware that it can be quite muddy here. Be sure to wear good water shoes, and bring a towel and a change of

Paddling downstream on Brandywine Creek is a quiet and scenic excursion.

DELAWARE

clothing. To avoid getting mud in your boat, walk out a few yards to where the bottom becomes gravel before rinsing your feet and getting in.

This is a popular destination for fly fishing, as the river is very shallow and narrow. Most fishing is done while wading in the water or from the shore. The most common fish include smallmouth bass, bluegill, and crappie.

You can paddle in either direction. Move slowly to avoid rocks and fallen tree branches. There is a large beaver lodge on the right side of the river as you go under Thompson Bridge. As you paddle along the creek look for ducks, geese, bluebirds, and other birds. Experience the tranquil creek waters and travel along the forested corridors. If you head upstream, you will pass by Ramsey's Farm, a privately owned farm. Downstream, you will head into Brandywine Creek State Park where you will see Piedmont wooded landscapes, wildflowers in spring, and possibly glimpses of wildlife.

The park maintains 14 miles of recreation trails including the inland Rocky Run Trail and Brandywine Trail, which winds along the creek. The open fields are prime spots for kite flying and disc golf. The nature center offers interpretive programs for individuals, school groups, and organizations. Civil War reenactments are held on site in spring. The Brandywine Valley is home to many historic homes, mills, and other landmarks that make this area a prime place for a day trip or extended visit. If you have time, tour one of the du Pont mansions such as Winterthur or Nemours Estate.

25 | Killens Pond

Traverse the perimeter of Killens Pond on the lookout for a variety of freshwater turtles.

Location: Felton, DE
Maps: Delaware State Parks: destateparks.com
Length: 2 to 4 miles
Time: 1.5 to 2 hours
Average Depth: 5 to 7 feet
Development: Rural
Access: Park entrance fee
Information: Delaware State Parks: 302-284-4526, destateparks.com
Camping: On-site, campgrounds and cabins available (see Appendix A)

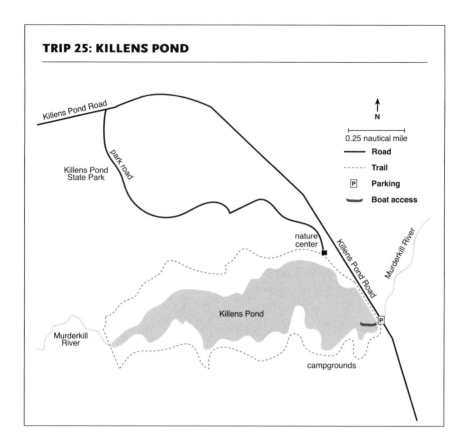

TRIP 25: KILLENS POND

Killens Pond Road

Park road

Killens Pond
State Park

N

0.25 nautical mile

— Road

----- Trail

P Parking

Boat access

nature
center

Killens Pond Road

Murderkill River

Killens Pond

Murderkill
River

campgrounds

P

Outfitters: On-site

Take Note: Electric motorboats only. The boat launch is at a separate location outside of the park entrance. Stay away from the drainage area just north of the boat ramp: surprisingly, it is not roped off and there are no warning signs.

GETTING THERE

To the Park: From US 50 East: Follow US 50 East toward Ocean City. Turn left onto MD 404 East and continue for 13.7 miles. Turn right onto MD 313 North, and then, after 0.8 mile (cumulative: 14.5 miles) turn right onto MD 317 East. Drive for 14.3 miles (28.8 miles), as the road becomes DE 14 East, and then turn left on US 13 North. After 4.3 miles (33.1 miles), turn right on Killens Pond Road. The park entrance is on the right.

    From I-95: Take DE 1 South for 42.1 miles to US 13 South. Drive on US 13 for 12.8 miles (cumulative: 54.9 miles), and then turn left on Killens Pond Road. The park entrance is on the right. (38° 59.418′ N, 75° 32.707′ W)

To the Boat Ramp: Continue as above, but before reaching Killens Pond Road, turn right on Paradise Alley Road. Drive for 2.2 miles, and then turn left on Killens Pond Road. The boat ramp is on the left.

From I-95: Continue as above, but turn left on Paradise Alley Road, and then turn left on Killens Pond Road. The boat ramp is on the left. (38° 58.839′ N, 75° 31.752′ W)

WHAT YOU'LL SEE

Killens Pond is a 66-acre millpond that was created in the late 1700s in Kent County, Delaware. It is surrounded by the Murderkill River, which flows for 20.5 miles through the central part of the state from Felton to Bowers, where it enters the Delaware Bay about 0.5 mile south of the mouth of the St. Jones River. Prior to the creation of Killens Pond, Native Americans lived along the Murderkill River and used the waters to transport important cargo such as meat, corn, flour, cheese, butter, tar, and hardwood boards.

Today, Killens Pond State Park is a year-round recreation area centered around the pond with boating, fishing, hiking, playgrounds, and picnic areas.

An eastern painted turtle suns itself near the western corner of Killens Pond.

Canoes, rowboats, kayaks, and paddleboats can be rented during summer. The Murderkill River Canoe Trail provides an extension to paddling the pond and opportunities to see a wide variety of wildlife. The rare but naturally occurring bald cypress tree is found along the shoreline. The pond is popular for fishing and is home to largemouth bass, catfish, perch, crappie, bluegill, and pickerel.

Launching from the boat ramp, stay to the left and follow the shoreline around the perimeter of the pond, where aquatic plants grow and attract shorebirds. While the park has many amenities, the pond is completely surrounded by woodlands and is very quiet. Be sure to paddle beyond the bridge on the western end of the pond where the Murderkill River begins and the waters narrow. Here you are likely to see a wide variety of freshwater turtles.

Common species you may see include the eastern mud turtle, a semi-aquatic species that prefers shallow water; the spotted turtle, which has spots that extend from the head to the neck and out to its limbs; the eastern painted turtle, an aquatic species with a distinct glossy black shell with seams that divide each scute and a yellow underbelly; the red-bellied turtle, an aquatic turtle with a dark, highly domed shell and a distinctive red belly; and the snapping turtle, one of the larger aquatic turtles at an average of 14 inches long and which is commonly found buried in the mud near shallow water. During the warmer months, you will see these reptiles swimming or basking on logs, slowing increasing their body temperature. Turtles are cold-blooded and so cannot control the temperatures of their bodies. They get their heat from the air, water, or ground around them.

The park offers a variety of recreational activities including hiking trails, a cross-country running course, and a fitness trail with twenty exercise stations. The 2.6-mile Pondside Trail winds along the banks of the pond. The park's campground and cozy cabins are open year-round and offer wonderful retreats for families. There is also an 18-hole disc golf course and a water park with slides and a waterplay system for all ages. A bike path from US 13 to the main entrance provides great access for bicyclists into and out of the park. The nature center is located alongside the pond and displays an extensive collection of native reptiles and amphibians.

For an additional place to kayak, drive 2.6 miles east of Killens Pond, where you will find the 58-acre Coursey Pond (off DE 15). The two ponds are connected via the Murderkill River but the dam between them makes the waters impassable.

4 | MARYLAND

Maryland lies at the center of the eastern seaboard, bordering
Washington, D.C.; Virginia; Pennsylvania; Delaware; and West Virginia. The
state's topography ranges from sandy dunes with low marshlands in the east to
gently rolling hills in the Piedmont Region to forested mountains in the west.
The Chesapeake Bay stretches across the state, with the Maryland Eastern Shore
running along the Atlantic Ocean. The population is densest in the center of the
state, in and around Baltimore and Washington, D.C. The western part of the
state is mountainous, with lakes, rivers, and trails ideal for outdoor exploration.

The state's dominating geological feature is the Chesapeake Bay. More than
two dozen tributaries provide Maryland with about 3,200 miles of shoreline and
a wide range of recreational activities, such as fishing, crabbing, swimming, boating, kayaking, and sailing. The bay and its surrounding creeks, salt marshes, and
small islands offer beautiful scenery and are excellent for canoeing and kayaking.

There are no natural lakes in Maryland, but there are more than 100 manufactured ones, most of which are smaller than 50 acres. The largest is Deep
Creek Lake, which covers nearly 4,000 acres near Oakland, in Garrett County.
The most significant river in Maryland is the Potomac, as it forms the entire
southern border, first between Maryland and Washington, D.C., and farther
south between Maryland and Virginia. There are many boating access points

along the river. Some sections of the Upper Potomac are whitewater and not advisable for kayaking. Many tributaries of the Potomac offer excellent quiet-water paddling and wildlife viewing.

More than 400 different species of birds can be found in Maryland. For many migrating birds on their journeys south, the Mid-Atlantic offers a convenient resting place. As you paddle the region, you will find an extraordinary diversity of waterfowl lingering along the shorelines.

Maryland is especially known for its blue crabs and oysters, and is also home to more than 350 species of fish, including the Atlantic menhaden and the American eel. Kayak fishing is very popular in the deeper waters.

Maryland's plant life is as diverse as its geography. Mid-Atlantic coastal forests of oak, hickory, and pine trees grow around the Chesapeake Bay and on the Delmarva Peninsula. A mixture of Northeastern coastal forests and Southeastern mixed forests cover the central part of the state. The Appalachian Mountains of western Maryland are home to mixed forests of chestnut, walnut, hickory, oak, maple, and pine. Maryland's state flower, the black-eyed Susan, grows in abundance throughout the state.

The Department of Natural Resources is working to build a statewide network of water trails, an ideal playground for boating and water sports. To date, there are more than 750 miles of designated water trails, and other projects are in development across the state. Many parks and outfitters offer rentals and guided excursions around the region. With so many Maryland waterways, there is always somewhere new and exciting to explore.

26 | Mallows Bay

Explore the Ghost Fleet of Mallows Bay, a unique graveyard of sunken ships in Southern Maryland with ample wildlife viewing.

Location: Nanjemoy, MD
Maps: National Marine Sanctuaries: sanctuaries.noaa.gov
Length: 1.5 miles
Time: 1 to 2 hours
Average Depth: 4 feet
Development: Rural
Access: No fees

TRIP 26: MALLOWS BAY

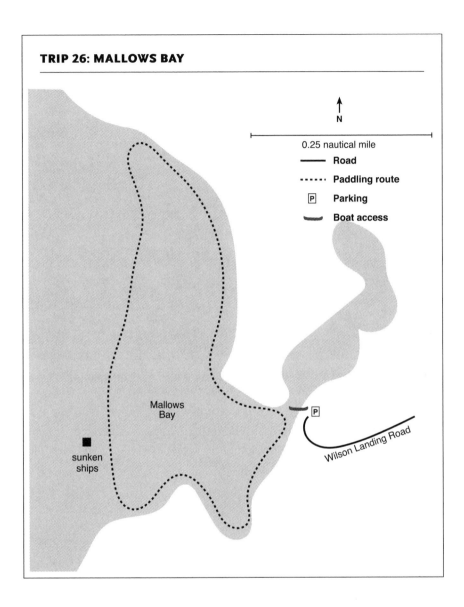

Information: Charles County Parks: charlescountyparks.com; National Marine Sanctuaries: sanctuaries.noaa.gov; Chesapeake Conservancy Itineraries: chescon.maps.arcgis.com
Camping: Goose Bay Marina and Campground, 12 miles east; Aqualand Marina and Campground, 28 miles east (see Appendix A)
Outfitters: Atlantic Kayak: atlantickayak.com

In the middle of Mallows Bay sits the remains of the *Accomac*, a ferry that was used to haul rubber from Brazil during World War I. It was brought to Mallows Bay in 1932.

Take Note: Unlimited horsepower. Swimming is not recommended as there are many metal obstructions throughout the area; be observant and careful as you explore this unique destination.

GETTING THERE

From the Capital Beltway (I-495), take MD 210 (Indian Head Highway) about 19 miles to MD 225, and then continue 2 miles (cumulative: 21 miles) to MD 224 (Chicamuxen Road). Continue south on MD 224, which becomes Riverside Road, for 16.5 miles (37.5 miles). Turn left onto Wilson Landing Road and follow it 0.7 mile to the end (38.2 miles). (38° 28.135′ N, 77° 15.817′ W)

WHAT YOU'LL SEE

Mallows Bay is a largely undeveloped tributary of the Potomac River and one of the most ecologically valuable landscapes in the state of Maryland. It is historically significant and a unique destination for kayaking, fishing, wildlife viewing, and hiking. Located on the Maryland side of the Potomac River in Charles County, the small bay is home to the World War I Ghost Fleet, the largest "ship graveyard" in the Western Hemisphere.

The diverse collection of nearly 200 historic vessels dates to the Revolutionary War and World War I. More than 100 of the ships are wooden steamships, part of the U.S. Emergency Fleet that was built between 1917 and 1919 to cross the Atlantic during World War I. Their construction at more than 40 shipyards in seventeen states was a massive national wartime initiative to expand the maritime industry and increase economic development. Most of the ships became obsolete after the end of the war. They were stored in the James River until they were sold to the Western Marine & Salvage Company, which towed the ships to Mallows Bay to attempt to salvage them for scrap metal. The company went bankrupt, and the ships were left in the bay. Today, the remains of dozens of decomposing ships can be seen in the shallow water.

The Charles County Parks and Recreation Department leases the land around the bay from the Maryland Department of Natural Resources. In 2010, a boat ramp and pier were built at the park to provide access for visitors to kayak among the ship ruins. A 0.8-mile walking trail loops around Mallows Bay Park and the salvage basin so you can get a glimpse of some of the wreckage from the shore. You can take a guided, narrated tour from Atlantic Kayak (advance reservations required) or set out on your own tour. The best time to visit is during low tide. You should use extreme caution during high tide when many of the ship remains lie just below the waterline and are not visible.

From the boat ramp, you can paddle just a short distance and inspect the remains of the ships. They form a reef that hosts an array of wildlife. The most prominent wreck is a rusty car ferry, the *Accomac,* that was used to haul rubber from Brazil during World War I. There is a large osprey nest on the shore-facing end of the wreck. Many of the wrecks have formed islands that support their own ecosystems. There are thriving populations of bald eagles, cormorants, herons, ospreys, beavers, river otters, deer, snakes, and turtles. The waters are home to striped bass, white perch, channel catfish, and other species of fish.

Many of the main wrecks are clustered together. As you paddle along, look into the skeletons of the ships to see tall grass, shrubbery, and even trees growing from the wreckage. (*Caution:* Do not get too close, as many vessel sites are quite fragile and have wood and steel protruding from their hulls and might cause damage to your canoe or kayak or personal injury.)

The Chesapeake Conservancy has created three paddling routes for exploring the sunken ships. The first itinerary, Burning Basin, runs in a circular cove near the boat launch and takes about an hour to complete. Among the wreckage is a wooden barge that was used by Bethlehem Steel as a work platform when the scrap metal from the ships was being recovered. Itinerary two, Ghost Fleet, is an inland passage that runs north along the shoreline, includes twelve stops along a variety of vessels, and takes about two and a half hours. One of the highlights on this route is the "The Flower Pot Wrecks," two cargo steamships that are overgrown with vegetation. Outer Passage, the third itinerary, follows the outer perimeter of Mallows Bay and continues farther north to Sandy Point. It takes an estimated one and a half hours. This route is rated for intermediate paddling experience as the waters can be challenging to navigate. On the northern-most section, "The Sentinel Wreck" is believed to have floated free from Mallows Bay and been towed back to the Maryland shore and abandoned.

In 2015, Mallows Bay was listed as an archaeological and historic site on the National Register of Historic Places. It has also been nominated to become a national marine sanctuary. The designation would help protect a 52-square-mile stretch of the tidal Potomac River and allow it to be better studied, interpreted, and protected. There are currently just fourteen national marine sanctuaries in the nation.

Mallows Bay Park has free parking, portable restrooms, picnic tables, and a walking trail that runs along portions of the bay. The park is an excellent place for wildlife viewing and has high-quality forest and marshlands. Forest interior nesting birds such as wood thrushes, northern parula warblers, acadian flycatchers, ovenbirds, hooded warblers, and scarlet tanagers have been seen in the park.

During the Civil War, these same shores were defended by thousands of Union troops to prevent a Confederate invasion of Southern Maryland. To learn more about the history of this historic site, check out the book *Ghost Fleet of Mallows Bay and Other Tales of the Lost Chesapeake* by Donald G. Shomette.

BALD EAGLE

The national emblem of the United States, the bald eagle was chosen to represent freedom due to its great strength and majestic looks. We see the eagle on our quarter, the half dollar, the silver dollar, and the Great Seal of the United States, our national coat of arms. And yet, its choice as America's national bird was a matter of concern for a least one founding father, Benjamin Franklin. He felt the bird was of bad moral character and too lazy to fish for itself. Franklin preferred the turkey, "a much more respectable bird."

Franklin wasn't wrong about the birds' opportunism. Rather than do their own fishing, they often go after other creatures' catches, harassing an osprey with prey until the latter bird drops its catch and then swooping in to steal it. While bald eagles mostly eat fish, they also eat smaller birds (including ducks, coots, and auklets), reptiles, amphibians, crabs, and small mammals, such as muskrat.

Eagles are a member of the *Accipitridae* family; which also includes hawks and turkey vultures, which are closely related and sometimes mistaken for bald eagles. Large and dark, turkey vultures have much smaller, darker heads and hold their wings in a pronounced V-shape when soaring.

Despite its moniker, the bald eagle is not really hairless. The name derives from an older meaning of the word: "white headed." The adult is primarily chocolate brown with a white-feathered head and tail; yellow feet, legs, and beak; and pale-yellow eyes. It has a heavy body, a large head, and a hooked bill. Males and females are almost identical, except for their size: Females are about 25 percent larger than males.

The bald eagle has a body length of 28 to 40 inches and a typical wingspan between 5.9 and 7.5 feet, enabling them to soar steadily through the air and to fly up to an altitude of 10,000 feet at speeds of 35 to 43 MPH, with diving speeds of 75 to 99 MPH. Young birds reach maturity at about 5 years. They are believed to mate for life, with an average lifespan in the wild of about 20 years. The oldest known eagle lived in captivity in West Stephentown, New York, to at least 48 years old.

They build nests in very tall trees, above a surrounding forest, 180 feet or more above ground. While nesting, the bald eagle is easily startled by human activity and most commonly is found near large bodies of open water, with abundant fish to eat and old growth, such as mature stands of coniferous or hardwood trees, in which to perch. In parks or forested environments, you may see them soaring in solitude, swooping down to snatch fish from the water or chasing other birds for their food. Bald eagles live throughout North America, including most of Canada, all of the continental United States, and in the northern areas of Mexico. Occupying varied habitats, from the southern reaches of Louisiana to the California desert and the eastern deciduous forests of Quebec and New England, northern birds are migratory, while southern birds remain in one place all year.

In the late twentieth century, these magnificent birds were on the U.S. government's list of Endangered and Threatened Wildlife. For many decades, environmental pollutants, such as mercury, persistent organic chemicals, heavy metals, and DDT weakened the birds' eggshells and severely limited their ability to reproduce. In recent years, environmental protective measures have helped populations to recover. The bald eagle was removed from the endangered species list in the lower 48 states in 2007. According to the 2015 North American Breeding Bird Survey, Partners in Flight estimates the global population of bald eagles at around 250,000. They remain most abundant in Alaska and Canada.

Look for bald eagles while you kayak or hike along lakes, reservoirs, rivers, and marshes. They are most easily seen perched on top of dead trees along the water's edge. To capture a photo worthy of these great birds, you will need a telephoto lens.

27 | Blackwater National Wildlife Refuge

This birders paradise is a gem of the Eastern Shore and one of the best places in the region to enjoy a peaceful paddle. Look for bald and golden eagles, ospreys, river otters, muskrat, dragonflies, and a wide variety of waterfowl.

Location: Cambridge, MD
Maps: Sketch map in brochure, U.S. Fish and Wildlife Service: fws.gov
Length: 3.5 to 4 miles or more if desired
Time: 2 to 3 hours
Average Depth: 2 to 5 feet
Development: Rural
Access: Park entrance fee
Information: U.S. Fish and Wildlife Service: fws.gov, Blackwater National Wildlife Refuge, 2145 Key Wallace Drive, Cambridge, MD 21613, 410-228-2677
Camping: Taylors Island Family Campground, 20 miles east (see Appendix A)
Outfitters: Blackwater Paddle and Pedal, 2524 Key Wallace Drive, Cambridge, MD 21613, 410-901-9255, blackwaterpaddleandpedal.com
Take Note: Electric motorboats only. Hunting is permitted for deer, turkeys, and waterfowl in select areas of the refuge; fishing and crabbing is allowed by boat, except in the waterway between MD 335 and Shorter's Wharf Road, which is closed October 1 through March 31 to protect migratory waterfowl.

TRIP 27: BLACKWATER NATIONAL WILDLIFE REFUGE

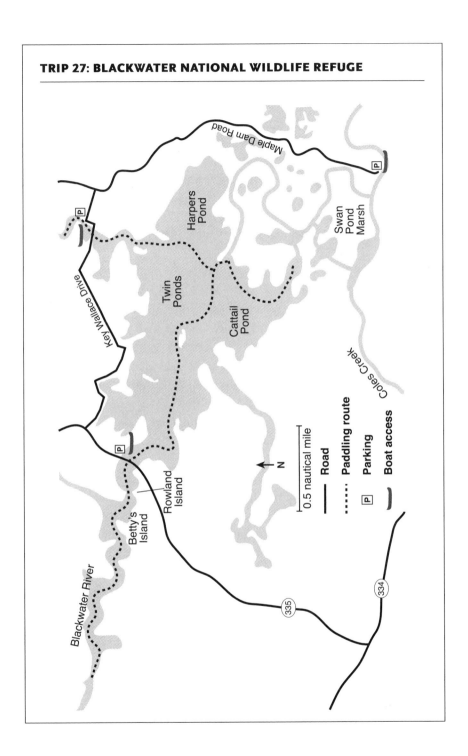

GETTING THERE

Take US 50 East and cross the Chesapeake Bay Bridge, then continue to Cambridge. After crossing the Choptank River Bridge into the city of Cambridge, continue on US 50 for approximately 4 miles and turn right at MD 16 West (Church Creek Road). Follow MD 16 for 2.8 miles (cumulative: 6.8 miles) before turning left onto Egypt Road. Continue 7.1 miles (13.9 miles) until the road dead-ends at Key Wallace Drive. Turn right onto Key Wallace Drive to get to the refuge office and to the visitor center. Pass the visitor center, cross the bridge, and you will see Blackwater Paddle and Pedal on the left.

To enter other waterways on the refuge, small boats may put in at the boat launch site on MD 335 or Shorter's Wharf Road. (38° 26.820′ N, 76° 4.881′ W)

WHAT YOU'LL SEE

As you arrive at Blackwater National Wildlife Refuge, you can tell that this is a special place: remote and tranquil and filled with stunning views and extraordinary nature-viewing opportunities. Established in 1933, Blackwater is a waterfowl sanctuary for birds and a prime destination for wildlife lovers. The property consists of more than 25,000 acres of tidal wetlands, open fields, and deciduous forests and is one of more than 540 units in the National Wildlife Refuge System that is managed by the U.S. Fish and Wildlife Service, a part of the Department of the Interior. The refuge is home to 250 species of birds, 35 species of reptiles and amphibians, 165 species of threatened and endangered plants, and numerous mammals. It is a great place for paddling as well as birding, photography, and bicycling. Visitors can drive, bike, or walk the approximately 4-mile paved Wildlife Drive, which travels along the Blackwater River and offers excellent views of the Refuge.

Blackwater National Wildlife Refuge has three marked water trails (green, purple, and orange) designated for kayaking. However, the trail markings are confusing, and it is easy to get lost along the Blackwater River. Susan Meredith, owner of Blackwater Paddle and Pedal, recommends kayakers follow the Green Trail only as it is the most navigable. Blackwater Paddle and Pedal is the only kayak outfitter along the refuge and guides trips north of the refuge along the Little Blackwater River. You may rent a kayak, take a guided trip, or launch your own kayak (with no fee) from the site at 2524 Key Wallace Drive. From the put-in spot, paddle to the right and you will easily navigate along these protected waters that are teeming with wildlife.

The refuge is home to 85 species of birds who specifically breed in the woodlands and surrounding habitat. The best time for viewing waterfowl is between mid-October and mid-March. Although most waterfowl migrate north in

Kayaks stand at the ready for a group tour of Blackwater National Wildlife Refuge.

spring, some remain through summer, using the protected areas of the refuge to raise their young. The most common ducks found here are mallards, black ducks, blue-winged teal, green-winged teal, and pintails. Other large resident birds include blue heron and bald eagles.

As you are paddling, be sure to look for bald and golden eagles, as they are commonly seen at Blackwater throughout the year. The refuge has the greatest density of breeding bald eagles on the East Coast, north of Florida. They are most often seen soaring over the marsh or perched in tall pine trees looking for a fish to snatch from another bird's talons. If you want to learn more about eagles and other birds on the refuge, stop by the visitor center, which has nature exhibits and TV monitors that broadcast live images from a bald eagle nest and an osprey nest onsite. The Friends of Blackwater operate raptor cams year-round and broadcast live images on their website as well. The visitor center is open Monday to Friday 8 A.M. to 4 P.M. and on Saturdays and Sundays from 9 A.M. to 5 P.M.

Ospreys, or "fish hawks," are common from spring through fall and conspicuously use nesting platforms that have been placed throughout the marsh at Blackwater National Wildlife Refuge. Osprey and eagle interactions are entertaining to watch due to the birds' lively competition for fish resources.

The largest natural population of formerly endangered Delmarva peninsula fox squirrels also lives on the refuge, although you will not likely see them on the water. The large tree squirrels live in mature hardwood and pine forests. To catch a glimpse of this steel-gray squirrel, take a walk along the Key Wallace Trail or the Tubman Road Trail, where they can often be seen foraging for food on the ground in the low branches of trees.

Blackwater kicks off each spring with its annual Eagle Festival in March, which features live birds of prey programs, an archery range, marsh hikes, and wildlife exhibits. In April, the refuge hosts an Earth Day celebration and litter pick-up day, and in June the annual Youth Fishing Day at Hog Range Pond includes a fishing event for kids with prizes, educational programs, and photos. Throughout summer, visitors enjoy guided bird-watching tours.

This land is also an important historic landmark. In March 2017, the Harriet Tubman Underground Railroad State Park and Visitor Center opened adjacent to the refuge to commemorate the life and legacy of the legendary abolitionist through state-of-the-art exhibits and educational programming. Harriet Tubman was born and raised in Dorchester County. The new state park, visitor center, and national monument will surely bring more visitors to explore the refuge and paddle on its waters. Cambridge, the nearest town, has a historic district that features brick-paved streets with parks, a marina, museums, and a lighthouse on the water.

28 | Little Seneca Lake: Black Hill Regional Park

Explore the convergence of three creeks in Little Seneca Lake via the self-guided Black Hill Water Trail.

Location: Boyds, MD
Maps: Montgomery Parks, montgomeryparks.org
Length: 5 miles
Time: 3 to 5 hours following the water trail markers
Average Depth: 32 feet
Development: Suburban
Access: Launch fee
Information: Montgomery Parks, montgomeryparks.org

TRIP 28: LITTLE SENECA LAKE: BLACK HILL REGIONAL PARK

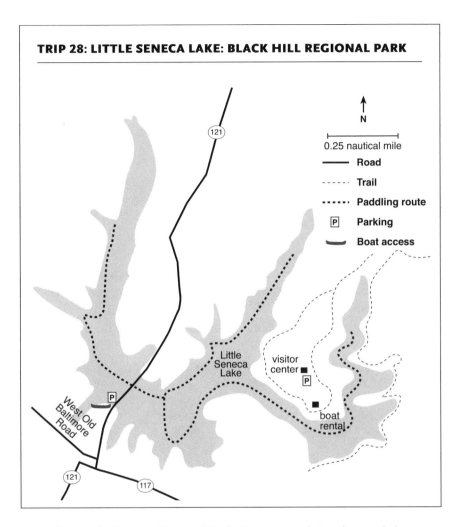

Camping: Little Bennett Regional Park Campground, 5 miles north (see Appendix A)

Outfitters: Onsite, 301-528-3466

Take Note: Electric motorboats only. Private boats are permitted on Little Seneca Lake from March 1 to December 15.

GETTING THERE

From the junction of I-495 (Capital Beltway) and I-270 spur in Maryland, head northwest on I-270 (toward Frederick) for about 18.5 miles. Get off at Exit 18 and turn left onto MD 121 (Clarksburg Road). Proceed generally southward for about 1.6 miles (cumulative: 20.1 miles). Then turn left onto West Old

Baltimore Road. Go east for 1 mile (21.1 miles), and turn right into the park. Turn right at Black Hills Road to follow the sign to the public boat ramp.

The public boat ramp and boat storage area are located off of Black Hills Road, across the Cabin Branch stretch of the lake. The boat rental facility is located further south, just below the visitor center off of Lake Ridge Drive. (39° 12.003′ N, 77° 17.655′ W)

WHAT YOU'LL SEE

The 505-acre manufactured Little Seneca Lake is the Washington, D.C., metropolitan area's largest lake, an irregularly shaped body of water formed by three creeks: Little Seneca, Cabin Branch, and Ten Mile. The creeks come together at Black Hill Regional Park and provide a healthy habitat for a wide array of wildlife and an ideal setting for boating and fishing.

Four decades ago, the area consisted of privately owned fields, woods, and streams. After drought struck the area in the 1980s, Montgomery County and the Washington Suburban Sanitary Commission agreed to create Little Seneca as an emergency water-supply reservoir and park. The three creeks were

Three turtles sun themselves in a protective cove of Little Seneca Lake.

dammed, stream valleys filled up, and farmers left. When the park opened in 1987, the land was still surrounded by farmland. Since then, residential development spreading westward has reached the park boundary. Today, water from the lake is released through the dam as needed to supplement water levels in the Potomac River and provide clean drinking water during times of drought.

While the park is just minutes away from a thriving suburban community, the lake is large enough that you will enjoy peace and quiet as you explore the small islands in each of its three branches. A self-guided water trail, created by the Maryland-National Capital Park and Planning Commission, includes eighteen markers to make it easy to learn about the region's flora and fauna along the route. To follow the water trail, pick up a map at the visitor center or print an online version.

The blue trail markers begin in sequence near the boathouse and rental facility and identify points of interest, geological characteristics, and potential wildlife that you may see in the specific area. Paddling the entire water trail can take up to five hours so you may want to explore just part of it and return another day to enjoy the rest of the lake. Launching from the public boat ramp, you will begin at the third marker. Next to the boat ramp you will see two silos. The barn was once used for dairy farming and today serves as a station for the Park Police Mounted Unit and their horses.

As you paddle along the water trail, you will see that Black Hill nurtures a rich population of plants and birds. The woodlands are predominately oaks, hickories, beeches, maples, tulip trees, and conifers. A variety of waterfowl can be seen; the ducks and geese are so used to humans on the lake that they are not easily scared off and may come close to you looking for food. In winter, fish-hungry bald eagles and ospreys can more easily be seen along the lake. There are also a number of active beaver lodges.

One of the most interesting sections of the lake is the cove at trail marker eleven. Approach the area slowly and quietly and you will likely see red-bellied cooters and smaller painted turtles sunning themselves on a log. This inlet is also home to a group of tall dead trees that tower over the water creating a beautiful and unique backdrop. When the stream valley was flooded to create the lake, many trees were left standing intentionally to provide a habitat for birds and fish. Fishing is popular here as the lake has a plentiful supply of largemouth bass, bluegill, tiger muskie, and catfish.

The park also features more than 10 miles of multiuse hiking, biking, and equestrian trails that go by historical areas. Near the park office and the start of Black Hill Trail, is an old gold mine that was used from the 1850s to the 1950s. Waters Mill dates to 1810 and still shows sign of the French Burr millstone used to grind flour on the site; it is located just off Black Hill Trail near Little Seneca Creek, just above the lake.

The visitor center provides exhibits and naturalist guided programs for children and adults, open Wednesday through Friday from 11 A.M. to 5 P.M. and Saturday and Sunday from 11 A.M. to 6 P.M. Park naturalists offer astronomy, fishing and kayaking programs, hikes, pontoon boat tours, and educational workshops throughout the year. There are also picnic areas, playgrounds, a fitness course, and volleyball courts.

29 | Piscataway Creek

Piscataway Creek provides a chance to see many types of birds, including ospreys, herons, loons, ducks, and bald eagles.

Location: Fort Washington, MD
Maps: National Park Service: nps.gov
Length: 5 miles
Time: 2 to 3 hours
Average Depth: 5 to 8 feet near marina, 2 to 3 feet in the narrowest sections
Development: Suburban
Access: Launch fee
Information: National Park Service: nps.gov; Accokeek Foundation at Piscataway: 301-283-2113, accokeek.org
Camping: Joint Base Andrews Family Campground, 13 miles northeast (see Appendix A)
Outfitters: Atlantic Kayak Company: atlantickayak.com
Take Note: Unlimited horsepower. Fort Washington Marina offers boat slip rentals and boat repair services and has a restaurant onsite. The grounds of the marina are open year-round and the marina is open May through October, Monday to Saturday 8:30 A.M. to 5 P.M., Sunday 9:30 A.M. to 4:30 P.M. Swimming and wading are not allowed in Piscataway Creek.

GETTING THERE
From I-495 South, take Exit 3 to MD 210 South (Indian Head Highway) and go approximately 4 miles. Take a right on Fort Washington Road and continue for 3 miles (cumulative: 7 miles), then turn left on Warburton Road

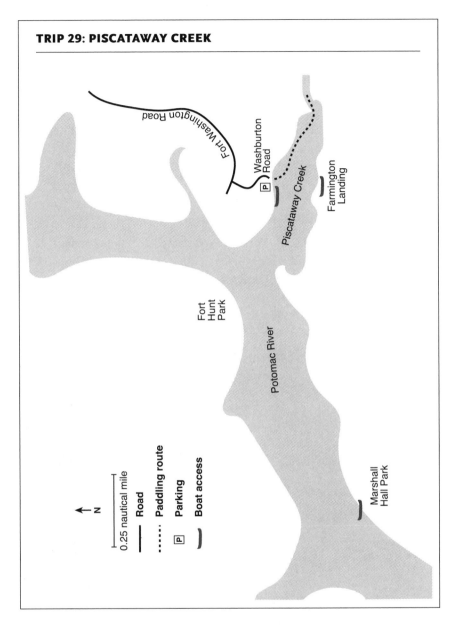

and continue into the entrance to Fort Washington Marina. (38° 42.194′ N, 77° 1.473′ W)

WHAT YOU'LL SEE

Fort Washington Marina is a part of Piscataway Park, located adjacent to Fort Washington Park, and provides access to Piscataway Creek and the Potomac

River in Prince George's County. The park is a great place to view wildlife as it is on the Atlantic Flyway, a migration route used by millions of birds each year. Some of the most abundant species include mourning doves, chimney swifts, red-bellied woodpeckers, blue jays, American crows, Carolina wrens, European starlings, and northern cardinals.

Launching from the marina, go to the left to approach the more sheltered waters of Piscataway Creek. You will paddle across a wide section for about 1 mile, and then the terrain will change dramatically becoming easier to paddle with shallow and still waters. Stay to the left as you proceed across the wider section and you may see a variety of birds. Follow the shoreline until you reach a large swath of water lotus. Go to the right to maneuver around the plants or paddle across some of the smaller patches of low-growing plants. On the right, you'll see a few houses. As you continue around to the left, the water lotuses begin to form a narrow and easy water trail that you can follow. These plants attract wildlife, so paddle slowly and look for beavers, herons, turtles, snakes, and possibly a bald eagle.

A great blue heron sits in a swath of aquatic plants, surveying the surrounding water.

If you continue paddling for another mile, the terrain changes again and narrows more becoming surrounded by woods. The creek eventually crosses under MD 210, where you will likely hear some road noise. Remember as you continue along that the return trip to the marina will require some harder paddling, so be sure to save some energy for the end of your excursion. As this area has a lot to explore, plan additional time following your kayak trip to visit Fort Washington Park and Piscataway Park.

Fort Washington was a defensive fort built along the Potomac River to protect the nation's capital. The original fort was completed in 1809 and destroyed during the War of 1812. The current fort, constructed in 1824, is maintained by the National Park Service. The grounds surrounding the fort offer extensive multiuse paths and river views and is an ideal setting for hiking, biking, picnicking, and fishing. Historical reenactments are held periodically at the park and there is a small museum that interprets the history of the area. The park grounds are open daily from 8 A.M. to sunset. The historic fort and the visitor center are open from 9 A.M. to 4 P.M. during winter months and 9 A.M. to 5 P.M. during summer.

Piscataway Park and Piscataway Creek are named for the Piscataway tribe, which was once one of the most populous tribes in the Chesapeake Bay region. The park extends along the Potomac River for about 6 miles and covers approximately 5,000 acres. Since 1957, the Accokeek Foundation, in partnership with the National Park Service, has managed about 200 acres within Piscataway Park at the National Colonial Farm, a historic farm museum. The property demonstrates eighteenth-century agriculture, including a reconstructed colonial-era farm featuring now-rare crops and livestock breeds, as well as a modern organic farm. Visitors can take a self-guided walking tour of the property, learn about its history, and observe an award-winning forest restoration project. Among its other attractions are views of George Washington's Mount Vernon Estate, a chestnut grove, an arboretum, and a marsh. The park's beautiful grounds, trails, and programs are open to the public year-round. The visitor center is open March 1 through November 30, Tuesday through Sunday from 10 A.M. to 4 P.M. and December 1 through February 28 from 10 A.M. to 4 P.M. on weekends only.

In addition to Fort Washington Marina, there are several boat ramps that can be used for kayaking. On the grounds of the National Colonial Farm, a fishing pier and a boat dock are both available for kayaking, although you have to carry your boat in a good distance from the parking lot. You can also launch from a dirt ramp at Farmington Landing at Wharf Road and from a concrete ramp at Marshall Hall Boat Ramp on Bryans Road, both in Accokeek.

OSPREY

For years, the osprey population suffered decline largely due to environmental pesticides and habitat destruction. Now, with the help of artificial nesting sites and a ban on DDT, they are making a tremendous comeback. Brown above and white below, the birds' most distinguishing marks are their broad, black cheek patches and black wrist patches.

A female osprey's wingspan averages 4 to 4.5 feet, with the male wingspan slightly smaller. Females choose partners based on nest location, favoring treetops near water, and the pair typically mates for life. While males and females may winter in different locations, they return to their nest within a few days of each other. Ospreys arrive in southern New Jersey around the end of March and in northern New Jersey a week or two later. Graceful touch-and-go aerial maneuvers, their courtship flights may be seen the first week or two after their arrival, as mating pairs are made or renewed. Part of the mating ritual entails the male catching fish for the female to prove he will be, or still is, a good provider. Both adults assist in building a new nest or repairing the old one, usually 3 to 5 feet in diameter, shoring up walls with fresh twigs and lining the bottom with mucky sod. While both contribute twigs, the female arranges the nest more often than not.

Also known as the "fish hawk," the osprey is the only raptor whose front talons turn backward and the only one that plunges feet-first into the water. Spines on the osprey's toes enable it to hold on to slippery fish, its main prey. They are also known to take an occasional small rodent or crustacean when fishing is extremely poor.

When not out hunting, the male can be found on his roost, about 100 yards away and within sight of the nest. At a hint of danger, such as human intrusion or blackbird mobbing, the female emits a high-pitched *eep, eep, eep,* a signal for the male to come to the rescue. As the female nears egg-laying time, she stays closer to the nest, leaving infrequently to stretch her wings. Once she lays her two to four eggs, she hunkers down in the nest, with only the top of her head visible to careful observers. She is the primary egg incubator but does trade off periodically with the male. From pairing to egg-laying, females are fed by the male. After catching a fish, the male eats the head and neck before bringing the remainder to the nest. He takes over incubation while the female feeds. After she has eaten and preened, she goes back to incubation duty, and the male returns to his proximal roost.

Young hatch about five weeks after the eggs are laid, but it will take an additional seven to eight weeks until they are ready to leave the nest. Even then, the parents must provide food for the first few weeks until the young can hunt well enough on their own. By mid-October, ospreys start heading south to their favorite wintering ground. Mating pairs usually split for the duration, only to meet again the following spring, when the courtship ritual plays out once again before actual mating takes place.

30 | Spa Creek

From your vantage point on this urban creek, check out some of Annapolis's most unusual waterfront properties.

Location: Annapolis, MD
Maps: Visit Annapolis: visitannapolis.org
Length: 3 miles
Time: 1 to 2 hours
Average Depth: 4 to 8 feet
Development: Urban
Access: Launch fee
Information: Truxtun Park, 273 Hilltop Lane, Annapolis, MD 21403, 410-263-7958; Spa Creek Conservancy: spacreek.net, 101 Spa View Avenue, Annapolis, MD 21401 410-353-6603
Camping: Annapolis Campground, 5 miles northeast (see Appendix A—the campground is open year-round to all active-duty, retired, and reserve military; Department of Defense employees and family members)
Outfitters: On-site, Kayak Annapolis: 443-949-0773, kayakannapolistours.com; Annapolis Canoe and Kayak: 410-263-2303, annapoliscanoeandkayak.com
Take Note: Unlimited horsepower; yield to all boats. Launch from Truxtun Park Boat Ramp.

GETTING THERE
On US 50 East, take Exit 22 for MD 665 toward Aris T. Allen Boulevard (Riva Road). Continue straight as MD 665 becomes Forest Drive and after approximately 2.6 miles, turn left onto Hilltop Lane and drive for 1.1 miles (cumulative: 3.7 miles). Turn left onto Primrose Road, and when the road forks after about

TRIP 30: SPA CREEK

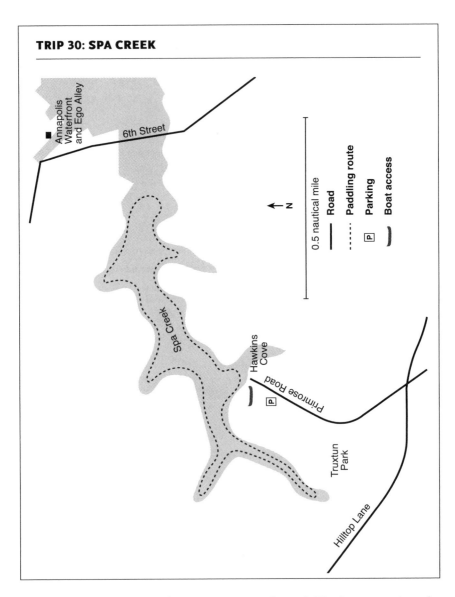

0.2 mile (3.9 miles), turn left onto Truxtun Park Road. The boat ramp is at the end of this road. Unload and then park your car in the lot 500 feet away near the restrooms. (38° 58.107′ N, 76° 29.912′ W)

WHAT YOU'LL SEE

Annapolis, the state capital of Maryland, is referred to as the sailing capital of the world and is an interesting place to explore by all kinds of watercraft. You can paddle a kayak along some of the creeks that surround downtown

Annapolis. One of the largest, Spa Creek, off the Severn River and the Chesapeake Bay, is an urban waterway and the gateway to Annapolis. While many paddling destinations are great for wildlife viewing, this one is usually more of a prime spot for people watching and marveling over waterfront properties and expensive boats.

From Spa Creek, you can stay in calm waters or paddle into more open waters in Annapolis Harbor. There, you will get a closer glimpse of the United States Naval Academy and other historic sites. You can get a real workout if you would like, as these waters continue on to wider and rougher sections of the Chesapeake Bay. Be aware of your own stamina and go only as far as you are comfortable.

The best place to launch into Spa Creek is from the public boat ramp at Truxtun Park, an 80-acre recreation area in the Eastport section of Annapolis. This tract of land was donated to the city in the 1930s by Truxtun Beale, a lawyer and a diplomat who was once the U.S. Ambassador to Persia and then to Greece, Romania, and Serbia. The park is run by the city and is home to Truxtun Park Municipal Swim Center, the only outdoor public swimming pool in Annapolis.

Kayakers share Spa Creek, near downtown Annapolis, with many other types of recreators.

Once a haven for fishing, crabbing, and boating, Spa Creek is unfortunately now classified as a highly impaired urban watershed. While it is currently unfit for swimming, and sediment buildup is reducing navigable waters for boaters, Spa Creek is still one of the easiest places to get out on the water from the Maryland suburbs.

The Truxtun Park boat ramp features two concrete launching ramps with adjacent finger piers. You can launch from the grassy area to the left of the ramp. As you leave the dock, head to the left and turn left again. You will see some beautiful homes lining the creek and the old oyster and crabbing boats docked along the shoreline. Paddle under the bridge at Pump House Road and continue around the bend to the left until you reach the end of the creek. Be mindful of shallow spots, as the depth in this area is inconsistent. Look for great blue herons, ducks, geese, and other shorebirds along the less populated coves. You are most likely to see wildlife as you paddle along the shoreline of the park.

After you turn around and head east, views of Annapolis Harbor and the United States Naval Academy are in the backdrop. Explore some of the smaller coves, such as Old Woman's Cove and Acton Cove, and you will see some interesting waterfront properties and massive watercrafts. If you have the energy, you can continue past the end of Spa Creek to Annapolis Harbor and Ego Alley, the city dock at the heart of historic Annapolis. The waters there are sometimes choppy and very busy with everything from dinghies to 100-foot-long ocean-going yachts. Avoid the main channel here when possible.

In addition to the boat ramp and swimming pool, Truxtun Park has hiking trails, a skate park, picnic areas, two playgrounds, twelve tennis courts, three baseball fields, and five basketball courts. The "Pip" Moyer Recreation Center is located here and offers an array of recreational and family activities such as indoor rock climbing, an indoor playground, three basketball courts, and a four-lane walking/jogging track.

After your paddle, explore Eastport, which features great seafood restaurants and the Annapolis Maritime Museum, where you can learn how to harvest oysters, climb aboard a locally built workboat, and engage in interactive experiences. You could also visit downtown Annapolis, which offers waterfront dining, shopping, and a variety of historic sites.

31 | Deep Creek Lake

Despite its many coves and inlets, Deep Creek is often thick with mountain tourists. To find a quiet escape from the bustling lake, meander up the narrow Meadow Mountain Run.

Location: Swanton, MD
Maps: Maryland Department of Natural Resources: dnr.maryland.gov
Area: 3,900 acres
Time: 2 to 3 hours or more
Average Depth: 16 feet in Deep Creek Lake; 2 to 3 feet in Meadow Mountain Run
Development: Rural
Access: Park entrance fee
Information: Maryland Department of Natural Resources: 301-387-5563, dnr.maryland.gov; Deep Creek Lake State Park, 898 State Park Road, Swanton, MD 21561
Camping: On-site: parkreservations.maryland.gov (see Appendix A)
Outfitters: On-site at the state park provided by Wisp Resort; around the lake, rentals are available from Aquatic Center, High Mountain Sports, Deep Creek Marina, and Bill's Outdoor Center. Many retail stores at the lake offer kayak rentals and some even provide delivery and pickup services.
Take Note: Unlimited horsepower. Park gate is open 8 A.M. to sunset. With 65 miles of shoreline, the lake has multiple places that you can launch; most of the marinas will let you launch your own kayak from their sites.

GETTING THERE
Travel west on I-70 to I-68 West, Exit 14A (for US 219 South Deep Creek Lake). Continue on US 219 South for 18 miles, and then turn left onto Glendale Road. Continue on Glendale Road for 1 mile (cumulative: 19 miles). Immediately after crossing the Glendale Bridge, turn left onto State Park Road. Continue for 1 mile to the park entrance (20 miles). If you bring your own kayak or canoe, park near the entrance gate and launch at the soft launch at the south end of the parking lot. Note, the kayak rental kiosk is located on the opposite side of the beach from the car top launch on the north (far right side) of the beach. (39° 30.712′ N, 79° 18.280′ W)

TRIP 31: DEEP CREEK LAKE

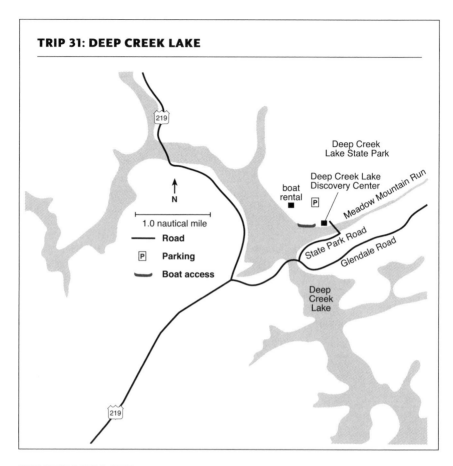

Deep Creek
Lake State Park

Deep Creek Lake
Discovery Center

boat
rental

Meadow Mountain Run

State Park Road

Glendale Road

Deep
Creek
Lake

N

1.0 nautical mile

— Road
P Parking
⌣ Boat access

WHAT YOU'LL SEE

Deep Creek Lake is the largest freshwater lake in Maryland and a popular four-season mountain resort area with breathtaking scenery. The 12-mile-long lake is located in Garrett County, just west of the Allegheny Front on a large plateau known as the Allegany Highlands. With 65 miles of shoreline, the area is one of the busiest boating destinations in the region.

Deep Creek Lake was artificially constructed as a hydroelectric project in the 1920s by the Youghiogheny Hydroelectric Company. Fed by natural springs, the lake continues to provide clean and clear water that is great for swimming. With a higher elevation, the climate tends to be much more temperate than in neighboring cities. In fact, the temperatures are usually 10 to 15 degrees Fahrenheit cooler than surrounding area.

You can launch a kayak from just about anywhere on the lake and take in panoramic mountain views, daydream about living in the luxury lakefront houses, and watch the lively activity of waterskis and jetskis. Beware, as the waters can get choppy from boat traffic, especially on weekends. To avoid boat traffic and have a better chance of encountering wildlife, set out early in the morning or go for an evening paddle. There are so many miles of shoreline that you can be sure to find some quieter coves and inlets to explore.

Launch from Deep Creek Lake State Park and you can easily reach one of the quietest corners of the lake. The state park boasts 1 mile of shoreline that is open to the public, with a public beach, kayak rentals, and a boat ramp. To launch your kayak from here, you will need to carry your boat down a short staircase and approximately 100 yards to the boat ramp. Paddle to the left and go under the State Park Road Bridge. The waters will narrow here, and boat traffic is significantly reduced in this area. Keep heading east and the lake leads to Meadow Mountain Run, a narrow, marshy creek with shallow waters and changing scenery. Quickly you will forget you were just in a busy resort area and you will enjoy the quiet natural environment.

The park offers a variety of recreational activities including boating, canoeing, swimming, fishing, hiking, hunting, mountain biking, horseback riding, and wildlife viewing. Facilities here include a Discovery Center that boasts a nature center and exhibits, campgrounds, picnic tables and shelters, restrooms, and playgrounds. The sandy, lifeguarded beach is a great place for young children to play and swim during the summer months.

Kayakers paddle along the shoreline of beautiful Deep Creek Lake.

After you paddle, spend some time at the beach or explore the miles of hiking trails at the state park. Interpretive walks are available near the Discovery Center and along the nearby Brant Mine Trail. For a longer, more challenging hike, try the rocky loop trails that ascend to the top of Meadow Mountain and provide an overlook of Deep Creek Lake.

The park consists of a maturing northern hardwood forest primarily consisting of oaks and hickories. The habitat has been preserved and managed over the past decades allowing the growth in numbers of wildlife species such as black bears, wild turkeys, and white-tailed deer. Small mammals include squirrels, chipmunks, raccoons, and opossums.

Stop by the Discovery Center, a 6,000-square foot interactive showcase with exhibits on turtles, foxes, black bears, and more. The center even has an on-site aviary full of rescued and rehabilitated birds of prey. Learn more about the natural and cultural resources of the park by attending interpretive programs such as talks, hikes, and evening campfire programs.

32 | Savage River Reservoir: Big Run State Park

Enjoy spectacular views, crystal clear mountain water, and the opportunity to see bald eagles and a variety of waterfowl.

Location: Swanton, MD
Maps: USGS Kitzmiller
Area: 360 acres
Time: 2 or more hours
Average Depth: 3 to 5 feet
Development: Rural
Access: No fees
Information: Maryland Department of Natural Resources: 301-895-5453, dnr.maryland.gov; Big Run State Park c/o New Germany State Park, 349 Headquarters Lane, Grantsville, MD 21536
Camping: On-site (see Appendix A)

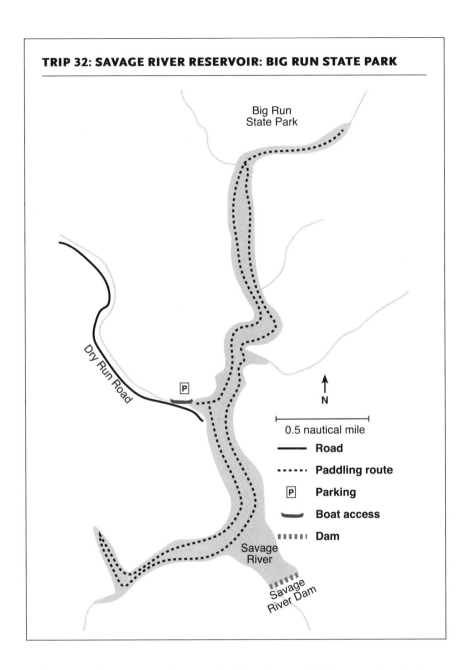

Take Note: Electric motorboats only. There is no cell phone service, food, water, restrooms, or other amenities, as the park is located in a very remote area, although it is just a 25-minute drive to the bustling Deep Creek Lake resort area; be sure to map out your route ahead of time as you will not be able to use a GPS to find your way.

The Savage River Reservoir offers a gorgeous mountain setting for paddling and is one of the quietest destinations in western Maryland.

GETTING THERE

From I-68, take Exit 22. Follow Chestnut Ridge Road south 2 miles to the end, and turn left on New Germany Road. Follow New Germany Road south for 5 miles (cumulative: 7 miles), and make a left on Big Run Road. Follow Big Run Road east for 5 miles (12 miles) to the end. Turn right on Savage River Road and continue for 2 miles (14 miles) to the intersection of Dry Run Road. The boat ramp is on the left.

From Deep Creek Lake, turn off US 219 onto Glendale Road. Cross the lake and continue for approximately 5 miles, and then turn right on North Glade Road. After 2.6 miles (cumulative: 7.6 miles), turn right on MD 495 and drive for 3.3 miles (10.9 miles). Go through the town of Swanton, turning left onto Swanton Road and continuing for 2.1 miles (13 miles). Pass over MD 135 onto Mount Zion Road. Follow Mount Zion Road for approximately 5.5 miles (18.5 miles) to the boat ramp. (39° 31.373′ N, 79° 8.630′ W)

WHAT YOU'LL SEE

Big Run State Park is a strikingly beautiful area located in the Allegheny Mountain region of northwestern Maryland and an ideal spot for boating, fishing, and hiking. The park is surrounded by Savage River State Forest and sits at the mouth of the Savage River Reservoir. The boat ramp is at the center of the reservoir and is surrounded by gorgeous scenery. The views are impressive, and it's hard to resist gasping at the natural beauty here. Since there are few amenities, this destination tends to be very quiet and a great locale for spotting wildlife. Take your time and paddle slowly to explore the coves and the rocky shoreline which is richly forested.

The Savage River Reservoir is one of the few places in the region you can kayak with mountain views along fresh, crystal clear waters that are easy to paddle. Look for bald eagles, great blue herons, vultures, beavers, turtles, frogs, and salamanders. The waters are flat and calm, so it is easy to traverse across much of the reservoir. At the far northern end, the water divides and narrows into a shallow creek where you will likely see waterfowl hiding along the sheltered waters.

At the southeast corner of the reservoir, you will approach the dam, a rock-filled, 184-feet-high, 1,050-feet-long structure that drains an area of 105 square miles. The land on the eastern side of the reservoir is the 2,000-acre South Savage Mountain Natural Area, a large forested landscape containing very steep inclines and forests that are a mix of oaks, with chestnut and white oaks dominating at the highest elevations, and northern red and white oaks on the lower terrain. This forest is home to a variety of nesting birds, including the rare cerulean warbler, which forages and nests in the tallest trees.

Created by construction of a dam in 1952, the Savage River Reservoir provides drinking water and controls flooding for the area. In 1982, the Maryland Department of Natural Resources documented the presence of a naturally reproducing wild trout population and later implemented policies to improve habitat conditions to ensure trout survival. Today, the reservoir produces the highest overall quality and abundance of wild brook and brown trout in the state of Maryland. Fishing is permitted year-round with a non-tidal fishing license. Other prevalent fish species found here include walleye, largemouth bass, black crappie, yellow perch, bluegill, catfish, tiger muskie, and suckers.

Mature mixed oak and northern hardwood forests provide a habitat to a plethora of wildlife species including black bears, white-tailed deer, bobcats, raccoons, wild turkeys, amphibians, and reptiles. Various species of hawks, owls, and songbirds can often be seen.

Big Run State Park is also a wonderful place for primitive camping, as there are 30 unimproved campsites and a youth group camping area. The park is the trailhead for a 6-mile hiking trail known as Monroe Run. The park is generally very quiet, but note there is a picnic pavilion onsite that can accommodate a crowd of 100 people.

Savage River State Forest offers a variety of outdoor recreational activities including hiking, mountain biking, snowmobiling, cross-country skiing, hunting, fishing, and boating. New Germany State Park is also located within the forest and features a 13-acre lake, providing additional paddling and fishing opportunities.

Several nearby trails are worth exploring and offer stunning scenery year-round. The 17-mile Big Savage Trail winds through forests of oak and hickory trees and terrain covered with thick stands of wild azaleas and rhododendron. There are a series of gravel roads for advanced cycling and a variety of loop trails that are ideal for bird-watching, mountain biking, and hiking.

33 | Sinepuxent Bay: Assateague Island National Seashore

See wild ponies and many species of birds on the beaches and marshes as you explore the extensive bay habitats of this barrier island.

Location: Berlin, MD
Maps: National Park Service: nps.gov
Length: 3 miles or more if desired
Time: 2 to 3 hours
Average Depth: 3 feet
Development: Rural
Access: Park entrance fee
Information: Maryland Department of Natural Resources: dnr.maryland.gov; National Park Service: nps.gov/asis, Assateague Island National Seashore, 7206 National Seashore Lane, Berlin, MD 21811, 410-641-1441
Camping: On-site (see Appendix A)
Outfitters: On-site: Assateague Outfitters: 13002 Bayside Drive, Berlin, MD 21811, 410-656-9453, mdcoastalbays.org/rentals; Ayers Creek Adventures: 8628 Grey Fox Lane, Berlin, MD 21811, 443-513-0889, ayerscreekadventures.com

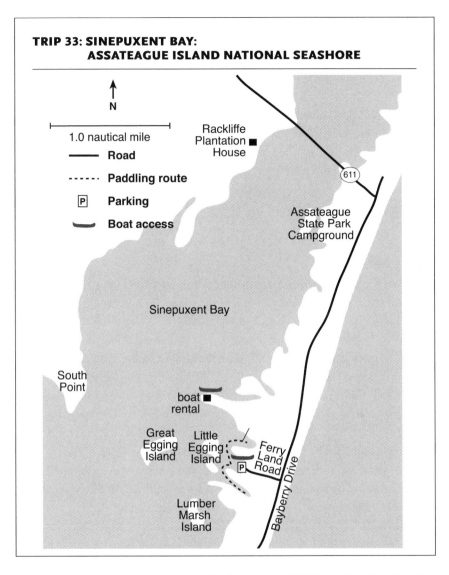

TRIP 33: SINEPUXENT BAY: ASSATEAGUE ISLAND NATIONAL SEASHORE

N

1.0 nautical mile

—— Road

----- Paddling route

P Parking

Boat access

Rackliffe Plantation House

611

Assateague State Park Campground

Sinepuxent Bay

South Point

boat rental

Great Egging Island

Little Egging Island

Ferry Land Road

P

Bayberry Drive

Lumber Marsh Island

Take Note: Electric motorboats only. Launch at Old Ferry Landing Road. If you paddle along the entire shore of the bay, you may see wild ponies, and you will definitely see them as you drive throughout the park. The ponies are wild animals: for your own safety, keep your distance and do not feed or pet them. Assateague is notorious for its mosquitoes, so be sure to protect yourself from bug bites, especially in summer. Stop by the visitor center and ask for a Sinepuxent Bay Water Trail brochure. Note that there is a sign for Old Ferry Landing Road at the park, but on Google Maps it is named Ferry Landing Road.

GETTING THERE

From the Chesapeake Bay Bridge, head east on US 50 toward Ocean City and turn right onto MD 611 (Stephen Decatur Highway) and continue for 102 miles. Before crossing the large bridge, after around 3.5 miles, there is a National Park Service visitor center on the right. Stop there to get maps or information. Continue on MD 611, and pass Bayside Drive, which is the location of the onsite rentals, and turn right at Ferry Landing Road. The boat launch is on the left.

From the Chesapeake Bay Bridge Tunnel, take US 13 north to Pocomoke City (91.3 miles). Turn right onto US 113 and head north toward Berlin. After approximately 28 miles, turn right onto MD 376 (Assateague Road). When it ends, after around 4 miles, turn right onto MD 611 and continue as above. (38° 12.008′ N, 75° 9.747′ W)

WHAT YOU'LL SEE

Assateague Island is one of Maryland's greatest natural treasures and a prime destination for kayaking and wildlife viewing. The 37-mile long barrier island, located off the coast of Maryland and Virginia, is most known for the more than 300 wild ponies who wander the beaches. It is a unique destination with breath-taking scenery and recreational opportunities including fishing, crabbing, clamming, kayaking, bird-watching, wildlife viewing, hiking, and swimming. Assateague Island consists of three public areas: Assateague Island National Seashore, managed by the National Park Service; Chincoteague National Wildlife Refuge, managed by the U.S. Fish and Wildlife Service; and Assateague State Park, managed by Maryland's Department of Natural Resources.

The island has miles of pristine beach, picnic areas, and designated areas for fishing and boating. Paddling is allowed anywhere in the Sinepuxent Bay. However, entrance to the bay can only be found in two locations: at the end of Bayside Drive and at the end of Old Ferry Landing Road. You can rent kayaks or take a guided excursion from Assateague Outfitters, launching from Bayside Road. This launch location opens to a portion of the Sinepuxent Bay that can be exposed to strong winds and currents. For an easier, more protected paddling spot, head a half-mile south to the public boat launch at Old Ferry Landing Road.

After you launch from the sandy beach, paddle to the left and explore the protected marshlands. Traverse around the cove in a clockwise direction and eventually make your way back toward Ferry Landing. Then turn right and proceed toward the Ferry Landing foot bridge. Stay to the left of the bridge and continue straight ahead. Stay to the right of Little Egging Island and follow the waters around to the right to explore several coves.

Assateague Island is among the best places to enjoy the Mid-Atlantic region's unique natural features and see a variety of birds and other wildlife.

During the summer months, this is a popular destination for bird-watching. Stay close to the shoreline and you may see gulls, great blue herons, tricolored herons, terns, semipalmated plovers, killdeer, sandpipers, mallards, geese, American oyster catcher, willet, cormorants, and many more species. To see the most wildlife and the fewest people, arrive early or late in the day.

The island's natural seashore is an important stopover for millions of migrating shorebirds. Thousands of acres of seagrass along the unspoiled beach make this area a haven for endangered birds, turtles, invertebrates, and insects. The conditions make this bay a perfect habitat for the growth of eelgrass and widgeon grass.

In late spring, adult horseshoe crabs migrate inland in search of sandy beach areas where they can dig nests and lay eggs. They frequently nest on the shoreline of Sinepuxent Bay and their eggs become an important food source for many migratory birds that stopover here.

Assateague boasts a rich history that dates back centuries. It is named for the tribe of native people who called this area home before European settlers colonized the Eastern Shore. The famous wild ponies of Assateague Island are descendants of ponies that were brought to the island more than 300 years ago. Although no one is certain how the ponies first arrived, most historians believe that seventeenth-century farmers abandoned them.

The state park is located at the end of SR 611 (just before the entrance to the National Seashore). It is composed of 680 acres of Assateague Island and offers separate swimming, surf-fishing, and surfboarding areas. Public access to the beach and the day-use parking lot is from 9 A.M. to sunset. A guarded swimming area is available daily during the summer months only from 10 A.M. to 5 P.M. Amenities at the park include a boat launch, a marina, campgrounds, a camp store, and a nature center.

After kayaking, stop by the historic Rackliffe House to learn about colonial life along Maryland's Eastern Shore. The restored eighteenth-century plantation house is located at the end of Tom Patton Lane, just a half-mile hike from the visitor center. Rackliffe House is open May through October.

The bustling Ocean City resort town is located approximately 9 miles north of the park offering endless family-friendly accommodations and activities. The historic town of Berlin is less than 8 miles away and features quaint shops, restaurants, and a hotel.

34 | Mattawoman Creek

This creek marks the spot where the Potomac River flows into a freshwater-tidal estuary. Look for osprey nests, beaver lodges, and an abundance of wildlife.

Location: Indian Head, MD
Maps: Maryland Department of Natural Resources: dnr.maryland.gov
Length: Up to 20 miles
Time: 2.5 hours or more
Average Depth: 8 to 10 feet
Development: Suburban
Access: Launch fee
Information: Maryland Department of Natural Resources: dnr.maryland.gov; Mattawoman Watershed Society, P.O. Box 201 Bryans Road, MD 20616, 301-751-9494, www.mattawomanwatershedsociety.org
Camping: Smallwood State Park (see Appendix A)
Outfitters: Atlantic Kayak: 108-A Mattingly Avenue, Indian Head, MD 301-292-6455, atlantickayak.com

TRIP 34: MATTAWOMAN CREEK

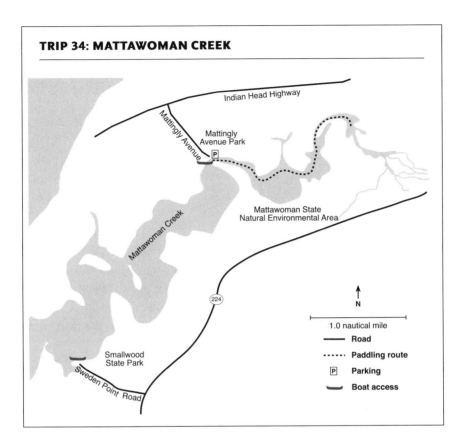

Take Note: Electric motorboats only. Atlantic Kayak offers rentals and tours, including twilight/moonlight tours where you can get out on the water at the perfect time for bird-watching and nature photography.

GETTING THERE
From I-95/I-495 (Capital Beltway), take Exit 3 to MD 210 (Indian Head Highway). Take MD 210 south about 18 miles to Indian Head. Proceed through town for about 2 miles (cumulative: 20 miles) and turn left onto Mattingly Avenue, just before the naval base gatehouse. Continue for 0.75 mile (20.75 miles) to the boat ramp. (38° 35.426′ N, 77° 9.663′ W)

WHAT YOU'LL SEE
Mattawoman Creek is a scenic freshwater-tidal estuary flowing into the Potomac River at Indian Head in Southern Maryland. The name Mattawoman comes from the Algonquin term *Mataughquamend*, translated as "where one goes pleasantly." With 20 miles of gorgeous scenery and the opportunity to

observe an abundance of wildlife, these wetlands are a favorite with paddlers from across the region.

At Mattingly Avenue Park, the kayak ramp has dual-side railings to hold onto and pull yourself up or down the slide, making it is very easy to get in and out of the water without getting your feet wet. From here, you can paddle in either direction. Across the creek is an osprey platform, and the shoreline is lined with marsh grass, wild rice, arrow arum, cattail, and spatterdock. Heading east (to the left of the launch) and across the waters is the Mattawoman State Natural Environmental Area, which includes more than 1,300 acres of mature forests that are protected by the Maryland Department of Natural Resources and serve as a prime habitat for forest interior dwelling species such as tanagers, warblers, and vireos, as well as woodpeckers, hawks, and owls.

The creek is home to some of region's finest tidal-freshwater marshes, with extensive beds of submerged aquatic vegetation and Maryland's only western-shore site harboring the American lotus, a perennial plant with large bluish-green colored leaves that is often confused with waterlilies. The American lotus contributes to the healthy ecosystem at Mattawoman Creek, as the submerged

The scenery along Mattawoman Creek is breathtaking and the waters are easy to paddle along.

stems provide food and shelter for invertebrates. July is the best time to see the blooming flowers.

This locale is a great for bird-watching, as large concentrations of waterfowl breed and feed here. The creek is home to Maryland's largest breeding wood duck population, nesting bald eagles, and unusually large concentrations of great egrets and great blue herons, as well as the most diverse amphibian populations in the state. You are also likely to see ospreys, barn swallows, red-winged blackbirds, fish crows, American crows, and sandpipers.

As you wind your way around the creek, you will come to a narrow section followed by several small islands. To the right, you will see the remains of a dredging operation with a beaver lodge and tall grass and shrubbery growing from the wreckage. (*Caution:* Do not get too close because wood and steel protrusions can result in damage to your canoe or kayak or in personal injury.)

The Mattawoman has the highest proliferation of largemouth bass in the entire Potomac River. It is an outstanding nursery for anadromous fish (especially herring, shad, and yellow perch) that spawn in fresh water after migrating from their home in the Atlantic Ocean or Chesapeake Bay. Along the western section of the creek, Smallwood State Park hosts many bass-fishing tournaments throughout the year.

You can also launch a kayak from the Sweden Point Marina on the opposite side of Mattawoman Creek and farther west at Smallwood State Park. The 628-acre park has lots of amenities including a marina, a boat ramp, a picnic area, campgrounds, a playground, a discovery center, and nature trails. The park is named for General William Smallwood, the highest-ranked Marylander who served in the Revolutionary War. His house, called Smallwood's Retreat, is open to visitors during the summer months. The Sweden Discovery Center offers interactive displays of snakes, toads, and turtles and learning stations such as a fossil dig sandbox. Children can enjoy nature programs year-round such as guided hikes, campfire programs, and Junior Rangers.

For a hike or a bike ride, explore the Indian Head Rail Trail, a 13-mile paved trail on an old Navy railroad bed that runs between the town of Indian Head and US 301 and offers views of the wetlands from the north side of Mattawoman Creek. On the south side, a walk on George Wilmot Trail leads to several vantage points along the creek.

35 | Tuckahoe Creek

Once a steamboat route, this shallow creek now provides abundant opportunities to view wildlife and a variety of habitats.

Location: Denton, MD
Maps: USGS Denton
Length: 2 to 3 miles or more if desired
Time: 2 hours or more
Average Depth: 3 feet
Development: Rural
Access: Launch fee
Information: Maryland Department of Natural Resources, 110 Fishing Lake Lane, Millington, MD 21651, 410-928-3643, dnr.maryland.gov
Camping: Tuckahoe State Park, 5 miles north (see Appendix A)
Outfitters: At the state park; canoes and kayaks can be rented for use on the lake
Take Note: Electric motorboats only. There are picnic tables but no bathroom facilities on-site. A permit is not required for kayaks and canoes that are transported without a trailer.

GETTING THERE
Take US 50 East to MD 404 East. Turn right at MD 309 (Main Street), then left onto MD 404/Alt Main Street. The boat ramp will be on the right. (38° 55.023′ N, 75° 56.683′ W)

WHAT YOU'LL SEE
Tuckahoe Creek is a 21.5-mile-long tributary of the Choptank River on Maryland's Eastern Shore on the border of Caroline and Queen Anne's counties. Its name comes from the abundance of arrow arum, a sturdy wetland plant with arrow-shaped leaves commonly called "tuckahoe." In the 1800s, steamboats regularly left the Chesapeake Bay to venture upstream along these waters. Tuckahoe Creek has changed since then. As with many tributaries of the bay, erosion has lined the creek bottom with sediment that has decreased water depth and left the waters unnavigable by large vessels.

Today, this quiet country stream is ideal for a secluded paddle, fishing, and wildlife viewing. The area has an abundance of wildlife, as it is bordered

TRIP 35: TUCKAHOE CREEK

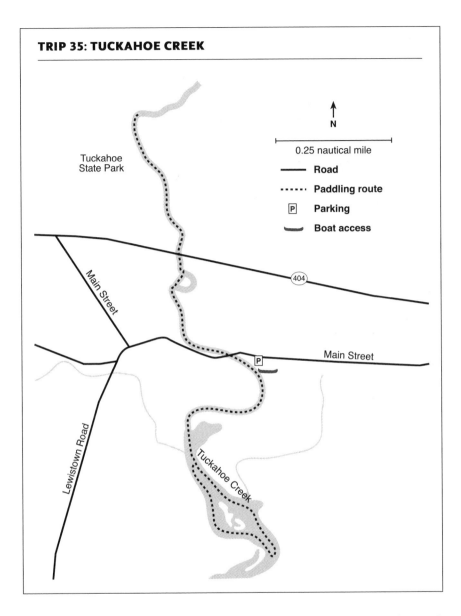

Tuckahoe State Park

0.25 nautical mile

— Road

····· Paddling route

P Parking

⌣ Boat access

N

Main Street

404

Main Street

Lewistown Road

Tuckahoe Creek

for most of its length by wooded marshlands running from the Choptank through Tuckahoe State Park. It is common to see bald eagles, ospreys, great blue herons, turtles, and a variety of amphibians and sometimes even beavers and muskrat.

Begin paddling at the Hillsboro boat launch. It is a very quiet destination near the historic town of Denton, the seat of Caroline County. The launch is easy, and the waters are calm. You can paddle in either direction. The creek

Sections of the 21.5-mile-long Tuckahoe Creek are rich with a diversity of plants and wildlife.

is very scenic with large expanses of aquatic vegetation and mud flats. To head toward the state park, go to the right. The creek is very narrow here and becomes tidal above Hillsboro, near the abandoned railroad bridge. You will pass under several bridges and see a variety of habitats as you work your way around many fallen and overhanging trees. They create interest, and sometimes a challenge, as you meander along the river. Look for painted turtles sunning themselves on the logs.

The bridge beneath MD 404 is quite loud, but the road noise will eventually fade away as the creek narrows and you enter the grounds to the state park. Paddle as far as you can and then return toward the boat access ramp. Paddling downstream from the boat launch, you will find that the creek is freshwater, wider, and deeper. This section meanders placidly past large tracts of marsh with little development; where you can, thread your way through large colonies of American lotus that provide food for ducks who eat the seeds, as well as beavers and muskrat who eat the rhizomes.

Fishing in the creek is best in spring when perch, shad, and herring are spawning. Tuckahoe Creek is home to a wide variety of fish, including largemouth bass, channel catfish, chain pickerel, redbreast sunfish, brown bull-heads, and other freshwater species.

After your paddle, you might visit Tuckahoe State Park, which has a 60-acre lake that offers boating and fishing, and more than 20 miles of recreation trails for hiking, biking, and horseback riding, picnic areas and a popular recycled tire playground for children. Canoes, kayaks, and mountain bikes can be rented on-site. The park offers activities and special events including day camps, canoe trips, educational presentations and displays, and Challenge Course programs. Hiking trails include a self-guided nature trail, a fitness trail, and a trail that traverses the lake.

Another nearby public boat ramp and kayak launching spot is located at Daniel Crouse Memorial Park, 6.5 miles east in downtown Denton. The town began as a tiny settlement in about 1781 and was a trade center for commerce between the Eastern Shore and Baltimore. Today, the town is one of the smallest in the region, and you will find it a rural and relaxing destination where you can paddle along the waters that some believe were part of the Underground Railroad system. Harriet Tubman, who escaped slavery on the Eastern Shore, might have used this stream corridor to lead enslaved people to freedom through these lands in the 1800s. From this location, you can kayak along the Choptank River to Martinak State Park, an area that that is popular for fishing and supports a variety of plants and wildlife.

36 | Potomac River and Seneca Creek: Riley's Lock

Explore two waterways in one trip, experience a lock, and see a variety of waterfowl and gorgeous scenery.

Location: Poolesville, MD
Maps: Interstate Commission on the Potomac River Basin: potomacriver.org
Length: 5 to 7 miles or more if desired
Time: 2 to 3 hours or more
Average Depth: 3 to 5 feet in Seneca Creek
Development: Rural
Access: No fees

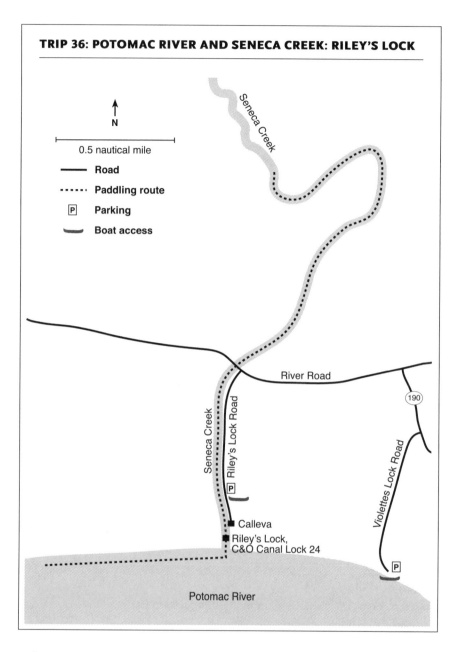

TRIP 36: POTOMAC RIVER AND SENECA CREEK: RILEY'S LOCK

N

0.5 nautical mile

——— Road

······· Paddling route

P Parking

⌣ Boat access

Seneca Creek

River Road

190

Riley's Lock Road

Seneca Creek

Violettes Lock Road

P

■ Calleva

■ Riley's Lock,
C&O Canal Lock 24

P

Potomac River

Information: National Park Service, Commission on the Potomac River Basin, 30 West Gude Drive, Suite 450, Rockville, MD 20850, 301-984-1908, potomacriver.org

Camping: Horsepen Branch Campsite, 3.8 miles west, along the canal towpath (see Appendix A)

Outfitters: Calleva Outdoors: Rileys Lock Road, Poolesville, MD 20837, 301-216-1248, calleva.org

Take Note: Electric motorboats only. The Potomac is subject to high winds and currents (especially after a rainstorm) so check the weather before your excursion.

GETTING THERE

Take I-495 to MD 190 (River Road) heading west. Continue for 11.5 miles, then turn left at a T intersection to stay on MD 190. At the bottom of the hill, in 0.7 mile (cumulative 12.1 miles), turn left onto Riley's Lock Road. Continue 0.7 mile (12.9 miles) and park on the left just before the canal and river. The boat ramp is located on the right, across the street from the first parking lot. (39° 4.247′ N, 77° 20.478′ W)

WHAT YOU'LL SEE

On this excursion, you can enjoy two completely different experiences at one destination. You can paddle along one of the calmest sections of the Potomac River and also wind your way up the narrow and scenic passages of Seneca Creek. The site is adjacent to the Chesapeake and Ohio (C & O) Canal towpath, a multiuse trail that is popular for hiking, biking, and picnicking. The canal and a series of locks were used from 1828 to 1924 to transport goods up and down the river by boat. Today, the canal is a part of a park that preserves the land, flora, fauna, and many historic sites along 185 miles of the Potomac River extending from Georgetown to Cumberland.

The C&O Canal Lock 24, known as Riley's Lock, is located at the mouth of the Great Seneca Creek, 8.5 miles above Great Falls. In 1830, this section of the canal was the farthest point west you could travel. The change in elevation required a lock to lift and lower the boats and an aqueduct to allow the boats to cross the creek safely. The aqueduct, the lock, and the lockhouse were built of Seneca red sandstone, the same distinctive material that was used to construct the Smithsonian Castle on the Washington Mall. Riley's Lock is named for John Riley and his family who lived for more than 45 years in the lockhouse and served as the lockkeeper here. On Saturdays during spring and fall, local Girl Scouts in period dress provide guided tours through the property.

Today the area is exclusively available for recreational use. The boat ramp is located just north of the canal along Riley's Lock Road and provides access to the Potomac and Seneca Creek for boating and fishing. Common fish found here include large- and smallmouth bass, crappie, channel catfish, perch, and bluegill.

To enter the Potomac River from the boat ramp, paddle to the left and go under the C & O aqueduct. The bridge is fun to paddle through, although the waters tend to be dirty where the two waterways merge. Beware of people fishing, and avoid the fishing lines. Enter the Potomac, turning right to stay on flat water. This is one of the easiest places to paddle on a wide and calm section of the Potomac River. Whitewater kayakers head downriver or begin their excursion half a mile to the east from Violetts Lock Boat Launch. Trump National Golf Club is located across the river on what's known as Lowes Island. As you paddle west you can see golf carts and the rolling terrain of the course.

There are many long islands to explore. You may see herons, ospreys, cormorants, ducks, and other waterfowl. There is the occasional beaver and bald eagle as well. Stay to the right and close to the shore to paddle most easily if there are strong currents. Paddle out as far as you are comfortable, and be sure to save some time to return and explore Seneca Creek. You don't have to paddle much on your return to the aqueduct, as the currents should guide you.

Paddling up the creek, pass by the boat ramp and keep heading north. The waters are shallow here, and while there is some road noise until you cross under the bridge at River Road, the paddling is easy and the scenery serene. You may see turtles sunning themselves on a log and a variety of other waterfowl. As the creek is narrow and surrounded by woodlands, you may be more likely

The aqueduct at Riley's Lock connects the Potomac River and Seneca Creek.

to see wildlife here than on the Potomac. The water is flat and easy to float much of the way back.

You may see groups venturing out with Calleva, a summer camp and outdoor adventure company located across from the boat ramp and the C & O Canal towpath. Calleva Liquid Adventures offers whitewater paddling classes for beginning, intermediate, and advanced levels.

Before or after your excursion, in July and August you can visit the nearby McKee-Beshers Wildlife Management Area and see more than 40 acres of sunflowers in full bloom. It is a rare thing to see as the vibrant flowers grow up to 10 feet tall with large yellow petals that are drawn toward the sun. Seven fields of flowers are planted each year by the Maryland Department of Natural Resources.

37 | Corker's Creek: Pocomoke River State Park

Watch for river otters, bald eagles, egrets, ospreys, great blue heron, and turtles in this cypress swamp.

Location: Snow Hill, MD
Maps: Maryland Department of Natural Resources, maps for sale in the camp store
Length: 2 miles
Time: 1 to 2 hours
Average Depth: 1 to 3 feet in Corker's Creek; 5 to 7 feet in Pocomoke River
Development: Rural
Access: No fees
Information: Maryland Department of Natural Resources, 580 Taylor Avenue, Annapolis, MD 21401, 410-632-2566, dnr.maryland.gov
Camping: On-site, Milburn Landing, 13 miles west (see Appendix A)
Outfitters: On-site by Maryland Department of Natural Resources: 410-632-2566; upriver, Pocomoke River Canoe and Kayak: 2 River Street, Snow Hill, MD 21863, 410-632-3971, pocomokerivercanoe.com
Take Note: Electric motorboats only. Launch from Shad Landing Marina and follow the Corker's Creek Canoe Trail.

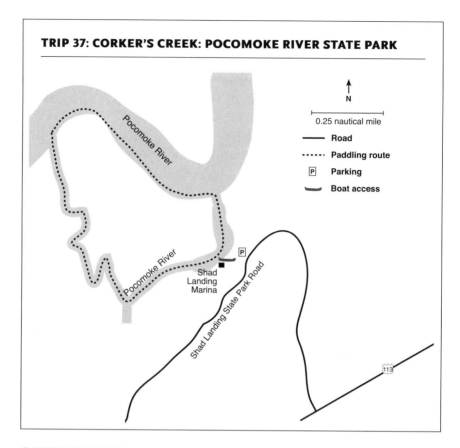

TRIP 37: CORKER'S CREEK: POCOMOKE RIVER STATE PARK

Pocomoke River

0.25 nautical mile

——— Road

••••• Paddling route

P Parking

⌣ Boat access

Pocomoke River

P

Shad
Landing
Marina

Shad Landing State Park Road

113

GETTING THERE

From US 50 East, take US 13 South for 3.3 miles to the MD 12 South/Snow Hill
Road exit. Continue on MD 12 South for approximately 15 miles (cumulative:
18.3 miles) to Snow Hill, and then turn right onto US 113 South. Drive for 4.2
miles (22.5 miles), and then turn right into the Shad Landing State Park.

From I-95, take DE 1 BUS South for 58.7 miles to US 113 South to Snow
Hill. Continue on US 113 for 67.3 miles (cumulative: 126 miles), and then turn
right into Shad Landing State Park. (38° 8.438′ N, 75° 26.405′ W)

WHAT YOU'LL SEE

Located within 15,000 acres of the Pocomoke State Forest in southwestern
Worcester County, this state park offers a wide range of outdoor activities,
including fishing, kayaking, hiking, hunting, and mountain biking. The forest
is well known for its loblolly pine and cypress swamps, which run along the
picturesque Pocomoke River. *Pocomoke* means "black water" in Algonquian, but

these black waters still boast good fishing. The river begins at the Great Cypress Swamp in Delaware and flows southwest for 45 miles to the Chesapeake Bay.

There are two sections of Pocomoke River State Park. Shad Landing is on the south side of the Pocomoke River off US 113. Milburn Landing is on the north side of the river on MD 364. Both areas have boat ramps and provide access to the river. Rentals are available only at Shad Landing. While you can paddle for miles along the Pocomoke River, an easy and scenic option is to follow Corker's Creek Canoe Trail, which traverses the island in front of the marina at Shad Landing.

Use the boat launch and paddle to the left to follow the trail clockwise. The park's combination of woodlands and swamp provides visitors the opportunity to view an array of the region's most common native plants and animals. In spring, white dogwood and pink laurel are in bloom. Throughout the year, you may get a glimpse of bald eagles, egrets, ospreys, great blue herons, river otters, turtles, and more than 50 species of fish.

On this gentle excursion, you will paddle along a very narrow creek past fallen logs, clusters of blossomed waterlilies, and the exposed "knees" of the bald cypress. Even though these majestic trees are coniferous and cone-bearing, they are not evergreens. The needles turn brown and drop off in fall, giving

A blue heron flies along the shoreline of Corker's Creek.

the tree a bald appearance. The trees here are 75 to 100 years old. During the nineteenth century, most of the trees were cut down for shipbuilding and to create shingles and home siding. Bald cypresses are slow-growing trees and long-lived due to their extremely hard wood.

When you reach the sign reading "Canoe Trail," turn right to continue around the island. Wood ducks and a variety of other wildlife feed on cypress seeds and various grasses. Due to the quality of the cypress swamp habitat, artificial nesting boxes have been installed along the waters. These boxes are used to replace disappearing natural nesting sites for wood ducks.

The yellow pond lily blooms throughout summer, providing food and shelter for fish and other wildlife. These plants have heart-shaped leaves and yellow flowers and are plentiful along the trail. The alder is a shrub found along the banks of the river. It produces miniature wood cones and twigs eaten by deer and other wildlife. It also provides excellent shade for fish. There are also peculiar knobby projections poking through the water at the base of the bald cypress trees. These are referred to as "knees." They are an extension of the tree's root system and help brace the cypress against high winds. They also are believed to provide oxygen to the submerged roots of the tree. Follow the canoe trail back to the marina.

If you are interested in a longer trip, you can paddle another 1-mile section of Corker's Creek from the marina south to the US 113 bridge.

Motorized jon boats, electric boats, canoes, and kayaks may be rented from the Shad Landing Marina. A sportfishing license is required to fish the Pocomoke River and nearby creeks. Common fish in these waters include largemouth bass, catfish, shad, perch, freshwater marlin, pickerels, and eels.

Pocomoke River State Park offers boat rentals, campgrounds, a park store, hiking trails, picnic areas and shelters, playgrounds, a swimming pool, and a nature center. The nature center is open during the summer season only and displays tanks containing fish, reptiles, amphibians, and other critters that are native to the Pocomoke River area. Park ranger programs and guided canoe and kayak trips are offered year-round. For an easy hike, take the 1-mile self-guided trail through the old-growth forest to the cypress swamp.

Janes Island State Park is another popular destination for kayaking and is located just a half-hour west, near Crisfield. Assateague and Chincoteague islands are also within a half-hour drive to the east.

CHESAPEAKE BAY WATERSHED

The Chesapeake Bay, the largest estuary in the United States, is the meeting point of rivers and streams (some stretching approximately 200 miles) with the Atlantic Ocean. The 64,000-square-mile area of land that drains into the bay known as the Chesapeake Bay watershed encompasses parts of six states: Delaware, Maryland, New York, Pennsylvania, Virginia, and West Virginia, as well as Washington, D.C.

The bay is 30 miles wide at its broadest and 2.8 miles at its narrowest. Water depth averages 46 feet, with a maximum depth of 208 feet. There are more than 100,000 streams, creeks, and rivers in the Chesapeake Bay watershed, including 150 major rivers. On the northern end of the bay, the Chesapeake Bay Bridge provides vehicle access between Annapolis and the Maryland Eastern Shore. On the southern end, the Chesapeake Bay Bridge Tunnel connects Virginia's Eastern Shore with the Virginia mainland. The cities and towns along the bay each have their own history and character, as first mapped 400 years ago by Englishman John Smith's documentation of nearly 3,000 miles of the bay and its rivers. Early European settlers used these waters as a transportation route and a major source of food, such as oysters, crabs, and fish.

Today's water trails throughout the region let you paddle many of these historic routes. In 2006, the National Park Service designated the first national water trail, the Captain John Smith Chesapeake National Historic Trail. This trail follows the route of Smith's first voyage along the East Coast during the seventeenth century and traces dozens of itineraries through the Chesapeake Bay and its rivers. The broader Chesapeake Bay Gateways Network collects water trails, as well as parks, museums, wildlife refuges, and historic landmarks, under its umbrella. The Susquehanna, Potomac, Rappahannock, York, and James rivers provide approximately 90 percent of the fresh water to the Chesapeake Bay and its watershed. These rivers and other smaller waterways serve as the habitats and nesting areas for more than 3,600 species of plant and animal life, including the Atlantic menhaden, the American eel, and about 350 other species of fish. Underwater bay grasses provide food and shelter for these fish, as well as for waterfowl, shellfish, and invertebrates. The more than 500 million pounds of seafood harvested from the bay every year—including blue crabs, clams, oysters, and rockfish (a regional name for striped bass)—contributes significantly both to our human diet and to the local economy. Bird predators include the American osprey, the great blue heron, the bald eagle, and the peregrine falcon. Larger creatures that thrive in the bay and on nearby land include bottlenose dolphins, river otters, the white-tailed deer, bobcats, muskrat, and red foxes. Other watershed inhabitants include turtles, more than 40 types of snakes and numerous varieties of frogs, toads, and salamanders.

Numerous flora make the Chesapeake Bay their home, on land and underwater. The tidal wetlands are dominated by nonwoody, or herbaceous, vegetation, with native perennials, such as smooth cordgrass, phragmites, and arrow arum, found in the low-lying saltwater marshes. The high marsh areas are dominated by saltmeadow cordgrass and marsh elder. Nontidal wetlands contain bulrush, broad-leaved cattail, jewel weed, spike rushes, and sedges. Trees commonly found in forested wetlands include red maple, loblolly pine, black gum, Atlantic white cedar, river birch, sweetbay magnolia, sassafras, and bald cypress. Shrubs in the forested wetlands include willows, alders, honeysuckle, and button bushes.

The watershed's multiple habitats are influenced by climate, weather, animal interactions, and human activities. The leading threat to the health of the Chesapeake Bay is excess nitrogen and phosphorus pollution from runoff sources including agriculture, sewage treatment plants, and urban and suburban development, as well as air pollution from automobiles, factories, and power plants. Efforts to restore the water quality—upgrading sewage treatment plants, using nitrogen-removal technologies on septic systems, and decreasing fertilizer use in lawns—have had mixed results to date.

The Chesapeake Bay Foundation (CBF) is a privately funded nonprofit dedicated to protecting and restoring the bay and its rivers and streams. With offices in Maryland, Virginia, Pennsylvania, D.C., and fifteen field centers, CBF engages in education, advocacy, and litigation to help the region leave a legacy of clean water for future generations.

The region offers prime conditions for outdoor recreation, including fishing, crabbing, swimming, boating, and sailing. The shallow, protected waters of the Chesapeake Bay and its tributaries are excellent for canoeing and kayaking, with plentiful launch points from boat ramps, beaches, and other shoreline areas. Conditions and experience requirements vary from place to place, so be sure to plan your excursion in advance and find out what you need to know before you go.

38 | Eastern Neck National Wildlife Refuge

Located on the Chesapeake Scenic Byway, this year-round paddling spot is a major layover for migratory waterfowl.

Location: Rock Hall, MD
Maps: U. S. Fish and Wildlife Service: fws.gov
Length: 10 miles or more if desired
Time: 2 hours or more
Average Depth: 5 feet
Development: Rural, island
Access: No fees
Information: U.S. Fish and Wildlife Service, 1730 Eastern Neck Road, Rock Hall, MD 21661, 410-639-7056, fws.gov
Camping: Bayshore Campgrounds, 4 miles north (see Appendix A)
Outfitters: East Neck Boat Rental: 2981 Eastern Neck Road, Rock Hall, MD 21661, 410-639-7100, eastneckboatrental.com
Take Note: Electric motorboats only. Kent County operates two boat launches within the wildlife refuge. The Ingleside Recreation Area, on the northwest side of the refuge, has facilities for crabbing and cartop boat launching from April 1 to September 30. On the east side of the refuge, the boat launch at Bogles Wharf Landing can also be used as a kayak launch. A waterproof, floating map and guide is available at the Friends of Eastern Neck Bookstore located at the visitor center. Be aware that mosquitoes and other biting insects are especially abundant during the summer months. There are no nearby stores to purchase repellent, water, or sunscreen. You should plan ahead and bring those items with you to the refuge.

GETTING THERE

Follow MD 20 into Rock Hall, and then turn left onto MD 445 (Main Street). Go 8 miles to the foot of the bridge, where the refuge entrance is. To reach Bogles Wharf, continue on MD 445, which turns into Eastern Neck Island Road, and turn left onto Bogles Wharf Road and follow it to the end. To reach Ingleside Recreation Area, turn right onto Ingleside Road and follow the road to the end.

Ingleside Recreation Area (39° 2.737′ N, 76° 14.103′ W); Bogles Neck (39° 1.954′ N, 76° 12.585′ W)

TRIP 38: EASTERN NECK NATIONAL WILDLIFE REFUGE

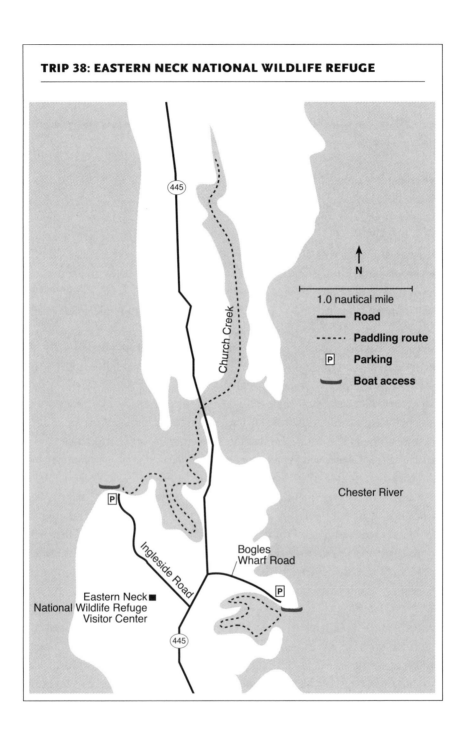

445

Church Creek

N

1.0 nautical mile

——— Road

------- Paddling route

P Parking

◡ Boat access

P

Chester River

Ingleside Road

Bogles
Wharf Road

P

Eastern Neck ■
National Wildlife Refuge
Visitor Center

445

WHAT YOU'LL SEE

With its prime location in Kent County, Eastern Neck is one of the lesser known paddling destinations along the Chesapeake Scenic Byway. The national wildlife refuge is an island located at the mouth of the Chester River with year-round opportunities for boating, fishing, hunting, environmental education, wildlife viewing, and photography. The 2,285-acre refuge is a major feeding and resting place for migratory and wintering waterfowl. It is also home to the southern bald eagle and the endangered Delmarva fox squirrel.

The 10-mile Eastern Neck Island Water Trail starts at Bogle's Wharf and loops around the entire refuge, connecting scenic, historic, and wetland restoration sites around the island. The trail includes long stretches of open, tidal water, which is affected by wind, weather, currents, and tidal changes. Circling the entire island is best suited for experienced kayakers and is most easily accomplished with an electric-powered boat. For a quiet trip, however, you can paddle some of the more protected sections of the trail and enjoy an easy and scenic excursion.

On the eastern side of the refuge, the waters are mostly calm due to their sheltered nature. The Ingleside Recreation Area has a picnic area, and the

A red-winged blackbird perches among waterside plants at Eastern Neck.

launch is down a slight hilly stretch of waterfront. For an easy excursion, paddle to the right and stay on the east side of the Eastern Neck Island Road Bridge, where you can explore Calfpasture Cove, Tubby Cove, and Long Cove. For a longer and more challenging trip, you can paddle under the bridge and then head north for 6 miles into Church Creek.

On the western side, the Chester River opens directly into the Chesapeake Bay, and the waters are subject to high winds and strong currents. However, you can easily launch from Bogles Wharf Landing and see plenty of interesting scenery and a variety of wildlife in the protected waters of Durdin and Shipyard creeks. The varied habitats include brackish tidal marsh, woodlands, grassy areas, and open waters. More than 240 species of birds and a variety of mammals, amphibians, and reptiles inhabit the island. In the coves and creeks, look for ospreys, bald eagles, red-winged blackbirds, common terns, herons, and egrets.

The most common species of waterfowl on the refuge include Canada geese, tundra swans, and mallards. A wide variety of ducks can be seen all over the island including canvasbacks, green- and blue-winged teal, American wigeons, northern pintails, ruddy ducks, long-tailed ducks, and others. The best time to visit is in fall and spring when birds are migrating. Bring binoculars as you may be lucky to get a glimpse of colorful birds such as warblers, tanagers, and flycatchers. In the tidal and marshy areas of the refuge you will likely see waterfowl that are most common in the Mid-Atlantic region such as great blue herons, green herons, and great and snowy egrets.

The refuge has nearly 9 miles of roads and trails that are open year-round. Seven trails and boardwalks are available for wildlife viewing. The Bayview/Butterfly Trail features an observation platform that offers spectacular vistas of the Chesapeake Bay. The Bayscape Garden demonstrates how bay-friendly native plants and shrubs attract butterflies and praying mantises. The Tubby Cove boardwalk extends over a diverse marsh through a stand of loblolly trees to two viewing platforms. The boardwalk is less than a quarter-mile round-trip, with the main path leading to an accessible viewing blind with an elevated viewing platform that provides a lookout over the bay and into Calfpasture Cove and Tubby Cove.

The visitor center is located on the south end of the island and features wildlife exhibits, a bookstore and gift shop, and restrooms.

39 | Piney Run Reservoir

Surrounded by woodlands and open spaces laced with trails, this easily navigable reservoir is a good close-to-home option.

Location: Sykesville, MD
Maps: Piney Run Park and Nature Center map available on-site
Area: 300 acres
Time: 2 hours
Average Depth: 26 feet
Development: Suburban
Access: Park entrance fee and launch fee
Information: Carroll County Department of Parks and Recreation, 30 Martz Road, Sykesville, MD 21784, 410-795-5165, ccgovernment.carr.org
Camping: Rambling Pines Campground, 5 miles southwest (see Appendix A)
Outfitters: On-site
Take Note: Electric motorboats only. Beware of restricted areas of the lake.

GETTING THERE

On I-695, take Exit 18 West to MD 26. Continue on MD 26 for 14 miles, and then turn left onto White Rock Road and continue for 1.8 miles (cumulative: 15.8 miles). Take a left onto Martz Road to the park entrance, 0.6 mile (16.4 miles) down the road.

From I-495, take Exit 31 North for MD 97. Continue north on MD 97 for 32.3 miles, and then turn right onto MD 26 East toward Eldersburg. Drive for 1.5 miles (cumulative: 33.8 miles) and turn right onto White Rock Road, then continue for 1.8 miles (35.6 miles). Take a left onto Martz Road to the park entrance, 0.6 mile (36.2 miles) down the road. (39° 23.897′ N, 76° 59.183′ W)

WHAT YOU'LL SEE

Piney Run Park is the oldest developed park in Carroll County, Maryland. It features a 300-acre lake and provides recreational activities such as fishing, boating, boat rentals, and park-sponsored fishing tournaments. The lake is relatively small, and you can explore most of it in just a few hours, but its location makes it an easy excursion for those who live in the area and a nice place to enjoy nature and bird-viewing opportunities. The lake is surrounded by 550 acres of woodlands and open spaces, which contain more than 5 miles

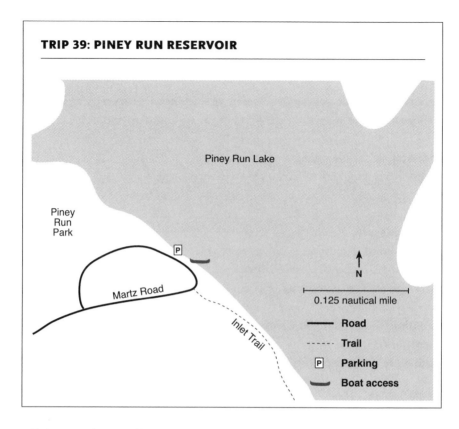

TRIP 39: PINEY RUN RESERVOIR

Piney Run Lake

Piney
Run
Park

P

Martz Road

Inlet Trail

N

0.125 nautical mile

———— Road
------ Trail
P Parking
⌣ Boat access

of hiking trails, as well as recreation areas, playgrounds, and picnic areas. The
Piney Run Nature Center offers year-round environmental education programs
for schools, organized groups, and mother nature programs.

While most parks in the area rent boats only between Memorial Day and
Labor Day, Piney Run offers rentals daily throughout the summer months and
on weekends from April 1 to October 31. The boat house offers rentals of
canoes, kayaks, rowboats, and paddleboats. Fishing is allowed with a permit.
The reservoir's fish are managed through the Maryland Freshwater Fisheries
Division. Fish species in the lake include black crappie, blue gill and sunfish,
yellow perch, trout, bullhead and channel catfish, large- and smallmouth bass,
striped bass, and tiger muskie. The most common birds that you will see on
the lake include Canada geese, tree swallows, wood ducks, woodpeckers, owls,
tree swallows, bald eagles, and Baltimore orioles.

There are two boat ramps in front of the main parking lot at the park. As
you head out into the lake, paddle to the right and pass some fishing platforms.
The open section of the lake tends to get windy and can be challenging when
paddling against the wind. When you reach the first cove, turn right into it and

proceed to the end. You will paddle along a more protected area, where it will be easier to maneuver. The nature center cove and Yak Shak are located on the right and may be busy with group activities. There are several active beaver lodges at Piney Run, though the easiest to spot is in the nature center cove.

Paddle back to the wider section of the lake, and then follow the lake to the right again and continue along this cove to the end as well. You will find a kayaker's picnic table at a point with the tree branch overhanging the lake on your right, making it a nice spot for a break if you feel like it. Continuing straight ahead, you will pass a large area of seedling trees that have been planted. The most interesting section of the lake is at the very end of the cove where the water becomes very shallow and covered with aquatic wetland plants.

There is a restricted wildlife management area on the northern end of the lake near White Rock Road. It is protected and set aside for the propagation of channel catfish and other wildlife. This area has excellent bird-watching opportunities; however, boats are restricted, and all observing must be done from White Rock Road.

Piney Run Park has 5 miles of hiking trails. The half-mile Lake Trail follows the perimeter of the lake from the boating area and playground to the nature center. The 3.5-mile Inlet Trail passes through a wide range of wildlife habitats

A female goose nests on the edge of Piney Run Reservoir, beside a beaver dam.

ranging from cultivated farmland to oak, hickory, and white-pine forests. Deer and fox may be seen on some of the more secluded sections of the trails. The Indian and Field trails offer additional opportunities to meander through the natural terrain surrounding the lake.

The park is known around the area for its annual fishing tournaments, including the PRP Panfish Tournament, the Catfish Shootout, the Youth Panfish Derby, and largemouth bass tournaments, where the person who catches the biggest fish wins a trophy. Cash prizes are awarded for some of the contests. Participants must preregister for the events.

For additional kayaking and fishing opportunities, travel 9 miles west to Liberty Reservoir. A seasonal permit is required prior to launching a boat there.

40 | Daugherty Creek: Janes Island State Park

A haven for waterbirds and avid paddlers, Janes Island provides expansive vistas and stunningly beautiful sunsets.

Location: Crisfield, MD
Maps: Maryland Department of Natural Resources map available to purchase at the camp store
Length: 30 miles, with a recommended first-time route of 2.75 miles
Time: 2 hours or more
Average Depth: 7 to 9 feet in Daugherty Creek; 1 to 3 feet in the interior water trails
Development: Rural
Access: No launch fee as long as you use the soft kayak ramp
Information: Maryland Department of Natural Resources, Janes Island State Park, 26280 Alfred Lawson Drive, Crisfield, MD 21817, 410-968-1565, dnr.maryland.gov
Camping: On-site
Outfitters: On-site
Take Note: Electric motorboats only. Janes Island has six water trails offering 30 miles of paddling opportunities. Check the water levels in advance, as the trails are subject to tidal changes. The red and blue trails are the most protected and easiest to paddle.

TRIP 40: DAUGHERTY CREEK: JANES ISLAND STATE PARK

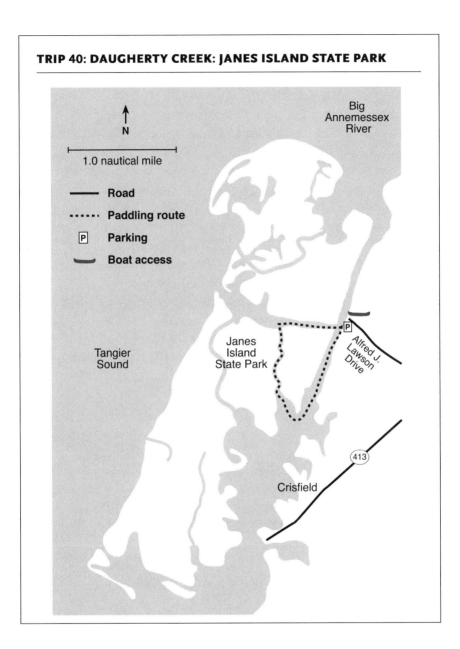

GETTING THERE

From US 50 East, follow MD 13 South to Westover, and then go south on MD 413 for 11.2 miles. Turn right onto Plantation Road, and then continue 1.5 miles (cumulative: 12.7 miles). Take a right turn onto Alfred Lawson Drive, and then enter the park. (38° 0.585′ N, 75° 50.878′ W)

WHAT YOU'LL SEE

Located near Crisfield on Maryland's Eastern Shore, this park offers a rare opportunity to enjoy a tranquil setting and the beauty of the Chesapeake Bay. Janes Island is probably one of the best parks in the region for kayaking, as it is well equipped for boating and features six water trails covering 30 miles in Daugherty Creek. There are 64 marked stops, allowing visitors to paddle at their own pace and follow a designated path to discover a variety of wildlife.

Maryland historians have determined that Paleo native people lived in this region approximately 13,000 years ago. At that time, sea levels were 350 feet lower than today and large mammals such as mammoths, horses, and bison roamed across what is now called Somerset County. Historic artifacts have been found along the shoreline of Janes Island that provide evidence that the lifestyle of the primitive people was very similar to the modern anglers, from hunting mammals to shucking oysters along the Chesapeake Bay.

Today, Janes Island is a state park and has a campground, rental cabins, a conference center, picnic areas and pavilions, a boat ramp, and marina. The island includes more than 2,900 acres of salt marsh, as well as miles of isolated beaches. A haven for birds, fish, crabs, and other salt marsh dwellers, the park offers the perfect setting for wildlife viewing.

The Janes Island marina has a floating dock that makes it easy to launch your kayak.

While paddling conditions vary depending on the weather and other factors, most of the water trails are protected from the wind and current. Both novice and experienced paddlers will enjoy hours of exploration here. The Janes Island water trail system is first-rate and was named in the American Canoe Association's inaugural list of recommended water trails. When you arrive, stop in the park store to pick up a map, or plan ahead and download the GPS waypoints for the six paddle trails through the Janes Island website.

The paddling trails are easy to follow in and around Janes Island, as they are posted with aluminum color-coded signs, each with a distinctive shape. The marina is located at the intersection of the brown and yellow trails. The interior trails can be very shallow in low tide so be sure to check the tide tables before you launch. Check with the staff on-site if you are uncertain.

The boat dock at the marina has a floating launch specifically for kayaks that makes it easy to get on and off of the water. For an easy first-time 2.75-mile trip, you can combine portions of a few of the trails, as described here.

After launching from the marina, paddle across the brown trail to the yellow trail and follow it until you reach the blue trail and then turn left. The trail is narrow and winds around several curves. The grass is just above your line of vision, so mostly you see the sky, which is especially soothing on a clear day. At marker three, you may see periwinkles, a species of small sea snail usually found on rocks, stones, marsh grass, or pilings between high- and low-tide levels. You will also see Virginia glasswort, annual plants that are native to salt marshes. The bright-green stems turn red or purple in fall.

Paddling along this route is very easy, and the scenery is lovely. The water is salt water, and the shores are mostly fine sand or tall grasses. At marker seven, turn left to stay on the trail. Stay alert as you may see deer, muskrat, ospreys, bald eagles, and a variety of waterfowl. As you paddle along, you will see the Crisfield windmill in the distance and, as the blue trail ends, you will see it more closely where the creek widens. Turn left on the brown trail and stay close to the left side. You will see the Crisfield skyline, including McCready Memorial Hospital, condominiums, and a few homes along the water. Follow the trail straight all the way back to the marina.

Anglers can fish in these waters for striped bass, bluefish, sea trout, croaker, flounder, and others. A sportfishing license is required for those 16 and older. The Chesapeake Bay blue crab is abundant in the waters surrounding the park. You do not need a license to catch crabs with a handline, but you are limited to catching two dozen. If you are lucky enough to catch anything, you can use the accessible fish-cleaning station at the marina to clean up your catch.

After your paddle, stop in the town of Crisfield. It is the southernmost town in Maryland and famous for its seafood—especially the Maryland blue crab—wildlife, and natural beauty.

Just a half hour drive to the north, you can also kayak at Pocomoke River State Park (see Trip 37).

41 | Dundee Creek

Dundee Creek offers the best kayaking and wildlife viewing within 18,000-acre Gunpowder Falls State Park.

Location: Middle River, MD
Maps: Available to purchase from the Maryland Department of Natural Resources
Length: 2 to 3 miles or more if desired
Time: 2 hours
Average Depth: 1 to 3 feet; deeper in the wider sections of the creek near the Dundee Natural Environmental Area
Development: Suburban
Access: No fees
Information: Maryland Department of Natural Resources, 580 Taylor Avenue, Annapolis, MD 21401, 410-335-9390, dnr.maryland.gov
Outfitters: Ultimate Watersports Dundee Creek: 7400 Graces Quarter Road, Middle River, MD 21220, 410-335-5352, ultimatewatersports.com
Take Note: Unlimited horsepower. The waters are too shallow for motorized boats in Saltpeter Creek.

GETTING THERE
From I-95, take Exit 67A for MD 43 East (White Marsh Boulevard) and continue for 1 mile. Turn onto US 40 East, and then, after 0.9 mile (cumulative: 1.9 miles) turn right onto Ebenezer Road and follow it for 4.5 miles (6.4 miles), past where the road turns into Graces Quarter Road. Go past the Hammerman entrance and enter the marina on the right. The kayaking launch is located just before the boat launch next to the Ultimate Watersports rental facility. (39° 21.124′ N, 76° 21.539′ W)

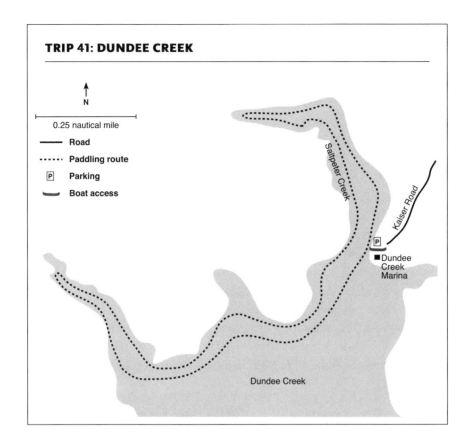

TRIP 41: DUNDEE CREEK

N

0.25 nautical mile

—— Road

••••• Paddling route

P Parking

⌣ Boat access

Saltpeter Creek

Kaiser Road

P

■ Dundee Creek Marina

Dundee Creek

WHAT YOU'LL SEE

Dundee Creek is one of the six areas that are part of Gunpowder Falls State Park. Established in 1959, the park is composed of more than 18,000 acres in Harford and Baltimore counties. With landscapes ranging from tidal wetlands to steep and rugged terrain, the state park features more than 120 miles of multiuse trails, protected wilderness, a swimming beach, and a marina. Each of the park areas offers something unusual to see and do. Dundee Creek is located at the mouth of the Gunpowder River and is the best spot for kayaking and wildlife viewing.

The kayak-launching area is located along Saltpeter Creek, just north of the marina where Ultimate Watersports rents kayaks and stand-up paddleboards. The launching beach offers ideal conditions. The parking is close, and the water is shallow. The landscape is gorgeous, with tall marsh grasses set in front of maples, oaks, river birch, and other hardwood trees that surround the waters.

As you get started, paddle to your right into the more protected waters toward the north end of the creek. This area is perfect for beginner kayakers and paddleboarders. The water is calm and shallow, and there are no rocks. If you touch the bottom with your paddle, you will notice it is soft and sandy. As you reach the far end of the creek, the water is only a foot deep.

Paddle lightly and float right over the water plants. The creek narrows and there are lots of small coves that you can paddle in and around. Move slowly through the marshlands and look for great blue herons, ospreys, bald eagles, cormorants, painted turtles, red-winged blackbirds, Baltimore orioles, tundra swans, and river otters.

After exploring the far end of the creek, turn around and proceed past the marina. Go out into the open waters, staying to your right. Continue around the curve. Straight ahead is Dundee Natural Environmental Area, a natural preserve encompassing more than 3,000 acres. You will see a small boat dock and a duck blind on your right. Paddle along the perimeter, and you may see a variety of wildlife. This area has a rich tradition of waterfowl hunting. Anglers have long explored this part of the Chesapeake Bay watershed in search of rockfish, chain pickerel, perch, catfish, and blue crabs.

The Marina Store rents motorboats and rowboats. Boats may be rented on an hourly basis during the marina store's normal operating hours. Ultimate Watersports rents kayaks, wind surfboards, and stand-up paddleboards at both

Dundee Creek is a beautiful and easy place to paddle in a marshland environment.

Hammerman Beach and Dundee Creek Marina. Dundee Creek has a designated fishing area at the end of Graces Quarters Road, as well as an archery range that is open year-round, 8 A.M. to sunset.

Located just across the creek, the Marshy Point Nature Center features more than 8 miles of hiking trails, its own canoe launch and pier, a wildlife observation area, and a butterfly garden. The nature center provides a variety of educational programs including summer camps, bird walks, guided boat trips, and seasonal festivals.

After your paddle, you can visit the Hammerman Area of Gunpowder Falls State Park, located 1.7 miles northeast of Dundee Creek. From I-95, take Exit 67A for MD 43 East (White Marsh Boulevard). Follow MD 43 to US 40 East. Turn right onto Ebenezer Road and follow it for 4.5 miles. The park entrance will be on your left. The Hammerman Area charges an admission fee and features a swimming beach, food concessions, picnic pavilions, playgrounds, and hiking trails. The Muskrat and Dogwood trails are both short hikers-only trails that wind through the woods and marsh.

5 | WASHINGTON, D.C.

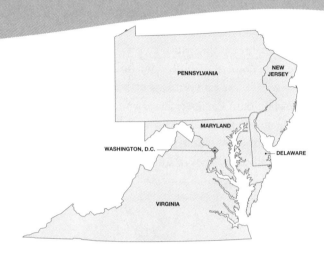

Kayaking is becoming very popular in the nation's capital. According to the American Fitness Index, Washington, D.C., is ranked as the fittest city in the United States, likely due to the growing population of young and active residents with an enthusiasm for outdoor recreation. The urban waterways are excellent places to paddle and are home to a wide range of wildlife.

The Potomac and Anacostia rivers played an important part in the history of Washington, D.C. President George Washington chose the federal city's site for its central location and access to the Potomac, facilitating commercial trade. To design the city, he appointed French-born architect Pierre Charles L'Enfant, who presented a plan of wide avenues, public squares, parks, inspiring buildings, and a system of canals to provide transportation along the Potomac watershed.

The Potomac flows more than 300 miles, from the Allegheny Mountains to the Chesapeake Bay and then into the Atlantic Ocean. On its way from the mountains to the ocean, the Potomac runs through West Virginia, Maryland, Virginia, and Washington, D.C. Today, the Potomac supplies water for most of the 6 million people who live in the capital area. Millions of people use the river and its adjacent land for boating, fishing, bird-watching, and paddling, although there are sections of the river where the water flows very rapidly, with waterfalls making spots dangerous for kayakers. As a novice paddler, be sure to stay in areas populated by other kayaks and canoes. The trips described in this book are along the calmest sections and best for quietwater paddling.

The Chesapeake and Ohio Canal, built in the eighteenth century, runs 184.5 miles along the north bank of the Potomac River, starting in Georgetown in Washington, D.C. and ending in Cumberland, Maryland. Over the years, advances in other forms of transportation led to the canal's abandonment as a shipping route. Today, the canal is a national park and is used for recreation. Canoeing and kayaking are popular in the sections from Georgetown to Violettes Lock (mile 22).

The 8.7-mile Anacostia River flows from Prince George's County in Maryland into Washington, D.C. From there, it joins the Potomac River, and the combined waters flow 108 miles to the Chesapeake Bay, at Point Lookout. Sadly, the Anacostia and its tributaries have been the victims of more than 300 years of abuse and neglect, resulting in pollution, loss of habitat, erosion, sedimentation, flooding, and wetland destruction. In recent years, private organizations and local businesses, as well as the D.C., Maryland, and federal governments, have formed a partnership to reduce pollution levels and protect the watershed's ecology. The Anacostia is slowly rebounding, and hundreds of acres of wetlands are under restoration. Today the river is a surprisingly great place to kayak, as Kenilworth Aquatic Gardens and Kingman and Heritage Islands Park offer wetland habitats for wide varieties of birds and other wildlife.

42 | Potomac River: Key Bridge and Georgetown

Enjoy the sights of the Potomac as you paddle past the Georgetown Waterfront, Roosevelt Island, and some of the quietest green space in the nation's capital.

Location: Northwest Washington, D.C.
Maps: Interstate Commission on the Potomac River Basin: potomacriver.org
Length: 4 to 6 miles
Time: 2.5 to 3 hours
Average Depth: 6 feet
Development: Urban
Access: Launch fee

TRIP 42: POTOMAC RIVER: KEY BRIDGE AND GEORGETOWN

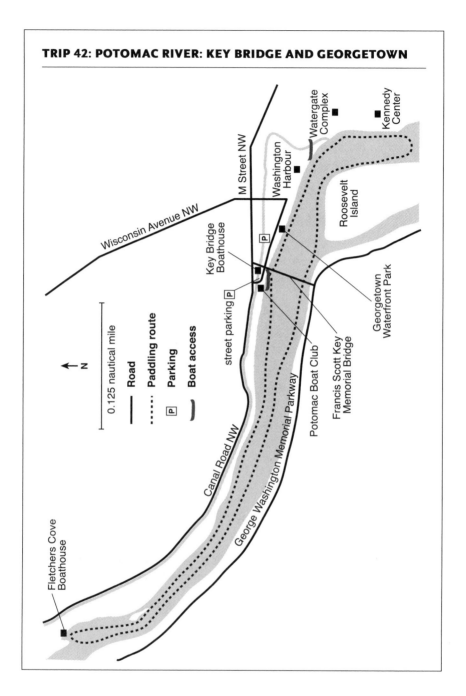

Information: Interstate Commission on the Potomac River Basin, 30 West Gude Drive, Suite 450 Rockville, MD 20859, 301-984-1908, potomacriver.org

Outfitters: Boating in D.C. at Key Bridge Boathouse: 202-337-9642, boatingindc.com

Take Note: Unlimited horsepower. Street parking is limited, and you may have to pay for garage parking.

GETTING THERE

From the George Washington Memorial Parkway: Cross the Francis Scott Key Bridge into Washington, D.C. Turn right on M Street Northwest 0.3 mile later. After 0.6 mile (cumulative: 0.9 mile) turn right onto Wisconsin Avenue Northwest. Drive 0.2 mile (1.1 miles), and then turn right onto K Street and follow it 0.4 mile to its end (1.5 miles). The boathouse is located on the left under the Key Bridge at 3500 K Street Northwest, Washington, D.C. (38° 54.252′ N, 77° 4.178′ W)

WHAT YOU'LL SEE

Paddling along the Potomac River near Georgetown is a great way to escape the bustle and to see some of the city's most stunning scenery. From iconic historic buildings to woodland and rocky shorelines, this destination offers a diverse and relaxing experience you can easily return to do again and again. On a nice day any time of the year, you will see many people engaging in paddle sports along this stretch of the Potomac. The river is popular for recreational kayaking and is also used for rowing practice and competitions. You will see everything from single watercrafts to eight-person sculls to wooden handcrafted kayaks to colorful painted dragon boats.

There is easy access from the street to the dock, although you have to carry your boat down twelve steps down to the water. Arrive early in the morning to snag a parking spot on the street or you will have to pay for garage parking farther down K Street. The dock is just above the water level so it is easy to step into your vessel when launching (it's a little more challenging to get out at the end of your excursion, but there is usually someone there to assist you).

When you depart from the dock, paddle downriver (to the left) and go under the Key Bridge. You will paddle past a great urban skyline with some of the area's most notable attractions. To your left, you will see Georgetown Waterfront Park, an urban park with flowering trees, walking paths, and park benches, and then Washington Harbour, Georgetown's multiuse waterfront development with boat docks, luxury condominiums, office space, a public boardwalk, and several restaurants. On your right is the skyline of downtown Rosslyn, a Northern Virginia neighborhood with modern high-rise office buildings, and Theodore Roosevelt Island, a 91-acre wilderness area that serves as a memorial to the nation's 26th president and is home to a variety of wildlife. Keep paddling straight ahead and you can see the famous Watergate Complex (known for its historic political scandal) and the expansive John F. Kennedy Center, the city's largest performing arts center. As you paddle toward the end of Roosevelt Island, you can even get a glimpse of the Washington Monument.

After taking in these impressive views, turn around and paddle upstream. As you go underneath Key Bridge, look to your right and you will see the boathouse for the Washington Canoe Club. The property is a National Historic Landmark, dating to 1904, and has been home to generations of paddlers, including Olympians. Keep paddling upstream and you will see the Georgetown University campus. Founded in 1789, Georgetown is the oldest Catholic university in the United States. The campus, with its collegiate Gothic and Georgian brick architecture, is situated on an elevated site about the Potomac River. If you paddle past it on the hour, you will hear the bell chiming from the Georgetown Cathedral.

As you continue upstream, the George Washington Memorial Parkway is on the left but the tree line will mask most of the automobile sounds. On the right, you may see people walking or biking along the Capital Crescent Trail,

Birds perch on a rock formation known as the Three Sisters in the Potomac River, just upstream from Georgetown University.

the multiuse trail that parallels the river and the Chesapeake and Ohio Canal. Approximately a half-mile upstream from Key Bridge, you will come upon three rocky islands known as the Three Sisters. Various local legends are associated with the Three Sisters, including a story of three nuns who drowned where the rocks are. Another story is that three Algonquin sisters drowned there while crossing the river in an attempt to win the release of their brothers, who had been kidnapped by another tribe. The Three Sisters are in the deepest part of the river and were a landmark even in colonial times and appeared on Pierre Charles L'Enfant's first map of the area. Today, birds are attracted to the islands. Move slowly through the rocks and look for great blue herons, cormorants, ducks, warblers, and other waterfowl.

Paddle upstream as far as you are comfortable. As you move farther west, you will reach large rock formations on the right. After approximately 2.25 miles, you will reach Fletcher's Cove where, if desired, you can continue upstream as far as Chain Bridge (see Trip 43: Potomac River: Fletcher's Boathouse for details).

You can also rent or launch a kayak from Thompson Boat Center, located just east of Washington Harbour at 2900 Virginia Avenue Northwest.

POTOMAC RIVER BASIN

The Potomac River is the fourth largest river along the Atlantic coast and the 21st largest in the United States. It runs more than 383 miles, from Fairfax Stone, West Virginia, to Point Lookout, Maryland, and drains 14,670 square miles of land area from four states (Maryland, Pennsylvania, Virginia, and West Virginia), as well as the District of Columbia. Flowing into the Chesapeake Bay, the Potomac affects more than 6 million people who live within the watershed.

"Potomac" was one of two Algonquin names for the river forming the northern boundary of Virginia, meaning "great trading place" or "place where people trade." The Potomac's common spelling through the eighteenth century was "Patowmack," with an earlier spelling of "Patawomeke." The spelling of the name was simplified over the years to Potomac.

The river's fascinating history continued in the ensuing decades. It was a transportation route and a food source for American Indians and the nation's earliest European settlers. George Washington chose the location for the nation's capital because the riverbank was already home to two major port towns: Georgetown and Alexandria. He knew the city would be the seat of the federal government, but he also envisioned it developing as a commercial center.

The Potomac River became the District of Columbia's main source of drinking water with the opening of the Washington Aqueduct in 1864. An average of approximately 486 million gallons of water is used daily in the Washington, D.C., area, with nearly 86 percent of the region's population receiving its drinking water from public supplies. Due to increasing urban development, the Potomac River and its tributaries are vulnerable to eutrophication, heavy metals, pesticides, and other toxic chemicals. The Potomac Watershed Partnership, a collaborative group of conservation organizations, works to protect the Potomac River watershed.

Major tributaries of the Potomac include the Anacostia River, Antietam Creek, the Cacapon River, Catoctin Creek, Conocoheague Creek, the Monocacy River, the North Branch, the South Branch, the Occoquan River, the Savage River, the Seneca Creek, and the Shenandoah River. Major cities in the basin include Washington, D.C.; Bethesda, Cumberland, Hagerstown, Frederick, Rockville, Waldorf, and St. Mary's City in Maryland; Chambersburg and Gettysburg in Pennsylvania; Alexandria, Arlington, Harrisonburg, and Front Royal in Virginia; and Harpers Ferry, Charles Town, and Martinsburg in West Virginia.

There are many boating access points along the river. Along the Upper Potomac, parking lots tend to be smaller with limited spaces but are usually free. (*Note*: Some access points are not ideal for launching, as they require carrying your craft for some distance.) In the tidal section of the river below Little Falls, more ramps are available for larger boats, as well as kayaks and canoes. In the lower Potomac, near Washington, D.C., many full-service marinas allow individuals to launch their own boats, kayaks, and canoes, sometimes requiring a small fee.

The Potomac River basin features free-flowing freshwater streams and rivers, as well as tidally influenced fresh and brackish waters. It is home to many national, state, regional, and local parks, and the Potomac River itself is a water trail. Popular recreational activities along the river include hiking, bicycling, picnicking, kayaking, rock climbing, and horseback riding. Major waterfront destinations include Great Falls National Park, the George Washington Memorial Parkway, Georgetown, the Southwest Waterfront and the Wharf, Alexandria, Mount Vernon, and National Harbor. Sightseeing cruises are available along the river, departing from Washington, D.C., as well as from Alexandria, Mount Vernon, and National Harbor.

The Chesapeake and Ohio (C & O) Canal, an engineering milestone of the nineteenth century, winds alongside the Potomac River for 184 miles. Begun in 1828, the canal took two decades to complete the 74 locks, eleven stone aqueducts, and seven dams that feed water from the Potomac. Today, the land surrounding the canal is a national historic park, protecting the history of the waterway, as well as places for hiking, biking, fishing, and horseback riding. The water levels of some areas of the C & O Canal are suitable for kayaking, while other sections are too low. Boating is not advisable between Great Falls and Chain Bridge, where currents are strong and many people have drowned. Swimming is prohibited in the canal and in the Potomac River.

Together, the Potomac and its related rivers and streams provide a habitat for a wide range of mammals and reptiles, more than 240 species of birds, and a variety of fish, including large- and smallmouth bass, shad, muskellunge, pike, catfish, walleye, and the northern snakehead. Keep an eye out for them as you explore.

43 | Potomac River: Fletcher's Boathouse

Less crowded than paddling spots downtown, this peaceful stretch is home to a boat rental and provides the opportunity to see birds and turtles.

Location: Northwest Washington, D.C.
Maps: Interstate Commission on the Potomac River Basin: potomacriver.org
Length: 2 to 4 miles
Time: 2 to 3 hours
Average Depth: 3 to 5 feet
Development: Urban
Access: No fees
Information: Fletcher's Cove Boathouse, 4940 Canal Road NW Washington, D.C. 20007, 202-244-0461, boatingindc.com
Outfitters: Boating in D.C.: 202-337-9642

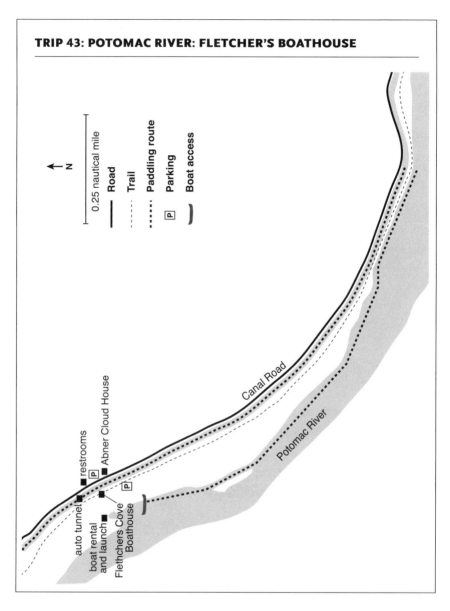

Take Note: Electric motorboats only. From Fletcher's Cove, you can paddle on both the Potomac River and the Chesapeake and Ohio (C & O) Canal (when there's been enough rainfall to fill the canal). To get there by car to the Potomac, you need to drive through a tunnel that is about 7 feet high; some vehicles may not clear the tunnel with kayaks on top. The dock near Fletcher's Boathouse is for use by renters only. To launch your own vessel in the Potomac, park at the far end of the parking lot and enter the water from there. It is not necessary to go through the tunnel if you want to paddle in the canal. There is a parking lot on the east side of the canal next to the Abner Cloud House. At times, such as after heavy rain, the river may be moving so fast that you cannot paddle back to Fletcher's Cove. Plan ahead and use your best judgment in these situations.

GETTING THERE

From I-495, take the Glen Echo exit onto the Clara Barton Parkway. Follow the Clara Barton Parkway until it becomes Canal Road, just past Chain Bridge, around 6.4 miles. Continue on Canal Road for 1 mile (cumulative: 7.4 miles) until the entrance at Canal and Reservoir. Fletcher's Boathouse is located on the right side of the road, and you will see the Abner Cloud House, an old stone building next to the canal. The entrance is a 180 degree turn, and you cannot enter the area southbound on Canal Road. From this direction, you have to pass the entrance and make a U-turn.

From I-66 East, take the Rosslyn exit to Key Bridge. Turn left onto Canal Road after crossing over Key Bridge. Bear left at Foxhall to stay on Canal Road, and continue 2.2 miles to the entrance of Fletcher's at Canal and Reservoir. The entrance is on the left and next to the Abner Cloud House, a historic building along the canal. Parking is available on both sides of the canal. To reach the west side parking lot next to the boat ramp, go through the auto tunnel and under the canal. (38° 55.030′ N, 77° 6.120′ W)

WHAT YOU'LL SEE

Fletcher's Cove is a lovely recreation area located in northwest Washington, D.C., that has been a renowned paddling and fishing destination since the 1850s. The park has unique access to both the Potomac River and the C & O Canal. The canal towpath and the Capital Crescent Trail merge here as well, making this an ideal location for hiking, biking, and picnicking. The on-site concessionaire, Fletcher's Boathouse, rents canoes, kayaks, and bicycles and sells fishing tackle and other accessories. This is a great destination for kayaking as it tends to be less crowded than the recreation areas near Georgetown, and you will likely see more wildlife.

As you pull into the parking lot, you will see the historic Abner Cloud House. It is the oldest building on the C & O Canal, dating to 1802, and was a residence and storeroom for the grains that were shipped to Georgetown. During the eighteenth and nineteenth centuries, the Potomac River was the main transportation route between Cumberland and the Chesapeake Bay. The canal was built with a system of locks that ran parallel to the river to provide a way to move goods down the river by boat. Hundreds of original structures, including locks and lockhouses, still stand along the river today. Since 1971, the canal has been a national park, providing a place to enjoy the outdoors and learn about the region's history. You can also paddle along the C & O Canal, launching in front of the Abner Cloud House at Fletcher's Cove. The waterway here is very narrow and shallow along this route, and the waters are often quite mucky. The water level in the canal is sometimes too low and unnavigable. Call Fletcher's Boathouse in advance to check on the depth.

To launch your own vessel in the Potomac, you have to carry your kayak in about 40 yards from the far end of the parking lot to the water. Pay attention to tidal pull and river levels because paddling upriver can be a workout during a strong outgoing tide or high-water flow (such as after a rainstorm). You can paddle upstream (to your right) 1 mile toward Chain Bridge before the river narrows and you feel a stronger current as you approach the bridge. Look up and you will see steep cliffs with some of D.C.'s most expensive homes. Paddling is not advisable beyond Chain Bridge, as it is an area where many have drowned. You may encounter whitewater paddlers here practicing their skills.

Heading downstream (to the left of Fletcher's), you will usually find a gentle stretch of water. Stay close to the shoreline and look for bald eagles, ospreys, ducks, geese, and other waterfowl. You will likely see turtles sunning themselves on rocks or tree branches. Stay close to the shoreline and continue paddling as far as you are comfortable. The Key Bridge and the beginning of Georgetown is just around 2 miles downstream. If the current is strong, be sure to save enough energy for your return trip.

Abner Cloud House, the oldest building on the C & O Canal, dates to 1802.

Following your paddle, hike or bike along the Capital Crescent Trail, which is built upon the former railbed of the 11-mile Georgetown Branch of the B & O Railroad. The scenery is shady and pleasant but heavily traveled on warm weekends. Head south on the trail for about 2.5 miles, and you will pass through the lushly landscaped promenade of Georgetown Waterfront Park. Continue along the waterfront to Washington Harbour, a multiuse development along the Georgetown waterfront where there are a variety of dining options and scenic views of the Potomac as well as the Kennedy Center and Roosevelt Island.

44 | Anacostia River: Anacostia Park

Once a neglected waterway, this rehabilitated urban wetland now provides habitat for numerous birds, fish, and other reptiles.

Location: Southeast Washington, D.C.
Maps: Kingman and Heritage Island Park: kingmanisland.org; Anacostia Watershed Society, Anacostia Water Trail Map and Guide download: anacostiaws.org
Length: 3.5 miles
Time: 2 hours
Average Depth: 3 feet
Development: Urban
Access: No fees
Information: Anacostia Watershed Society, 4302 Baltimore Avenue, Bladensburg, MD 20710, 301-699-6204, anacostiaws.org
Outfitters: Anacostia Watershed Society, tours only: 301-699-6204
Take Note: Electric motorboats only. The waterways surrounding the islands are tidal; check current tide data before planning your trip at freetidetables.com. The Anacostia Park Boat Ramp is located on the east side of the river.

GETTING THERE
From I-295: Take the eastbound Pennsylvania Avenue exit and turn right onto Fairlawn Avenue Southeast, heading south. Drive 0.1 mile and turn right onto Nicholson Street Southeast to enter the park. Turn right toward the skating pavilion. The boat ramp is on the left.

From Suitland Parkway/South Capitol Street: Follow Suitland Parkway west toward Washington, D.C. Turn right onto Firth Sterling Avenue, and then take the next left turn on Howard Road. When you approach the Douglass

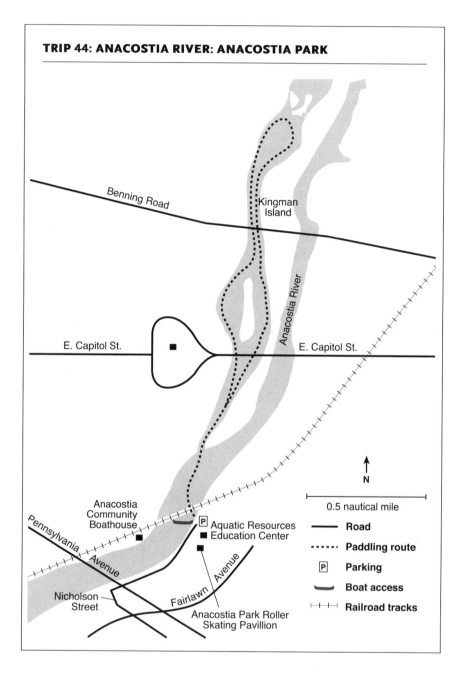

TRIP 44: ANACOSTIA RIVER: ANACOSTIA PARK

Benning Road

Kingman
Island

Anacostia River

E. Capitol St.

E. Capitol St.

Anacostia
Community
Boathouse

Pennsylvania
Avenue

P Aquatic Resources
Education Center

Nicholson
Street

Fairlawn Avenue

Anacostia Park Roller
Skating Pavillion

N

0.5 nautical mile

——— Road

····· Paddling route

P Parking

⌣ Boat access

+−+− Railroad tracks

Bridge, the lanes will split and the park entrance is to the right. Turn right toward the skating pavilion. The boat ramp is on the left. (38° 52.782´ N, 76° 58.227´ W)

WHAT YOU'LL SEE

The Anacostia River has changed dramatically over the years. The 8.7-mile river that flows through Washington, D.C., was long known as one of the nation's most neglected and polluted urban waterways. Now, though, you may be surprised by the acres of forests, wetlands, and wildlife you will encounter when paddling here.

Historians estimate that native people lived on the Anacostia for approximately 10,000 years. In colonial times, English settlers cleared forests in the watershed to grow tobacco and use the river as a port and commercial center. Over the last two centuries, development caused pollution, loss of habitat, erosion, sedimentation, and flooding. The river was neglected, and water quality suffered for a number of years. In the 1980s, the community took on a cleanup initiative to protect and restore its natural resources, and restoration of the Anacostia began.

Today, the river is beginning to rebound. Eagles and ospreys circle overhead. Fish have returned to their ancestral spawning grounds, and beavers navigate the deep channels of the river. Native plants, grasses, and trees line the river, helping to provide a healthy habitat for wildlife. In 2007, the National Park Service established the Anacostia Water Trail to provide a boating or paddling route to explore the sites along the 9-mile stretch of the Anacostia River, running from Bladensburg, Maryland, through Washington, D.C. (see Trip 45: Anacostia River: Bladensburg Waterfront Park).

This paddling route begins in Washington, D.C., toward the southern end of the river. Anacostia Park is a 1,200-acre national park with a public boat ramp, a roller skating rink, swimming pool, ball fields, trails, and picnic areas. There is plenty of available parking. Unfortunately, litter is still a problem here, and trash tends to float up onto the boat ramp. While conditions are not ideal, it at least is easy to get out onto the water quickly. Once you paddle out a short distance, the waters become cleaner and more appealing.

From the boat ramp, paddle to the right and go underneath the Anacostia Railroad Bridge and you will immediately see Robert F. Kennedy (RFK) Memorial Stadium on your left. Cross the river to the left side and proceed along the western shoreline as it runs parallel to the Anacostia Riverwalk Trail toward the East Capitol Street Bridge. On your left, you will notice a narrow entrance with a large cement structure that look to be the remains of an old bridge. The land to your left is the RFK Festival Grounds and, after passing through the narrow entrance, the large tract of land to your right is Kingman Island.

As you paddle north, you will enter the 110-acre Kingman Lake, which was built as part of a restoration project. The landscape changes from an urban setting surrounded by woodlands to marshlands with an abundance of native plants and grasses. These wetlands provide a habitat for 188 species of birds and nearly 50 species of fish. Look for bald eagles, ospreys, cormorants, great blue herons, turtles, great egrets, river otters, and other waterbirds. After crossing under the East Capitol Street bridge, stay to the left, passing by the small Heritage Island on your right.

Kingman Island and its adjoining Heritage Island were artificially constructed and completed in 1916. Both islands were federally owned property until 1995 when the city began the river cleanup initiative. Now, they are a part of the Anacostia Riverwalk Trail that is owned by the District of Columbia and managed by the Living Classrooms Foundation. After paddling, you might return here to explore the islands on foot. The only public access to Kingman Island and Heritage Island Park is from the west bank of the river, from the back of RFK Memorial Stadium's parking lot 6. There is a low-clearance boardwalk that crosses to the recreational area and provides access to more than 1.5 miles of trails used for hiking, biking, birding, and educational programs.

After paddling past the bridge at Benning Road Northeast, the waters become very shallow and, depending on the amount of recent rainfall, may

A cormorant spreads its wings as it sits on a rock in Anacostia River.

be impassable. When you are ready, turn around and paddle back to the boat ramp. You can paddle on either side of Heritage Island.

Once you return to the park, you can also walk or bike along the Anacostia Riverwalk Trail. The paved walkway continues across the bridges into downtown D.C., with access to the Navy Yard and Capitol Hill neighborhoods.

You can sometimes launch a kayak from the western shore, opposite the boat ramp, from the Anacostia Community Boathouse at 1900 M Street Southeast. The dock is open to the public, but available only when member groups are running their programs. The boathouse provides a home for the National Capital Area Women's Paddling Association, Capital Rowing Club, and D.C. Strokes Rowing Club. The Anacostia Watershed Society periodically sponsors paddling tours that depart from here.

45 | Anacostia River: Bladensburg Waterfront Park

This historic waterway crosses between two of D.C.'s most beautiful natural settings, but parts of the route are only navigable at high tide. Plan ahead.

Location: Bladensburg, MD, to Northeast Washington, D.C.
Maps: Anacostia Watershed Society: anacostiaws.org
Length: 6 miles or more if desired
Time: 2.5 to 3 hours
Average Depth: 2 to 3 feet
Development: Urban
Access: No fees
Information: Prince George's County Department of Parks and Recreation, Bladensburg Waterfront Park, 4601 Annapolis Road, Bladensburg, MD 20710, 301-779-0371, pgparks.com; Anacostia Watershed Society, 4302 Baltimore Avenue, Bladensburg, MD 20710, 301-699-6204, anacostiaws.org
Camping: Greenbelt Park, 5 miles northeast (see Appendix A)
Outfitters: On-site
Take Note: Electric motorboats only. Check tide charts before launching. Access to the lower portions of the Anacostia River may be limited due to changes in the tide and the depth of the water. Paddling into Kenilworth Park and Aquatic Gardens is best when it is close to high tide.

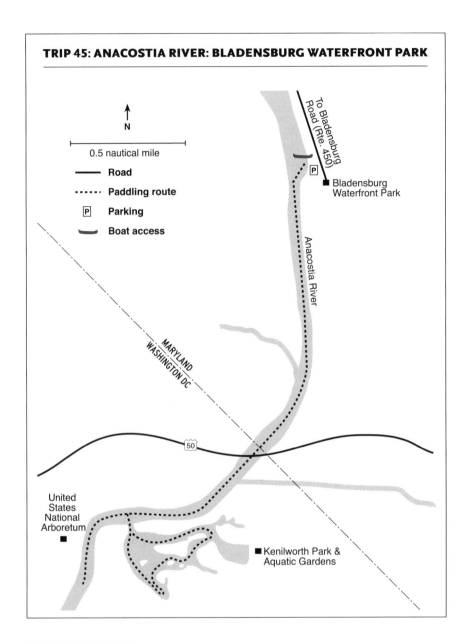

GETTING THERE

From Washington, D.C., take New York Avenue East. Turn north on US 1 Alt N (Bladensburg Road) and continue for 2.4 miles. After passing Peace Cross, take the first right into the park.

From I-495, take Exit 23 for MD 201 South (Kenilworth Avenue) toward Bladensburg and drive for 5 miles. After the traffic light at Upshur Street, turn right onto MD 450 (Annapolis Road). Go left at the end of exit ramp onto MD 450 West. The park entrance is on the left.

From Virginia, take Kenilworth Avenue North. Take the exit ramp on the right to MD 450 West. Turn right at the stop light onto MD 450 West. The park entrance is on the left. (38° 56.007′ N, 76° 56.282′ W)

WHAT YOU'LL SEE

This paddling route begins at Bladensburg Waterfront Park at the northern end of the Anacostia River in Prince George's County, Maryland, and crosses into the District of Columbia between two of the city's most beautiful natural settings: Kenilworth Aquatic Gardens and the United States National Arboretum. Near Bladensburg, the river has a 3-foot tidal range which means that there are places on the Anacostia that are available only at high tide. It is always best to explore the wetlands on an incoming tide to ensure that there is enough water to paddle your way back to your starting point. Check on the tide schedule before heading out by visiting saltwatertides.com.

While the water quality of the Anacostia River has improved dramatically in the last two decades, it is still rather muddy and unsafe to swim in. When you launch a kayak from Bladensburg Waterfront Park, you will notice that trash tends to collect near the boat ramp. It is a bit unsettling, but once out on the water, you will see that the river is slowly rebounding from the centuries of pollution and neglect. Hundreds of acres of wetlands are being restored, and aquatic life is starting to reemerge. You will be amazed how much wildlife you can see in such an urban locale.

The kayak ramp is set up for wheelchair access, as it has dual side railings to hold onto and rollers that allow you to slide, making it is very easy to get in and out of the water without getting your feet wet. After you launch, turn left to head south toward D.C. The Anacostia Riverwalk Trail, a new multiuse hiker/biker trail runs on the left side parallel to the river from Bladensburg Park to Benning Road Northeast. To date, 19.5 of the ultimate 28 miles of the Riverwalk Trail are open and heavily used. As you paddle along the river, you will see pedestrians and bicyclists enjoying the scenery along the shoreline. Much of this route is surrounded by parkland on both sides, so be sure to enjoy the natural surroundings. Look for turtles sunning themselves on tree limbs as you proceed downriver.

When you cross under MD 50, you are entering the District of Columbia. Continue under the MARC train bridge and keep paddling. When you see a new redwood walking bridge on the left, which is a part of the Anacostia Riverwalk Trail, you have arrived at Kenilworth Park and Aquatic Gardens.

A great egret stands on the shoreline of the aquatic gardens.

Turn left and the scenery will immediately become marsh-like. Wind your way through the garden water trails and move slowly to observe waterfowl or sun-worshipping turtles. While Kenilworth is best known for its exotic water lotus and lilies that flower in summer, you must visit the interior sections of the park to see them. By kayak, you can see a variety of grassy areas as well as marsh plants and wildflowers. These wetlands attract more than 40 species of birds, including ospreys, herons, and bald eagles. A variety of turtles, dragonflies, butterflies, and snakes can also be found.

After completing a loop around the gardens, work your way back to the Anacostia River. Turn left and paddle approximately one-third of a mile, crossing over to the west bank to the grounds of the National Arboretum. Here you will find a floating dock that you can tie your kayak or canoe to, or you can easily drag it up onto the grassy area. This is a great place for a picnic or a side trip to explore the lush bamboo forests of the Asian gardens. When you are ready, paddle back to Bladensburg.

After your paddle, spend some time exploring Bladensburg Waterfront Park. The waterfront is newly revitalized with a fishing pier, playground, and a community boathouse. The park and its visitor center are part of the Star-Spangled

Banner National Historic Trail. Photos, artifacts, and other exhibits tell the story of the people, places, and events of the Battle of Bladensburg, which occurred here on August 24, 1814, and allowed the British to attack Washington, D.C., burning the White House and U.S. Capitol.

You may also visit the town of Bladensburg, which has its own interesting history dating to 1742. Named after Maryland Governor Thomas Bladen, the town was a tobacco inspection port and the original terminus of the Baltimore and Ohio Railroad. Some of the historic properties still exist, such as Magruder House; Free Hope Baptist Church and The George Washington House, a tavern during colonial times and currently the headquarters for the Anacostia Watershed Society.

6 | VIRGINIA

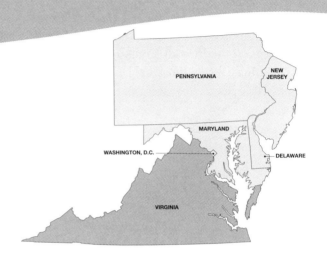

History and nature make Virginia a great place to enjoy the outdoors.
The site of the first permanent English settlement in the Americas, the commonwealth is home to many historic landmarks. Although increasingly metropolitan, much of Virginia is heavily forested, descending from the mountains and valleys in the west to the beaches of the Atlantic coast. With 37 state parks and hundreds of bodies of water, there are endless places to kayak, canoe, hike, and camp. Significant rivers include the Potomac, Shenandoah, Rappahannock, James, and York. Large lakes include the John H. Kerr Reservoir, Lake Moomaw, and Smith Mountain Lake.

Virginia's geographic regions are defined primarily by a combination of geology and topography. The Appalachian Plateau, the Valley and Ridge, and Blue Ridge provinces in the western part of the state are mountainous; the Piedmont consists of rolling terrain; and the Coastal Plain is flat and low-lying. Most of Virginia's rivers rise in the mountains and flow east-southeast to the Atlantic Ocean or west-southwest into the Tennessee and Ohio River basins. Shenandoah National Park and the George Washington National Forest provide vast protected lands with beautiful trails, waterfalls, and vistas. There is some flat water along the Shenandoah River (see Trip 46), although the water conditions are predominantly Class II and higher, so paddlers should be sure to learn about the area before launching.

To the east, the low-lying Tidewater region is deeply influenced by tidal rivers and is dominated by the Chesapeake Bay. Virginia's Eastern Shore, a 70-mile peninsula surrounded by the bay and the Atlantic Ocean, is home to small maritime towns, including Cape Charles and Onancock. South of the James River, coastal communities include the Norfolk region, Virginia Beach, and the Great Dismal Swamp. The Potomac River and its tributaries offer extensive paddling opportunities in the most populated part of the state: northern Virginia near Washington, D.C., where the land is relatively flat.

Virginia's plant life is as diverse as its geography. Coastal forests of oak, hickory, and pine trees grow around the Chesapeake Bay. Western Virginia is home to mixed forests of chestnut, walnut, hickory, oak, maple, and pine trees. The American dogwood, which is both Virginia's state flower and state tree, grows in abundance throughout the state.

More than 472 species of birds have been identified in Virginia, making it a destination for bird-watching, and its 200-plus species of freshwater fish— Walleye, brook trout, Roanoke bass, blue catfish—make it popular with fishers, as well. That diversity increases in the tidal Chesapeake Bay, which is home to more than 350 species of fish, as well as the beloved blue crabs and oysters. While paddling near Chincoteague Island, you may be lucky enough to catch a glimpse of other famous area residents: the island's wild horses. With numerous lakes and rivers throughout the state, Virginia offers plenty of unusual destinations to explore.

46 | Shenandoah River: North Fork

One of few rivers in the nation that flows south to north, this Shenandoah route sticks to a narrow waterway from start to finish.

Location: Mount Jackson, VA
Maps: Virginia Department of Game & Inland Fisheries; dgif.virginia.gov
Length: 3 to 6 miles
Time: 2 hours or more
Average Depth: 1.5 to 4 feet, depending on rainfall and time of year

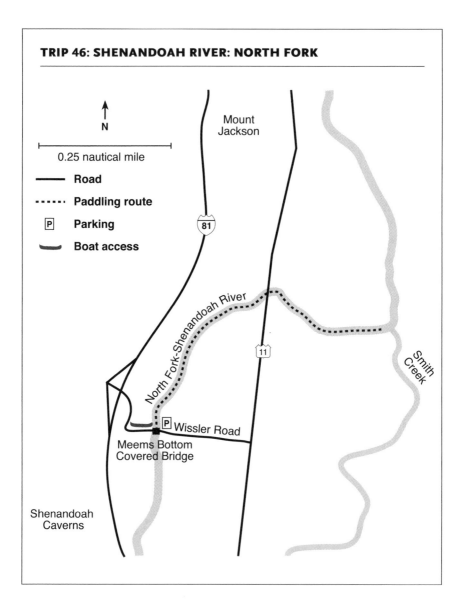

TRIP 46: SHENANDOAH RIVER: NORTH FORK

N

0.25 nautical mile

—— Road

······ Paddling route

P Parking

Boat access

Mount Jackson

81

North Fork-Shenandoah River

11

Smith Creek

P Wissler Road

Meems Bottom Covered Bridge

Shenandoah Caverns

Development: Rural

Access: No fees

Information: Virginia Department of Game & Inland Fisheries: dgif.virginia.gov; Friends of the North Fork of The Shenandoah River: fnfsr.org; Gateway to Shenandoah Visitor Center: 33229 Old Valley Pike, Strasburg, VA 540-465-5884; USGS Water Resources: waterdata.usgs.gov

Camping: Shenandoah Valley Campground, 1 mile south (see Appendix A)

Outfitters: Route 11 Outfitters: Woodstock, VA 540-459-8823, route11outfitters.com; Skyline Canoe Company: 541 South Royal Avenue, Front Royal, VA 22630, 540-305-7695, skylinecanoe.com; Front Royal Outdoors: 8567 Stonewall Jackson Highway, Front Royal, VA 22630, 540-635-5440, frontroyalcanoe.com

Take Note: Most of the land adjacent to the North Fork of the Shenandoah River is privately owned. There are just three public access sites along the North Fork: Meems Bottom, Chapman's Landing, and Riverton. The water depth is variable due to rainfall. The best time to paddle here is spring and early summer.

GETTING THERE

From I-81, take Exit 269 and turn left on VA 730 (Caverns Road). Drive 0.5 mile, and then turn left onto US 11 North; continue for 0.9 mile (cumulative: 1.4 miles). Turn left onto VA 720 (Wissler Road). The entrance is on the east bank under the covered bridge on the east side of the river, just under a half-mile down Wissler Road (1.9 miles). You'll see a small gravel parking lot on the south side of the road. Follow a small path about 100 feet down to the river bottom. (38° 43.243′ N, 78° 39.302′ W)

WHAT YOU'LL SEE

The Shenandoah River and its two major tributaries, the North Fork and the South Fork, are scenic jewels of Virginia's Shenandoah Valley. The river is one of the few in the nation that flows from south to north, and its gentle nature makes it ideal to float by kayak or canoe. The North Fork begins in the mountains of Rockingham County and flows north through beautiful countryside for 116 miles to the town of Front Royal where it joins the South Fork. Of all the routes in this book, this is one where you will be paddling along a very narrow waterway from start to finish. The river is about 120 feet at its widest point.

Most people book livery service along the Shenandoah River so that they can paddle one-way. Canoe outfitters provide a shuttle service, drop you off, and let you float back a chosen distance to the outfitter headquarters. Canoes, kayaks, inner tubes, rafts, and paddleboards may be rented. You can launch your own kayak too.

Meem's Bottom Covered Bridge is one of the best places where the water flow is usually slow enough that you can enjoy a round-trip excursion, easily returning to your starting point. Be sure to check water conditions before launching at waterdata.usgs.gov. Beware that low water flows during the summer months may require you to walk your boat through shallow areas. Be sure to wear sturdy

The river typically runs shallow enough under Meem's bridge to allow paddling against current.

shoes. Excessive nutrients in the watershed promote the growth of aquatic plant vegetation that can become very dense during the summer months and sometimes impede paddling. You should avoid boating when the river is more than 4 feet on the USGS Mount Jackson North Fork Shenandoah River gauge or when there are large objects floating in the river.

From Meem's Bottom, you can paddle in either direction, although it is easier to go toward Mount Jackson when the water level is low. It is about a 3-mile trip one-way. When levels are under 2.5 feet, the river becomes rather shallow. Proceed with caution as you may have to portage your boat around rocks.

The Meem's Bottom Covered Bridge is on the National Register of Historic Places and is the largest covered bridge still in use in Virginia. The current bridge is the fourth structure to be built at this location since 1867 as earlier iterations were destroyed by fire and floodwaters. The current structure was constructed in 1894. The bridge provides an interesting and scenic vantage point to start a kayaking trip along the North Fork. You can walk or drive across the bridge, but check your clearance in advance if you have a kayak atop your vehicle.

Launch from the grassy area to the left of the bridge on the east side of the river. You will have to carry your kayak down a short incline to the water. The waters are clear, and the river is surrounded by an abundance of forested scenery with opportunities to see waterfowl and wildlife. Look for great blue herons, wood ducks, painted turtles, and damselflies. The North Fork is a popular destination for fishing, as it supports a diverse fish population including largemouth bass, bluegill, redbreast sunfish, channel catfish, and muskellunge. This route is very quiet, and you probably won't encounter many other kayakers or canoeists.

Across from the parking lot on Wissler Road is the Bridgemont Farm, home to a popular corn maze, which is open during the fall season.

The Shenandoah Valley is known for its hundreds of miles of hiking trails with spectacular views, lush forests, streams, and wildlife. For a nearby hike, drive south on VA 11, and turn left on VA 211 to the Bird Knob–Emerald Pond Trail (about 9 miles from Meem's Bottom). Emerald Pond is a beautiful spring-fed swimming hole off the 8.3-mile Bird Knob Trail. After some significant climbing early in the hike, most of the terrain is easy ridge walking.

Also nearby, Shenandoah Caverns offers a one-hour, 1-mile guided tour on crushed gravel pathways through seventeen underground rooms.

47 | Occoquan Reservoir

Explore a variety of coves along the Occoquan Water Trail and enjoy its breathtaking views.

Location: Lake Ridge, VA
Maps: NOVA Parks: novaparks.com
Area: 2,100 acres
Time: 2.5 hours or more
Average Depth: 5 to 7 feet
Development: Suburban
Access: Launch fee
Information: Lake Ridge Golf & Marina: 12350 Cotton Mill Drive, Woodbridge, VA 22192, 703-494-5288, pwcgov.org
Camping: Prince William Forest, 9 miles south (see Appendix A)
Outfitters: On-site
Take Note: Electric motorboats only. You can purchase a waterproof paddler's guide and water trail map online from the park authority.

TRIP 47: OCCOQUAN RESERVOIR

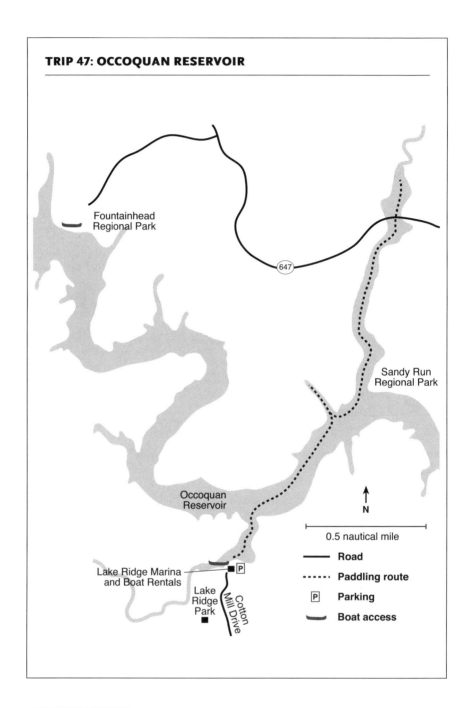

GETTING THERE

From I-95: Take Exit 160 to VA 123 North in Occoquan. Drive 0.4 mile and turn left onto Old Bridge Road. After 3.7 miles (cumulative: 4.1 miles), turn right onto Hedges Run Drive. Take the next life onto Cotton Mill Drive. You will pass the entrance to Lake Ridge Park on the left. Continue to the end of the road, and then turn right into the marina parking lot. (38° 41.793′ N, 77° 19.123′ W)

WHAT YOU'LL SEE

Bordered by wooded parkland to the east and mostly undeveloped tracts of land to the west, when paddling along the Occoquan Reservoir, you will hardly know you are in the midst of two of the most populous counties in Virginia. The Occoquan is a 2,100-acre water impoundment, which forms the boundary between Fairfax and Prince William counties in Northern Virginia. It supplies water to the residents of Fairfax County and the City of Alexandria. The scenery is beautiful here, and several public parks along the route provide recreational facilities and access for boating.

Occoquan is from an Algonquin Doeg word meaning "at the end of the water." Before colonial times, the native Doeg tribe farmed, fished, and hunted on this land. Early in the 1600s, Captain John Smith sailed and explored the Occoquan River. During the eighteenth century, the waters were used to operate a gristmill, and early colonists relied on the river for transportation and trade. Over the past two centuries, despite development taking over much of the region, the waterway has retained much of its beauty. It is an alluring fishing spot. Fly fishers and anglers reel in a diverse range of fish including largemouth bass, catfish, and perch.

In recent years, the Chesapeake Bay Gateways and Watertrails Network developed the Occoquan Water Trail to guide recreational paddlers in their exploration of this major tributary. Boats are available to rent for fishing, canoeing, kayaking, and sailing. With the close proximity to Washington, D.C., many of the parks with boat ramps fill to capacity during the summer on nice-weather days, especially holiday weekends. Access to the water with public parking can be found at Occoquan, Fountainhead, and Bull Run regional parks.

You can avoid the crowds at the regional parks by beginning your paddle from the lesser-known Lake Ridge Park, a small recreation area run by the Prince William County government. The marina here offers boat rentals and has a public boat launch, as well as a concession booth, bait sales, and boat rentals. The park also has a golf course, mini-golf, and picnic areas.

The launch at the Lake Ridge Park marina is in a protected cove with a fishing pier. Paddle straight ahead, and you will see a small island and a condominium complex on the left. As you continue past the island, you will reach the Occoquan Reservoir. You can paddle for miles from here in either direction. Fountainhead Regional Park is approximately 2.5 miles to the west, and Bull

A stand-up paddleboarder and a kayaker paddle quietly along the Occoquan Reservoir.

Run Regional Park is another 5 miles beyond. The reservoir winds around many bends along the way. Occoquan Regional Park sits approximately 4 miles to the east. Below the Occoquan Reservoir Dam, the reservoir opens into the brackish Belmont and Occoquan bays and farther into the Potomac River.

For a nice 5-mile round-trip excursion from the marina, head to Sandy Run. After launching from the boat ramp and paddling out of the cove into the Occoquan Reservoir, turn right. Paddle slowly along the shoreline and look to your right at the brightly colored rocks painted with high school rowing team emblems. If you wish, take a detour to explore the small coves along the way, where you are more likely to see shorebirds. After about a quarter-mile, you will reach a large, odd-looking modern structure with a red roof. That is the Sandy Run Boathouse, also known as the Occoquan Boathouse, which is home to the area's scholastic rowing facility and racecourse. The 2,000-meter Class A racecourse provides a venue for rowing crew education, training, and competitions. The boat launch and facility are open to registered crews and their personnel only.

Turn left as you approach the boathouse, passing the rowing-competition floating viewing dock on your left, and follow the creek to the end. Here the waters narrow, and it is easy to paddle. Common wildlife you may see along this route include ducks, bald eagles, red-tailed hawks, turkey vultures, great blue herons, Canada geese, beavers, bullfrogs, black rat snakes, and painted and box turtles. When you reach the bridge over VA 647 (Hampton Road), check out the architecture of the few but luxurious waterfront properties off to the right. After passing the bridge, the creek narrows and eventually becomes too shallow to paddle. Be sure to check out the gorgeous Spanish-style mansion on your right before turning around to head back to the boat ramp.

For hiking nearby, you can explore the trails at Occoquan, Fountainhead, or Bull Run regional parks or head to the quieter Occoquan Bay National Wildlife Refuge. You may also enjoy visiting the historic waterfront town of Occoquan. Once an industrial settlement with a gristmill and tobacco warehouses, the town is now an interesting place to explore and has restaurants, shops, and a town boat dock.

48 | Powell's Creek: Leesylvania State Park

Powell's Creek is a birder's paradise. Move slowly through these waters and you will see eagles, ospreys, ducks, cormorants, and herons.

Location: Woodbridge, VA
Maps: Virginia Department of Conservation and Recreation: dcr.virginia.gov
Length: 3 miles
Time: 1 to 2 hours
Average Depth: 3 to 5 feet
Development: Suburban
Access: Park entrance fee
Information: Virginia Department of Conservation and Recreation, Leesylvania State Park, 2001 Daniel K. Ludwig Dr., Woodbridge, VA 22191, 703-730-8205 or 800-933-PARK, dcr.virginia.gov
Camping: On-site (see Appendix A)
Outfitters: Woodbridge Sailing School: 703-963-3151, sailwoodbridge.com
Take Note: Unlimited horsepower. There's a large marina on-site and a separate cartop launch for smaller boats, such as canoes and kayaks. Guests may rent canoes, tandem kayaks, and stand-up paddleboards at the Breakwater Marina store from Memorial Day to Labor Day.

TRIP 48: POWELL'S CREEK: LEESYLVANIA STATE PARK

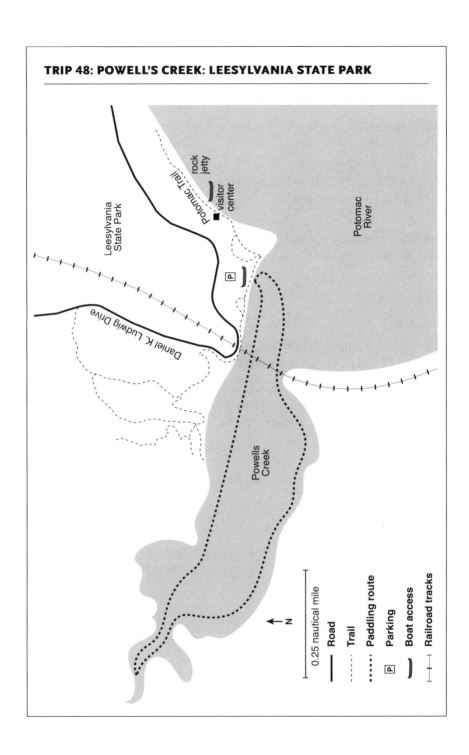

Potomac River

rock jetty

visitor center

Potomac Trail

Leesylvania State Park

Daniel K. Ludwig Drive

Powells Creek

0.25 nautical mile

N

Road
Trail
Paddling route
P Parking
Boat access
Railroad tracks

GETTING THERE

From I-95, take Exit 156, then go east on Dale Boulevard to US 1 (Jefferson Davis Highway). Turn right onto US 1, drive 1 mile, and then turn left onto SR 610 East (Neabsco Road). You will enter the park after about 2 miles (cumulative: 3 miles); drive under the railroad bridge and turn right at the sign for Bushey Point. Follow the sign to the cartop boat ramp. If you have reached the marina, you have passed the entrance to the kayak launch area. *Note*: the Bushey Point parking lot has limited parking and may be busy on holiday weekends. (38° 35.087′ N, 77° 15.590′ W)

WHAT YOU'LL SEE

Leesylvania State Park occupies 542 acres along the Potomac River between Neabsco and Powells creeks and features wetlands, forests, a sandy beach, and hiking trails. The line dividing Virginia from Maryland comes so close to the shore here that visitors can cross from one state to the other simply by walking down the fishing pier. The scenic marshlands are among the best for kayaking and wildlife viewing in the region. The park is also one of the top destinations in Virginia for eagle spotting.

Leesylvania is listed on the National Register of Historic Landmarks and is named for Virginia's legendary Lee family. Henry Lee II, the grandfather of General Robert E. Lee, lived on the property from 1747 until his death in 1787. The property was eventually donated to the Commonwealth of Virginia and opened as a state park in 1989. Today, the park offers recreational activities, including boating, hiking, picnicking, and fishing.

The kayak launch is located in an open stretch of some of the calmest waters off of the Potomac River. Paddle just a short distance to your right and go under the railroad bridge to Powell's Creek, where you will find an amazing natural wonderland. As you begin your excursion, trains may run over the tracks, and you might also hear hikers or anglers along the adjacent walking path. After you cross beneath the bridge, stay to the right and the sounds of nature will begin to dominate. You will see huge swaths of water lotuses and arrowhead arum on the side of the creek. The shoreline has begun eroding, so Virginia is building jetties parallel to the shoreline and covering them with aquatic plants. As the roots grow, they'll hold the sand in place, protecting the shoreline from additional erosion. These plants provide the perfect habitat for a wide array of birds and other wildlife.

The water is shallow throughout Powell's Creek. Be sure to approach the area slowly and listen to the sounds of singing birds, jumping fish, and mating bullfrogs. You can paddle right over the water lotus to get an up-close view

The still waters of Powell's Creek make it ideal for wildlife photography.

of ospreys, ducks, cormorants, and herons. As you move to the far end of the creek, you may even see a bald eagle. *Note:* water striders, a non-biting insect, may cling to your boat since they tend to surround the water plants. Don't be alarmed, as they are harmless.

Of all of the many places in the Mid-Atlantic region, Powell's Creek is one of the best spots for photography. The waters are still, and there are tons of birds. You can easily spend a few hours exploring the creek. Take your time and meander along the water foliage.

For a longer paddle, you can head east to the marina area and the busier section of the park. Leesylvania is a very popular warm-season destination for boaters and beachgoers. Swimming from the shore is not allowed. The waters are choppier and rougher along the coastline near the marina. This section of the Potomac River is excellent for fishing for largemouth bass, bluegill, channel catfish, perch, and striped bass.

From the kayak-launching area, you can walk along a wooded footbridge to the main areas of the park where you will find amenities including a boat launch, snack bar and store, visitor center, and rest rooms.

The park offers four hiking trails that lead to scenic overlooks of the Potomac River including one on the remains of a Civil War Confederate gun battery. Visitors can also enjoy guided history and nature walks, fishing tournaments, and other programming. Four tents-only primitive camp sites are available only for guests arriving by canoe or kayak. Advance reservations are required.

49 | Pohick Bay

Look for bald eagles, great blue herons, ospreys, and other wildlife as you paddle through this vast protected landscape.

Location: Lorton, VA
Maps: NOVA Parks, novaparks.com/parks
Length: 4 to 5 miles or more if desired
Time: 2 to 3 hours
Average Depth: 5 feet in the bay; 1 to 3 feet in the creek
Development: Suburban
Access: Park entrance fee
Information: NOVA Parks, Pohick Bay Regional Park, 6501 Pohick Bay Drive, Lorton, VA 22079, 703-339-6104, novaparks.com
Camping: On-site (see Appendix A)
Outfitters: On-site
Take Note: Unlimited horsepower. Guided nature kayaking and stand-up paddleboarding tours are offered on select dates throughout the summer and fall.

GETTING THERE
From I-95 South of the Capital Beltway, exit at Lorton. Turn left on Lorton Road, drive 0.6 mile and turn right on Armistead Road. Continue just 0.2 mile (cumulative: 0.8 mile) farther, and then turn right on US 1. Drive 0.9 mile (1.7 miles) and turn left on SR 242 (Gunston Road). Continue 1 mile (2.7 miles) to the golf course on your left or 3 miles (4.7 miles) to the main park. (38° 40.516′ N, 77° 10.022′ W)

TRIP 49: POHICK BAY

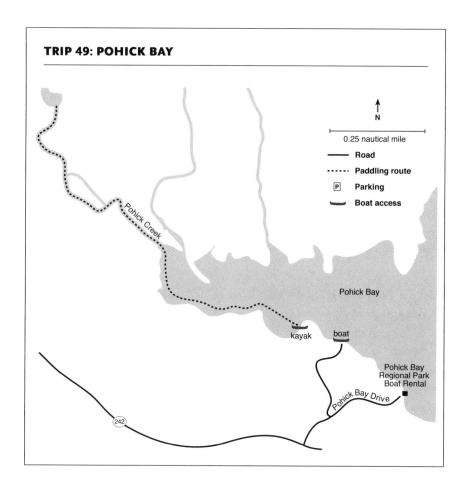

0.25 nautical mile

—— Road

----- Paddling route

P Parking

Boat access

Pohick Creek

Pohick Bay

kayak   boat

Pohick Bay
Regional Park
Boat Rental

Pohick Bay Drive

242

WHAT YOU'LL SEE

Pohick Bay is a part of the Occoquan Water Trail, which traces a 40-mile route on two tributary waterways of the Potomac River. As you paddle along Pohick Bay and the connecting Accotink Bay, you will explore a vast and changing landscape, past thousands of acres of public lands dedicated to resource conservation.

Located on Mason Neck Peninsula, Pohick Bay Regional Park provides an ecologically diverse land that shelters an abundance of wildlife, including the bald eagle. The bay attracts a variety of shorebirds and waterfowl, American toads, Eastern box turtles, various salamanders, and millipedes. Fox, deer, raccoons, and black rat snakes also frequent the area.

The 1,004-acre regional park is owned and operated by the Northern Virginia Park Authority (NOVA Parks) in southern Fairfax County, located 25 miles south of Washington, D.C. The park offers a variety of water-oriented and other recreational facilities. Amenities include a public boat ramp and marina with kayak, canoe and paddleboard rentals, family and group camping, rustic cabins, Pirate's Cove waterpark, 12 miles of equestrian and hiking trails, miniature and disc golf, and picnic areas. Guided nature walks, canoe and kayak tours, stream and pond studies, and other interpretive programs are available. While the park has many public facilities, the boat launch is situated at the far western corner of the park and offers a quiet destination for paddling and wildlife viewing.

If you have your own boat, note that the kayak launch area is located more than half a mile west of the boat rental kiosk. There is a ramp for motorboats and a separate shore launch for kayaks and paddleboards with a shallow gravel bottom. Motorboats are allowed on the bay, but most of the boat traffic goes the opposite direction into the deeper waters of the Potomac River. Paddle to the left and follow the shoreline to traverse Pohick Bay in a clockwise direction, and then head north up to Accotink Bay if time allows. You can stay in the wide-open waters of Pohick Bay or follow the narrow sections of the bay to

An osprey perches on a tree limb overlooking Pohick Bay in Lorton, Virginia.

Pohick Creek, which continues north for several miles. As you leave the boat launch, you will pass by a few private homes and boat docks on the left. Bird nesting boxes and some very large duck blinds are strategically scattered along the boundaries of the bay.

Continue paddling across the bay to the left. As you proceed to the far western section of the cove, the waters are filled with water lotuses, which provide a great habitat for a variety of wildlife. Wind your way through the narrow openings between the acres of plants. The most common marsh plant here is the yellow pond lily or spadderdock, a plant with very large leaves coming right out of the water. There is also an abundant amount of hydrilla, a non-native aquatic plant you will see underwater in the marsh. Many of the largest trees you will see along the banks are American sycamore. There are also a variety of oak species, tulip poplar, sweetgum, and maples.

Continue to your left toward the far west corner of the bay where there are groups of standing dead trees that serve as a critical habitat for numerous wildlife and forest invertebrate species. Look at these towering bare trees and you are sure to see ospreys; they also tend to attract bald eagles. There are many nests along the shorelines. You may also see great egrets and great blue herons.

As you paddle through swaths of aqua plants, the bay eventually narrows and becomes Pohick Creek. The water is very clear and shallow here, and you can see the plant life growing on the bottom. The shores are covered in pickerelweed, a beautiful perennial aqua plant that can grow up to 3.5 feet tall. Its leaves are shiny green, heart- or lance-shaped, and attached to a long blue petiole, which grows in a rosette from the roots. Submerged portions of all aquatic plants provide habitats for many invertebrates. Be careful paddling here, as there are some branches sticking out of the waters. You can continue along the creek for several miles before turning back.

When you return to the bay, head north (to your left) and the waters deepen. Paddle to the left and around the perimeter of the bay to see another stand of dead trees with osprey nests. In the center of the bay is a small island with a duck blind. Circle around the island, and look for birds such as migrating warblers and red-winged blackbirds. This is also an excellent place to enjoy a day of fishing for largemouth bass, catfish, striped bass, and perch.

50 | Dyke Marsh
Wildlife Preserve

Explore one of the region's most biodiverse areas in an urban setting close to Washington, D.C.

Location: Alexandria, VA
Maps: National Park Service: nps.gov
Length: 4.5 miles
Time: 2.5 to 3 hours
Average Depth: 1 to 3 feet
Development: Urban
Access: Launch fee
Information: National Park Service, George Washington Memorial Parkway Headquarters, 700 George Washington Memorial Parkway, McLean, VA 22101, 703-289-2500, nps.gov; Friends of Dyke Marsh, P.O. Box 7183, Alexandria, VA 22307, fodm.org
Outfitters: Bell Haven Marina, George Washington Memorial Parkway, Alexandria, VA 22307; 703-768-0018, saildc.com
Take Note: Unlimited horsepower. Launch from Belle Haven Marina. Check tide charts before launching, since the interior sections of the Dyke Marsh may be limited due to changes in the tide and the depth of the water. To paddle into the marsh, you should plan your excursion close to high tide. For tide information, go to tides.willyweather.com.

GETTING THERE
From the George Washington Memorial Parkway: Travel south toward Mount Vernon. After crossing the stone bridge at Hunting Creek, after about 1 mile, take the next left onto Driveway to enter Belle Haven Park and Marina/Dyke Marsh Wildlife Preserve.

From I-495: Take US 1 South. Stay in the right lane and follow the signs for Fort Hunt Road. At the end of the golf course, after about 0.7 mile, turn left onto Belle Haven Road. Drive 0.5 mile (cumulative: 1.2 miles) and turn right on the George Washington Memorial Parkway. After 0.2 mile (1.4 miles), take the first left at Driveway to enter Belle Haven Park and Marina/Dyke Marsh Wildlife Preserve. Proceed straight to the marina. (38° 46.657′ N, 77° 2.940′ W)

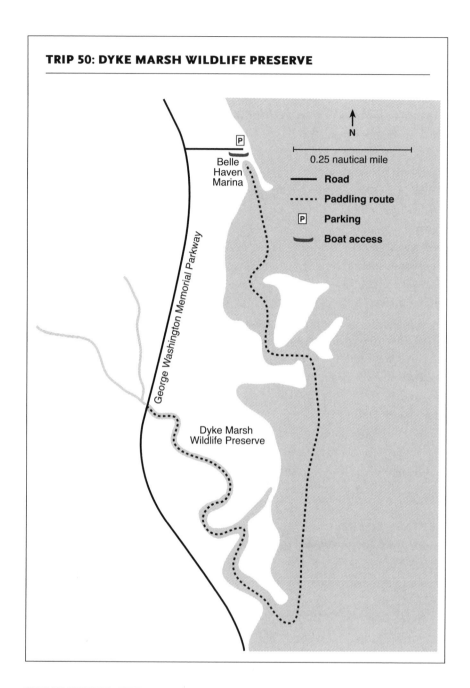

WHAT YOU'LL SEE

Surprisingly, you will find one of the region's most biodiverse areas in this urban setting close to Washington, D.C. The Dyke Marsh Wildlife Preserve is a 485-acre freshwater tidal wetland that runs along the western shoreline of the

Potomac River south of Alexandria, Virginia. It is one of the largest, most significant tidal marshes in the Washington metropolitan area and home to a wide variety of plants and aquatic birds. The preserve is managed by the National Park Service and is a unit of the George Washington Memorial Parkway.

The kayak launch at Belle Haven Marina is located at the far end of the parking lot next to the kiosk that rents kayaks, canoes, stand-up paddleboards, sailboats, and jon boats. The launch is a soft artificial turf, which makes getting in and out of the water easy. As you get started, you will be in an open area of the Potomac River where many boats are anchored. Stay to the right and paddle between the sailboats to reach a protected wetlands area. As you paddle across this short distance, to the left you will see the Woodrow Wilson Bridge and the skyline of National Harbor. Looking to your right, the landscape is forested marshland. After you paddle past the first section of the marsh, you will see a long boardwalk over the marsh. Pass the walkway and turn right.

You will be paddling in one of the calmest sections of the open waters of the Potomac River. The waters are also very shallow here and overridden with hydrilla, a submersed perennial herb commonly called water thyme. The plant is rooted in the riverbed and has long stems, up to 25 feet in length, that branch at

A cormorant sits on a log in the center of the Potomac River.

the surface and becomes horizontal, forming dense mats. These plants are very invasive and, when the water level gets low, it can be difficult to paddle through them. The shallow water depth and the health of the habitat make this water very clear, so you can easily see the plants and the areas to avoid. This is a great place for bird-watching and photography as the plants attract a diverse population of birds. Look for gulls, ducks, geese, cormorants, finches, and others.

Continue paddling along the Potomac toward a small island on the left. When you come to an opening to the protected wetlands, turn right to get a closer look and wind your way through this amazing water trail. Dyke Marsh provides a habitat to many species of plants, fish, reptiles, and amphibians that can only survive in wetlands. It is home to more than 270 known species of birds, and at least 20,000 species of insects.

As you wind your way through the Dyke Marsh, you will paddle parallel to the popular multiuse Mount Vernon Trail and the George Washington Memorial Parkway. You may see some bikers and will definitely hear some road noise. But listen closely to the sounds of nature and keep your eyes to the right, where you will surely see lots of birds. The most abundant species include Canada goose, American crow, European starling, song sparrow, a variety of gulls, white-throated sparrow, rock dove, red-winged blackbird, and American goldfinch. Great egrets, great blue herons, ospreys, cardinals, and woodpeckers are commonly seen as well. Look also for snapping turtles, northern water snakes, beavers, and muskrat swimming in the marshy areas. Frogs are also commonly seen here including the green frog, bullfrog, and southern leopard frog. Two dozen species of dragonflies and damselfies have been seen here as well.

As you paddle farther north, the waters eventually become surrounded by narrowleaf cattail, a plant more common to saltwater marshes. Other plants along the waters include arrowhead, wild rice, arrow arum, pickerelweed, and spatterdock. The marsh does not reconnect with the Potomac, so when you reach the Mount Vernon Trail footbridge, turn around and retrace your path back to the marina. As you return to the open waters of the Potomac, be sure to enjoy the panoramic views of National Harbor and Alexandria.

After your paddle, head to the adjoining Belle Haven park for a picnic along the waterfront, take a walk on the Dyke Marsh Trail to see the habitat on foot, or take a bike ride along the scenic Mount Vernon Trail. The trail runs parallel to the George Washington Memorial Parkway and is just 6.6 miles to George Washington's Mount Vernon Estate with many interesting points of interest along the way.

51 | Rappahannock River

Parts of this river verge on whitewater, but this quiet stretch offers the chance to view river otters, great blue herons, ospreys, screech owls, and turtles.

Location: Fredericksburg, VA
Maps: Virginia Department of Game & Inland Fisheries, dgif.virginia.gov
Length: 3 to 5 miles
Time: 2 to 3 hours
Average Depth: 2 to 3 feet
Development: Urban
Access: No fees
Information: Fredericksburg Government, City Dock, 2017 Sophia Street, Fredericksburg, VA 22401, 540-372-1086, fredericksburgva.gov; Greater Fredericksburg Tourism Partnership, Fredericksburg Visitor Center, 706 Caroline Street, Fredericksburg, VA 22401, 540-373-1776, visitfred.com
Camping: Fredericksburg, VA/Washington, D.C., South KOA, 14 miles south (see Appendix A)
Take Note: Electric motorboats only. Launch from the City Dock Park at 207 Sophia Street. There are two ramps perfect for motorboats, kayaks, or stand-up paddleboards. In addition, there are several fishing piers. There is ample parking, and the grounds are well maintained.

GETTING THERE
From I-95, take US 17 BUS South (Warrenton Road). Drive for 1.3 miles, and then turn right onto Washington Street. When the street ends after 0.2 mile (cumulative: 1.5 miles), turn right onto West Cambridge Street and then continue onto King Street, which then becomes VA 607 (River Road). After around 1.3 miles (2.8 miles), turn right onto Kings Highway. Turn left at the first cross street, after 0.2 mile (3 miles), onto Sophia St. The City Dock and parking lot will be on the right. (38° 17.821′ N, 77° 27.230′ W)

WHAT YOU'LL SEE
The Rappahannock River is the nation's longest free-flowing river. It runs 184 miles from the Blue Ridge Mountains in the west to the Chesapeake Bay in the east. Although the river is beautiful and seems calm and easy-flowing in most

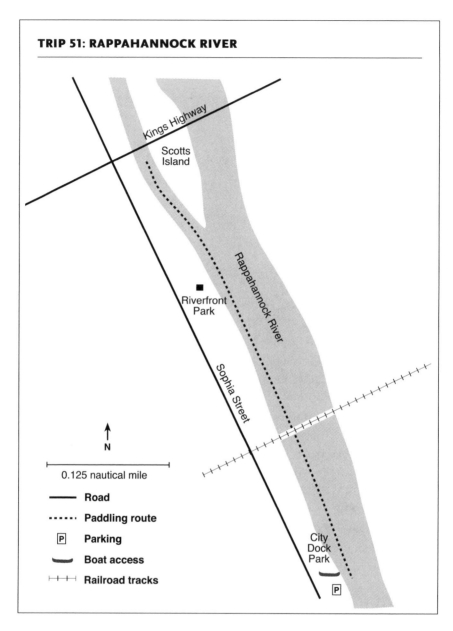

TRIP 51: RAPPAHANNOCK RIVER

Kings Highway

Scotts
Island

Rappahannock River

Riverfront
Park

Sophia Street

N

0.125 nautical mile

——— Road
······· Paddling route
P   Parking
⌣   Boat access
┝┿┿┥ Railroad tracks

City
Dock
Park

P

places, there are some Class I to III rapids along the river, and it can be dangerous in some areas. Around the city of Fredericksburg, the Rappahannock drops
off the Piedmont onto a long boundary between the two geographic provinces
where creeks tumble off old Appalachian rocks onto the flat sediments of the
plain. The City Dock area of Fredericksburg is one of the easier places to kayak.

The name "Rappahonock" comes from an Algonquian word, *lappihanne* (also recorded as toppehannock), meaning "river of quick, rising water." The river is affected by tides and currents here so be sure to check the water level and flow rate before heading out, and only tackle stretches you feel comfortable and experienced enough to handle. You can check the water level by visiting water.weather.gov.

The City Dock in Fredericksburg dates back to George Washington's day. Although Fredericksburg is more than 125 miles south of the Mason-Dixon line, some historians believe the Rappahannock served as a boundary between the North and the South during the Civil War. The battles of Fredericksburg and at Rappahannock Station were both fought across this waterway in 1862. Ferry Farm, the boyhood home of George Washington, is located directly across the river from the Fredericksburg City Dock. You can see the gardens and the archaeological site when paddling down the river.

After launching from the City Dock, paddle to the left and proceed toward the Fredericksburg train bridge. Keep heading north and stay to the left. You may see a variety of wildlife along the secluded reaches of the river, including river otters, great blue herons, ospreys, screech owls, and turtles. The river is surrounded by American sweetgum trees, sassafras, black elderberry, lamb's quarters, and swamp rose. Although a great deal of the watershed along the Rappahannock is undeveloped woodlands and farmland, recent growth in the area is changing the appearance of the river and its impact on the area.

Near Fredericksburg, multiple bridges cross the Rappahannock River.

As you paddle north, you will eventually pass by Scotts Island on your right. Today there is no access to the island from land or the river. According to an article by Roy Butler in the *Fredericksburg Times*, in the 1920s Scotts Island was home to a carnival on Saturday nights with "comedians, minstrel troupes, Dixie jazz bands, dancing, boxing and wrestling, shooting galleries, and wheels of fortune, and side shows." The island was described as "where the birds sing and the cool breezes blow."

In 2011, the City of Fredericksburg acquired the riverfront property at 609 Sophia Street to create a new park and provide a space for outdoor public events. Riverfront Park in Downtown Fredericksburg has a single, stationary dock that River Rock Outfitter uses for kayak rentals and instruction. This is a public dock; however, depending on the tide, it can be a tricky entry and exit. In addition, there is no parking adjacent to the dock. This is a beautiful area to paddle, but it is recommended that you use the livery service for assistance getting in and out of the water and you will also be able to paddle one-way to experience more of the river.

After paddling, visit the historic city of Fredericksburg. The charming town was a major port during the colonial era and the site of several battles during the Civil War. The 40-block historic district contains 350 original eighteenth- and nineteenth-century buildings and is home to living history museums, restaurants, shops, and art galleries.

A water trail is currently being developed by the Friends of the Rappahannock in cooperation with the Virginia Department of Conservation and Recreation. When completed, the trail will provide suggestions for paddling trips from Kelly's Ford to the Fredericksburg City Dock, highlighting the best spots along the middle section of the river.

52 | Diascund Creek Reservoir

This quiet reservoir offers an expansive area to explore with calm waters and pristine scenery.

Location: Lanexa, VA
Maps: USGS Walkers Quadrangle
Area: 1,110 acres
Time: 2 to 3 hours or more

TRIP 52: DIASCUND CREEK RESERVOIR

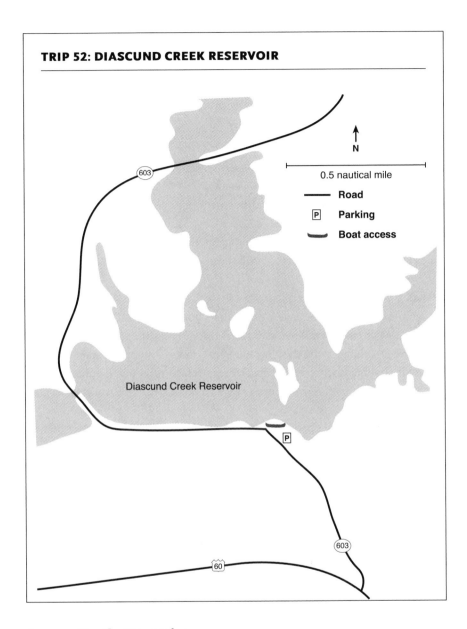

Average Depth: 10 to 12 feet
Access: No fees
Development: Rural
Information: Virginia Department of Game and Inland Fisheries, 3801 John Tyler Highway, Charles City, VA 23030, 804-829-6580, Ext. 129, dgif.virginia.gov

Camping: Rockahock Campgrounds and Ed Allen's Campgrounds, Chickahominy Riverfront Park, and Riverside Camp, all of which are 3 to 5 miles south (see Appendix A)

Take Note: Electric motorboats only. Enter the reservoir from the boat ramp at Diascund Reservoir Park.

GETTING THERE

Take Exit 214 on I-64 East to SR 155 South toward Providence Forge. Continue on SR 155 South for 3.8 miles, then turn left onto US 60 East (Pocahontas Trail). Follow US 60 East for 8.9 miles (cumulative: 12.7 miles) through the town of Lanexa, then take a left onto SR 603. Continue straight until you reach a stop sign and turn right, and then take an immediate left. Stay on SR 603 for 0.5 mile (13.2 miles). The boat ramp is on the left. (37° 25.725′ N, 76° 53.423′ W)

WHAT YOU'LL SEE

Located just 20 miles northwest of Williamsburg, Diascund Creek Reservoir offers miles of easy kayaking. The reservoir supplies the water for Newport News and is situated along the New Kent and James City county line. Diascund Creek drains into the Chickahominy River before reaching the James River. The watershed is very lightly developed and is mostly rural residential, with forested pastureland.

The reservoir is operated jointly by Newport News, James City County, and the Division of Game and Inland Fisheries and is open to the public for boating access and fishing. Powerboats are not allowed, so it is a kayak-friendly body of water. While you can enter the water from other points around the area, the best way is from the Diascund Reservoir Park. The public boat ramp is located in the center of the reservoir, just outside the town of Lanexa.

There are no public facilities other than the boat dock and parking lot, so the area is generally very quiet. With more than 1,100 acres, you will find many interesting coves and islands to explore. The largest creeks are Diascund Creek, Beaverdam Creek, Timber Swamp, Wahrani Swamp, and Barnes Swamp. The deepest waters are approximately 24 feet and located near the pump house.

As you paddle, you can see for long distances across the still waters. In the flats, you will see lots of hydrilla, an invasive bay grass that grows in freshwater portions of the Chesapeake Bay and most of its tributaries. The surrounding lands are rich in diverse vegetation and provide idyllic woodland habitats for birds, reptiles, and mammals. Hardwood trees include white and red oaks, tulipwood, hickory, pine, maple, and black walnut.

The reservoir is irregularly shaped, with three major creek arms. You can easily spend many hours here taking in the pristine scenery and lovely sounds of nature. From the boat dock if you paddle to the right creek branch, you can travel 2 miles to the I-64 bridge where the creek narrows considerably before entering the Wahrani Swamp. If you take the center branch, you can paddle up to 2.7 miles to the Beaverdam Creek, a Civil War battlefield site. If you decide to take a longer excursion, turn left after heading out from the boat dock and paddle for up to 5 miles to the Diascund Creek going under the bridges for SR 603 and SR 627. Beware that while paddling across the reservoir, you will be mostly in wide-open spaces with full exposure to the sun and wind, where small whitecaps are common. Be sure to apply sunscreen to protect yourself from UV exposure and be prepared for a bit of a work out to cross to the opposite shoreline.

The water is clean, and the reservoir is full of fish. This beautiful site attracts many birds and other wildlife. Diascund is a prime place for fishing as the waters have abundant populations of largemouth bass, sunfish, crappie, bluegill, chain pickerel, and perch. An average fish caught here weighs 3 to 4 pounds.

Different seasons bring different birds to the area. Some species are residents and remain throughout the year. Others are seasonal, migrating from the north in winter to warmer climates. Then, in spring, southern species migrate to the area to take advantage of the food resources as plants and insects emerge from winter dormancy. Birds you are likely to see during the prime paddling season include pied-billed grebes, eastern screech owls, mute swans, mallards,

Diascund Reservoir is a quiet kayaking destination with many narrow coves to explore.

wild turkeys, great egrets, little blue herons, red-shouldered hawks, red-bellied woodpeckers, house finches, blue jays, and European starlings.

For more kayaking and additional outdoor recreation options, head 22 miles south to Chickahominy Riverfront Park where you will find a boat ramp with kayak and paddleboard rentals, a golf driving range, picnic areas, a playground, and a swimming pool that are available for use by campers and visitors.

Lanexa is an unincorporated town located partially in New Kent County and partially in James City County. Rockahock, a nearby campground overlooking the Chickahominy Lake, is home to many festivals and concerts. Located near Virginia's Historic Triangle (Williamsburg, Jamestown, and Yorktown), you can easily visit these areas and experience the living history programs that include trilling fifes and drums, firework displays, theatrical programs, and interpretive characters of eighteenth-century America.

53 | Chincoteague National Wildlife Refuge

Paddle close to the famous Chincoteague ponies, as well as dolphins and the widest variety of native birds on the East Coast.

Location: Chincoteague Island, VA
Maps: U.S. Fish and Wildlife Service, fws.gov
Length: 7 miles
Time: 2 to 3 hours
Average Depth: 10 to 15 feet
Development: Rural, island
Access: Permits are required at city boat ramps and the National Seashore has an entrance fee.
Information: Chincoteague Chamber of Commerce, 6733 Maddox Boulevard, Chincoteague Island, VA 23336, 757-336-6161, chincoteaguechamber.com; U.S. Fish and Wildlife Service, Chincoteague National Wildlife Refuge, 8231 Beach Road, Chincoteague Island, VA 23336, 757-336-6122, fws.gov
Camping: Toms Cove Park, Chincoteague Island KOA, and Pine Grove Campground (see Appendix A)
Outfitters: Assateague Tours: 712 East Side Road, Chincoteague Island, VA 23336, 757-336-6176, assateaguetours.com

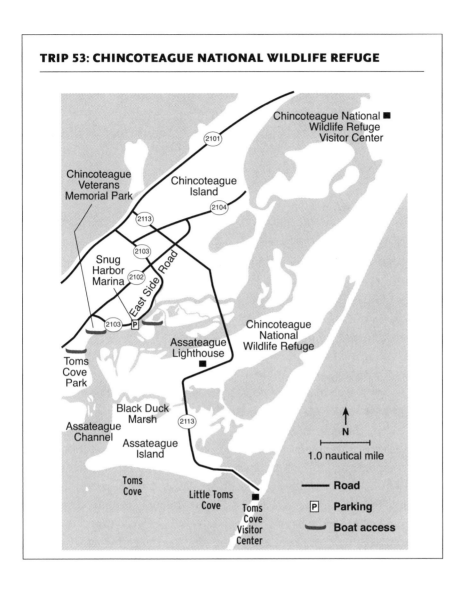

TRIP 53: CHINCOTEAGUE NATIONAL WILDLIFE REFUGE

Chincoteague National Wildlife Refuge Visitor Center

2101

Chincoteague Veterans Memorial Park

Chincoteague Island

2104

2113

2103

Snug Harbor Marina

2102

East Side Road

2103

P

Toms Cove Park

Assateague Lighthouse

Chincoteague National Wildlife Refuge

Black Duck Marsh

Assateague Channel

2113

Assateague Island

N

1.0 nautical mile

Toms Cove

Little Toms Cove

Toms Cove Visitor Center

——— Road

P Parking

⌣ Boat access

Take Note: Unlimited horsepower. Kayaks can be launched from Snug Harbor Marina, Toms Cove Hook, East Side Boat Ramp, and Memorial Park. Conditions vary and are subject to strong currents. While you can kayak on your own, the best way to experience Chincoteague is to take a guided tour. Snug Harbor Marina and Hotel offers waterfront accommodations, motorboat rentals, kayak rentals, and boat tours around the islands. There are two visitor centers on the island: Chincoteague Wildlife Refuge Visitor Center, operated by the U.S. Fish and Wildlife Service, and Toms Cove Visitor Center, operated by the National Park Service.

GETTING THERE

Take US 50 East and cross over the Chesapeake Bay Bridge; continue on US 50 for 68.1 miles, and then go south on US 13. Continue on US 13 for 38.9 miles (cumulative: 107 miles), and then turn left on SR 175 (Chincoteague Road). Drive 11.5 miles (118.5 miles) and turn right onto Main Street. After 0.3 mile (118.8 miles), turn left onto Church Street and continue for 1.8 miles (120.6 miles) as the road becomes East Side Road. Snug Harbor Marina is located on the left. (37° 55.022′ N, 75° 22.407′ W)

WHAT YOU'LL SEE

Chincoteague is one of the most memorable places you can kayak on the East Coast. World-famous for its wild ponies, Chincoteague National Wildlife Refuge includes more than 14,000 acres of beach, dunes, marsh, and forest, which provides a protected habitat for hundreds of species of animals and migratory birds. Visitors enjoy the peaceful environment and recreational activities including hiking, biking, boating, swimming, fishing, crabbing, clamming, bird-watching, and wildlife viewing.

Chincoteague is both a town on the Virginia Eastern Shore and an island that stretches 7 miles long and 1.5 mile wide. Chincoteague Island is connected via a bridge to Assateague Island (see Trip 33: Assateague Island National Seashore), a 37-mile long barrier island that is also a national wildlife refuge and is maintained by the National Park Service. The waters between Chincoteague and Assateague are among the best places to get up close to the famous Chincoteague ponies, dolphins, and the biggest selection of native birds on the East Coast.

The wild ponies of Assateague Island are descendants of ponies that were brought to the island more than 300 years ago. Although no one is certain how the ponies first arrived, a popular legend is that they escaped from a shipwreck and swam ashore. Most historians believe that seventeenth-century farmers used the island for grazing livestock to avoid taxation and then abandoned the horses.

Departing from the marina at Snug Harbor, paddle across Chincoteague Bay to your left. The shoreline is lined with oyster reefs. The salty ocean water provides an ideal habitat for the growth of oysters and other shellfish. Oysters and Chincoteague have a long history, as the island is a major producer of them and the industry is thriving. Virginia is the largest producer of fresh, farm-raised oysters, so you may see artificially constructed oyster beds that are commercially owned.

As you tour the marshlands of Chincoteague, you will see the Assateague Lighthouse, maintained by the Coast Guard for many years. It is still operational

The wild ponies of Assateague are a treat to see up close. They are said to be descendants of ponies brought to the island more than 300 years ago.

and is in the National Register of Historic Places. Paddle toward the lighthouse and get an up-close view of the 142-foot high structure. If it is windy and the currents are strong, you can stay close to the waters' edge to keep yourself from drifting.

Stop along the marshes and watch the birds. More than 300 species inhabit the island. While kayaking, you may see great blue herons, egrets, piping plovers, golden plovers, black bellied plovers, terns, oyster catchers, laughing gulls, black skimmers, and other wading birds. The National Wildlife Refuge restricts visitors to certain areas of the park. It is illegal to get out of your kayak and walk the grounds. If you would like to spend time on land, explore the designated walking trails at another time. Keep in mind that the ponies are wild animals and for your own safety, keep your distance.

Fishing, crabbing, and clamming are also popular activities here. Blue crabs are easy to catch, and refuge law sets limits on the size and number that you may catch. Anglers 16 and older must possess a valid fishing license.

Virginia's ponies are owned by the Chincoteague Volunteer Fire Department. Each year on the last Wednesday of July, the herd is rounded up and swum from Assateague Island to Chincoteague Island in the annual Pony Penning. The next day, some ponies are sold at auction to control the herd's population and raise money for the fire company. A crowd of approximately 50,000 people attends the annual event.

The Wildlife Refuge is open November through March from 6 A.M. to 6 P.M., April and October from 6 A.M. to 8 P.M., and May until September from 5 A.M. to 10 P.M. The Assateague Lighthouse is open for visitors each weekend from April through November from 9 A.M. to 3 P.M. A variety of tours and interpretive programs are available. There are two visitor centers, Tom's Cove, operated by the National Park Service, and Chincoteague Wildlife Refuge Visitor Center, operated by the U.S. Fish and Wildlife Service. The refuge maintains several miles of trails for hiking and biking.

Wild Beach stretches north 11 miles and is a hiker's paradise. Vehicles are not permitted here. As you walk north you will see fewer and fewer people, and, if you go during winter, you can have the beach virtually to yourself. You can also walk the 5-mile stretch of beach between Tom's Cove Hook and Fishing Point. In order to protect threatened and endangered species, the hook (from the Coast Guard Station to Fishing Point) is closed from March 15 to August 31. The interior dunes along the hook are closed restricted areas.

The town of Chincoteague has unique shops, museums, fine restaurants, and a wide variety of accommodations including hotels, bed and breakfasts, vacation rental homes, and campgrounds.

54 | Potomac River: Algonkian Regional Park

Experience the wonders of the Potomac River and explore its many islands where you may see a variety of waterfowl and amphibians.

Location: Sterling, VA
Maps: Interstate Commission on the Potomac River, basinpotomacriver.org
Length: 2 to 3 miles or more if desired
Time: 2 hours
Average Depth: 5 to 8 feet
Development: Suburban
Access: Launch fee
Information: Nova Parks, Algonkian Regional Park, 47001 Fairway Drive, Sterling, VA 20165, 703-450-4655, novaparks.com
Camping: Cabins on-site (see Appendix A)

TRIP 54: POTOMAC RIVER: ALGONKIAN REGIONAL PARK

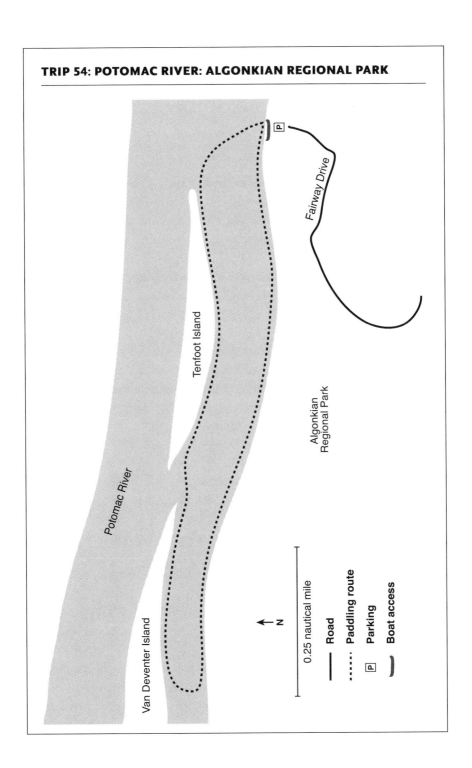

Fairway Drive

Tenfoot Island

Algonkian Regional Park

Potomac River

Van Deventer Island

0.25 nautical mile

N

Road
Paddling route
Parking
Boat access

Outfitters: On-site kayak rental available for guided tours only on select dates

Take Note: No boat restrictions. This area can be subject to strong currents, so be sure to check the weather.

GETTING THERE

From I-495 (Capital Beltway), take Exit 45A to merge onto VA 267 toward Dulles Airport. Continue for just under 2 miles, and take Exit 16 to merge onto VA 7 (Leesburg Pike) toward Leesburg (both are toll roads). Drive for 8.2 miles (cumulative: 10.2 miles), and then take the ramp onto SR 6220 (Algonkian Parkway) and continue for 4 miles (14.2 miles). Turn right onto Cascades Parkway; it merges into Fairway Drive. At the stop sign, turn left into the park and follow the signs to the boat ramp. There is a large parking lot designated specifically for boaters. (39° 3.730′ N, 77° 22.702′ W)

WHAT YOU'LL SEE

The boat launch at the 838-acre Algonkian Regional Park is an easy entry point to explore the Potomac River, the longest and most diverse river in the capital region. Located in Loudoun County, Virginia, about 20 miles northwest of Washington, D.C., this part of the river is quiet and has many islands to explore. The waterfront area of the park is a popular picnic spot that attracts a crowd on summer weekends.

The currents can be swift shortly after rainstorms, so be sure to check the weather before setting out and paddle upstream first to test the current. This is an interesting place to kayak and can be challenging depending on the weather. Stay close to the shoreline, as paddling will be easier and there is a greater chance of observing wildlife. Powerboats are allowed here, but the water traffic in the area is generally low.

Named for the Algonquian-speaking native tribes, the Powhatans, the park was once a major route for European settlers between Alexandria, Virginia, and the Shenandoah Valley. A part of the Virginia Birding and Wildlife Trail, these wetlands are an excellent place to spot bald eagles, herons, hawks, kingfishers, turkeys, songbirds, dragonflies, butterflies, river otters, and other wildlife. There are also vernal pools and a swamp that attracts a variety of amphibians.

From the launching area, paddle upstream to the left and across to Tenfoot Island. This 15-acre tract of land contains a floodplain forest with many mature deciduous trees and rare herbaceous plants. The island provides an excellent habitat for waterfowl, amphibians, and reptiles.

If you continue farther upriver (west) you will come to a larger tract of land, Van Deventer Island. The island is slightly less than 2 miles long and has many overhanging birches and sugar maples. You will likely see a variety of waterfowl such as wood ducks, great blue herons, and double-breasted cormorants. This is also a good area for fishing. Common fish include large- and smallmouth bass, bluegill, chain pickerel, chain pickerel, tiger muskie, American eel, sunfishes, bluegill, bullheads, black crappie, channel catfish, and yellow perch. Freshwater clams can be found on the beach along the outskirts of the island.

Continue paddling as far as you have energy for, and then proceed across to the opposite shore to return to the boat ramp. Alternatively, you may choose to traverse around Van Deventer Island or Tenfoot Island, but beware that the north side of the islands is situated along a wider section of the Potomac with stronger currents. You may also venture farther east to explore Sharpshin Island. This smaller island is about 200 yards long and very narrow. It has a small beach with an open area that is a perfect place to rest before paddling back to shore.

Algonkian Regional Park is one Northern Virginia's most popular parks, with activities including fishing, boating, golf, tennis, soccer, and hiking. Guided paddle tours are offered on select dates during summer and early fall.

The Potomac River offers miles of shoreline and interesting flora and fauna.

The park rents two- to five-bedroom furnished cabins with kitchens, scenic decks, and a lovely view of the Potomac River.

There are a variety of trails within the park, including accessible trails, paved trails, hiking trails, and a designated horseback-riding trail. Families enjoy gathering at the large playground and picnic shelters. Guided programs are available, including nature walks, hikes, boat tours, stream and pond studies, and educational talks. The island-themed Volcano Island Waterpark (open May to September) is located here as well, attracting families to hang out in the giant wading pool and water-play structures during the warmest days of summer. The Woodlands is an event space on-site that is available to rent for weddings and other large gatherings. It can accommodate up to 200 guests.

The park is located adjacent to Lowes Island, home to the 800-acre Trump National Golf Club, a private golf club purchased by Donald Trump in 2009. If President Trump is at the golf course, there are security restrictions that may limit access to the riverfront, and kayaking may not be allowed.

Just east of the golf club is Seneca Regional Park, an equestrian-friendly park that is bisected by the Potomac National Heritage Trail and follows the same routes explored by George Washington. Hiking trails here run along the Potomac River extending to Riverbend Park and farther south to Great Falls, where the trails connect with the Fairfax Cross County Trail.

55 | Lake Drummond: Great Dismal Swamp

The lake and wildlife refuge is rich in history and a haven for a large variety of birds, flowering plants, and butterflies.

Location: Suffolk, VA
Maps: U.S. Fish and Wildlife Service, fws.gov
Area: 3,100 acres
Time: 2 hours or more
Average Depth: 3 feet
Development: Rural
Access: Park entrance fee
Information: U.S. Fish and Wildlife Service, Great Dismal Swamp National Wildlife Refuge, 3100 Desert Road, Suffolk, VA 23434, 757-986-3705, fws.gov
Camping: Davis Lakes Campgrounds, 13 miles northwest (see Appendix A)

TRIP 55: LAKE DRUMMOND: GREAT DISMAL SWAMP

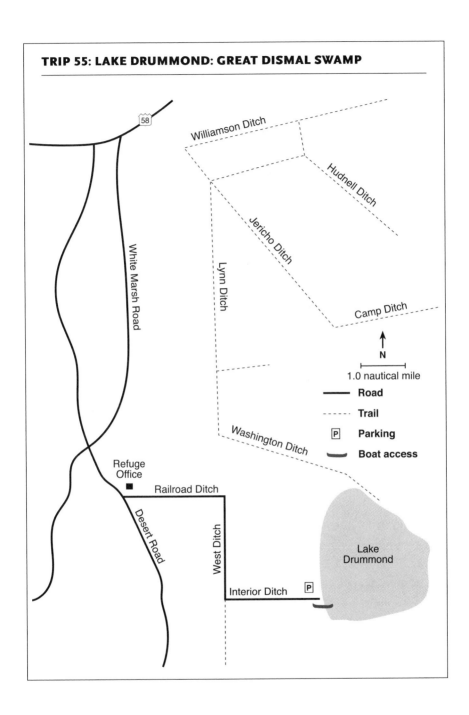

Outfitters: Adventure Kayak Tours: 757-237-8776; Kayak Nature Tours: 757-480-1999

Take Note: No boat restrictions. Vehicle access to Lake Drummond is via the Railroad Ditch entrance. Seasonal hours are April 1 to September 30, 7 A.M. to 7 P.M., and October 1 to March 31, 7:30 A.M. to 5 P.M. The gate closes one hour earlier to allow all vehicles to leave the area on time. The self-serve permit and fee envelope can be found at the Permit Station on Railroad Ditch Road, a half-mile from the entry gate. The lake is open for boaters and anglers from sunrise to sunset. There is limited parking space and no restroom facilities.

GETTING THERE

On I-64 toward Suffolk, Virginia, take Exit 299B onto I-664 North toward US 13/Bowers Hill/US 58/Suffolk/US 460/Newport News. Move to the right two lanes and take Exit 13A toward Suffolk onto US 460 West/US 58 West/US 13 South. Exit onto US 58 toward downtown Suffolk. Drive for approximately 5.2 miles, and then exit onto US 460. Drive for another 0.9 mile (cumulative: 6.1 miles), then turn right onto SR 13 (East Washington Street). Continue for another 3.2 miles (9.3 miles), and then turn right onto SR 642 (White Marsh Road) and drive for 6.4 miles (15.7 miles). Turn left onto Desert Road, drive for 2.8 miles (18.5 miles), and then turn left onto Railroad Ditch Road. The refuge headquarters will be on your left. Railroad Ditch Road becomes West Ditch Road, and then turns left and becomes Interior Ditch Road. Note, the 6 miles from the permit station to the lake is along a narrow gravel road. Drive slowly and look for wildlife. (36° 35.493′ N, 76° 29.278′ W)

WHAT YOU'LL SEE

Lake Drummond at the Great Dismal Swamp is a special place for boating and fishing. The national wildlife refuge serves as a vast habitat for more than 200 species of birds and nearly 100 species of butterflies and skippers. It is home to one of the largest black bear populations on the East Coast. The refuge is also an important historical site as it is an official stop on the Underground Railroad Network to Freedom.

At 3,100 acres, Lake Drummond is the largest natural lake in Virginia. When you look at a map, the lake looks miniscule. That's because the undeveloped land that it sits on is massive, occupying 112,000 acres of contiguous forest consisting of red maple, pine, sweetgum, oak, poplar and Atlantic white cedar. The lake was formed about 4,000 years ago after a wildfire burned away several feet of the swamp's peat soil. The soil gives the lake's water a dark-brown, almost black color. Despite its murky appearance, the water is home to several species of fish, including mud sunfish, yellow perch, brown and yellow bullhead catfish, bowfin, and crappie.

Lake Drummond is the main source of water for the Dismal Swamp Canal. The historic canal borders the eastern edge of the refuge. Initially proposed by George Washington and excavated by enslaved people, it was an important strategic holding during the American Civil War.

"The Lake of the Dismal Swamp" is a well-known myth of the swamp described by Irish poet Thomas Moore in his 1803 poem. It tells the story of a young native woman who died just before her wedding day and her ghostly white canoe is sometimes seen paddling across the water of Lake Drummond. Her bereaved lover followed her to the dismal swamp and never returned.

There is only one boat launch onsite, located on the western shore of the massive circular Lake Drummond. You can paddle in either direction and easily navigate the waters, but beware that after a while much of the scenery looks the same and you will need to see across the lake to locate the boat ramp. It is a good idea to bring a set of binoculars on this excursion. The distance across the lake is 2.5 to 3 miles so if you want a short paddle stay close to the water's edge. Along the shoreline, you will see lots of bald cypress trees with massive trunks.

Bald cypress on Lake Drummond are a striking sight.

In recent years, two wildfires have made an impact on the swamp. The 2008 South One Fire lasted for 121 days and burned 4,800 acres. In 2011, the Lateral West Fired burned 6,300 acres. The wildfires have left scars along the forest near the boat ramp at Lake Drummond. As you paddle to the south, you will see sections of burned trees and the beginnings of regrowth. Fire has always been a part of the Dismal Swamp history. Extreme heat and dry weather dries the peat soil, which becomes highly flammable and produces thick smoke as it burns. The fires burn deep in the soil, making them very hard to contain. Fire prevention has become a priority for the refuge management.

In winter, the lake provides a resting place for thousands of migratory birds including tundra swans and snow geese. In summer, it is home to great blue herons and great egrets. Look for northern harriers, northern parulas, and prothonotary warblers darting in the brush. Bald eagles have productive nests around the lake's shoreline and can be seen fishing for their young. Common birds seen here include warblers, wood duck, barred owl, and pileated woodpecker.

The Great Dismal Swamp has lured amateur and professional entomologists to observe nearly 100 species that have been recorded within the boundaries of the refuge. Several species are completely dependent upon vanishing food sources that can be found within the swamp.

After your paddle, take a short walk on the boardwalk to the Underground Railroad Pavilion, which was built to showcase the Great Dismal Swamp's role as a stop on the Underground Railroad and as a home for a hidden community of freedom seekers and escaped enslaved people known as Maroons.

At the intersection of Railroad and West Ditch roads lies an area where the dense forest is replaced by tall marsh grass and cypress trees. The 10-acre marsh is home to several beaver lodges, including one visible from West Ditch Road. It is also possible to see river otter, turtles, wood ducks, herons, and mallards.

At the Washington Ditch entrance, you might enjoy a walk on the three-quarter-mile, accessible boardwalk or the 4.5-mile hiking and biking trail that leads to the lake. From the Jericho Ditch entrance, you can enjoy many miles of hiking and biking. You can also reach Lake Drummond by water through the Feeder Ditch entrance on the east side of the refuge; however, there is no accessibility by car. The lake connects to the canal with water-only access. It takes several hours to paddle from the start of the canal to the lake.

56 | First Landing State Park

Paddle along a sandy beach, a saltwater marsh, and a residential lake all in one excursion. Look for waterfowl near the luxury waterfront homes.

Location: Virginia Beach, VA
Maps: Virginia State Parks, dcr.virginia.gov
Length: 5 miles or more if desired
Time: 2 to 3 hours or more
Average Depth: 3 to 5 feet
Development: Suburban
Access: Park entrance fee; free soft launch from the Narrows; boat ramp has a launch fee
Information: Virginia Department of Conservation and Recreation, First Landing State Park, 2500 Shore Drive, Virginia Beach, VA 23451, 757-412-2300, dcr.virginia.gov
Camping: On-site at the Shore Drive Entrance (see Appendix A)
Outfitters: On-site
Take Note: Unlimited horsepower. The launching area is located off of 64th Street, at a separate location approximately 6.5 miles from the Visitor Information Center and campground.

GETTING THERE

To the Narrows and 64th Street Boat Ramp: From I-64, take Exit 282 to US 13 North (Northampton Boulevard). Drive 4.4 miles, and then turn right onto US 60 (Shore Drive), which is the last exit before the tunnel. You will pass the visitor center on the left after 4.6 miles (cumulative: 9 miles). Drive for a total of 9.2 miles (13.6 miles), as the road changes name to Atlantic Avenue, and then turn right onto 64th Street and follow it to the end to the park entrance. The Narrows and beach launch area are to the left. The boat ramp is at the far end of the parking lot. (36° 53.432′ N, 76° 1.041′ W)

WHAT YOU'LL SEE

First Landing State Park offers an ideal environment for kayaking and wildlife viewing and is a great place to escape the crowded nearby Virginia Beach resort areas. Located on the north end of Virginia Beach, the quiet bayside setting is

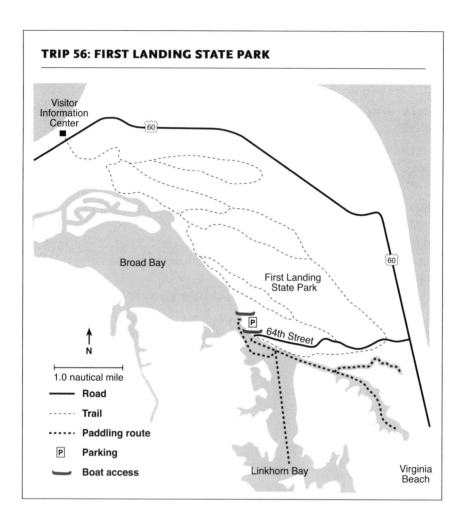

TRIP 56: FIRST LANDING STATE PARK

Visitor Information Center

60

Broad Bay

First Landing State Park

60

P

64th Street

N

1.0 nautical mile

Road

Trail

Paddling route

P   Parking

Boat access

Linkhorn Bay

Virginia Beach

an unexpected gem with recreational opportunities and camping areas. The park is located where the Chesapeake Bay and the Atlantic Ocean merge, so for easy paddling you need to head to the western borders of the park where the bays and creeks offer calmer, more approachable waters.

The park contains 2,700 acres of protected salt marsh habitat, bay and dune maritime forests, and freshwater ponds. Chesapeake native people inhabited this area from about 800 BCE to 1600 CE. As the site of the first landing of Jamestown colonists in 1607, First Landing is a National Historic Landmark and the most visited state park in Virginia.

The best place for launching a kayak at the park is from the beach area at the Narrows off 64th Street on the south end of the park, 6.5 miles from the main entrance. There is plenty of parking and a restroom. There is also a boat ramp on the opposite side of the parking lot; however, there is a $4 fee for launching, and the soft launch at the beach is easier, as it gives you quicker access to calmer waters. To launch from the beach, you have to carry your boat a short distance across the sand. Canoes, kayaks, and other watercraft may be rented from the park concession.

Both launch areas offer direct access to Linkhorn and Broad bays, which have many small coves to explore. This area provides a variety of paddling experiences, as you can choose to spend your time exploring the wider sections of Broad Bay and Wolfsnare Creek or wander into numerous smaller creeks.

To quickly reach the easiest paddling area, go to the left of the beach. As you enter Rainey Gut, the shoreline alternates between salt marsh and sandbars. The waters are very shallow here. Turn to the left and explore the narrow cove where you will see many tall dead trees with osprey nests. Look for blue herons, ospreys, great white herons, kingfishers, black nocturnal herons, crabs, and oysters. Seeing eagles here is uncommon, but the park has the highest concentration of ospreys in the area. Paddle back to the main route and keep heading east. You will reach Crystal Lake, a marsh-lined, oyster-rich ecosystem surrounded by expensive waterfront properties and boat docks. Paddle as far as you would like and spot your dream home. Turn around and return to the beach.

Crystal Lake is a marsh-lined, oyster-rich ecosystem.

After your paddle, explore the hiking or bike trails. The Cape Henry and Long Creek trails both connect with the 64th Street park road. Or drive to the main park entrance off of Shore Drive. The park visitor center and the main area of the park have a beach (on the Chesapeake Bay), restrooms, an information center, an Environmental Education Center, and campgrounds. To reach the visitor center from the boat launch, follow 64th Street for 1.7 miles, and turn left on Shore Drive/60. Continue for 3.5 miles. Turn left into the park entrance is on the right. *GPS Coordinates:* 36° 55.092′ N, 76° 3.193′ W.

The park has 20 miles of trails and 1.5 miles of sandy beach frontage. Fishing and crabbing are popular as well. Common animals you may see include lizards, salamanders, toads and frogs, birds, squirrels, turtles, and snakes.

Just a few miles south of the park, the bustling Virginia Beach resort area has a 3-mile boardwalk that stretches along its beach-lined oceanfront. The 14 miles of white sandy beaches, oceanfront hotels and restaurants, historic landmarks, and family-friendly attractions offer endless opportunities for recreation including fishing, golf, and whale- and dolphin-watching.

57 | Back Bay National Wildlife Refuge

View a variety of wildlife and habitats along the secluded coves of a large wildlife refuge.

Location: Virginia Beach, VA
Maps: U. S. Fish and Wildlife Service, Virginia Beach Visitor Information Center: vbgov.com
Length: 2 miles or more if desired
Time: 2 hours or more
Average Depth: 3 to 5 feet
Development: Rural
Access: While an entrance fee is required to enter the refuge grounds, Back Bay is free from many locations on the western shore of the North Bay section
Information: U.S. Fish and Wildlife Service, Back Bay National Wildlife Refuge, 4005 Sandpiper Road, Virginia Beach, VA 23456, 757-301-7329

TRIP 57: BACK BAY NATIONAL WILDLIFE REFUGE

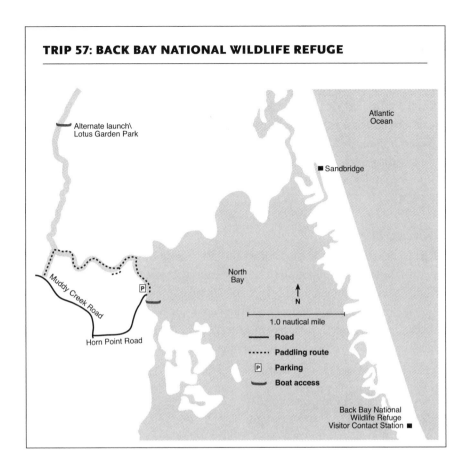

Camping: North Bay Shore Campground, False Cape State Park, and Indian Cove Resort (see Appendix A)

Outfitters: Adventure Kayak Tours: 3985 West Neck Road, Virginia Beach, VA, 757-237-8776 adventurekayaktours.net; Kayak Nature Tours: 89th Street, Virginia Beach, VA 23451, 757-480-1999, kayaknaturetours.net; Surf & Adventure Co.: 577 Sandbridge Road, Virginia Beach, VA 23456, 800-695-4212, surfandadventure.com

Take Note: Electric motorboats only. When launching from Horn Point, beware that when water levels are high, the road can be significantly washed out. Check the water levels before driving to the end of the road. During summer months, bug repellent is highly recommended as biting insects are plentiful this time of year.

GETTING THERE

From I-264 East, take Exit 22 to Birdneck Road and head south onto Birdneck Road. Travel 3.1 miles then turn right onto General Booth Boulevard. Continue for 3.9 miles (cumulative: 7 miles), and then turn left onto Princess Anne Road. After 0.9 mile (7.9 miles), the road turns into Sandbridge Road, so turn right to stay on Princess Anne Road. Continue for 2.2 miles (10.1 miles) then turn left onto Indian River Road. Drive for 1.6 miles (11.7 miles), and then turn left onto North Muddy Creek Road. Follow this road for 1.4 miles (13.1 miles). Turn left onto Horn Point Road and follow it to the entrance of the launch site. (36° 42.414′ N, 75° 58.197′ W)

WHAT YOU'LL SEE

Virginia Beach has developed one of the first comprehensive water trail networks in the state. At the southern end of Virginia Beach, the Back Bay National Wildlife Refuge is a prime place to kayak, thanks to the endless opportunities to explore and view wildlife. The refuge contains more than 9,250 acres of barrier islands, dunes, freshwater marshes, maritime forests, ponds, and ocean beaches that provide a protective habitat for a variety of wildlife, including

Back Bay offers miles of unspoiled habitat to explore.

migrating waterfowl and endangered species. Visitors can also hike and bike along the scenic trails and participate in educational programs. The refuge shares a border with the 4,321-acre False Cape State Park in North Carolina, featuring miles of unspoiled beaches in an ocean-to-freshwater bay habitat.

Many put-in and takeout points are located throughout the Sandbridge area. Horn Point is one of the recommended spots to launch, leading to the secluded section of Ashville Bridge Creek south toward Muddy Creek. The kayak launch site includes a parking area and restrooms. The U.S. Fish and Wildlife Service has begun plans for a living shoreline stabilization project at this site. Looking out from the launching area, you will see the Sandbridge resort in the distance to the right.

The refuge is composed of thousands of acres of mixed pine forest that provides habitats for white-tailed deer, owls, squirrels, woodpeckers, and a wide variety of birds.

Launch from the shoreline, paddle to the left, and keep heading left past the house into the narrow cove surrounded by tall grasses. Throughout this excursion, keep turning left to stay on the main route and take additional left turns into narrow passageways to explore as often as you would like. Most of the smaller coves do not connect to the main trail so you will have to turn around to continue along the route. The first cove is one of the largest and becomes pond-like surrounded by beautiful scenery.

Head back out to the main trail and then continue left and when you see houses on your right, turn left again to stay on the main trail. You can paddle right up to Blue Pete's Restaurant, a local favorite with outdoor dining and picnic tables.

Arriving at Muddy Creek, you will enter an area that locals refer to as "Cypress Alley," a woodland marsh that is home to great blue herons, white egrets, songbirds, turtles, and snakes. Paddle through an extensive phragmites marsh; as you weave your way up the creek, the salinity decreases and the bald cypress become more prolific.

The wildlife refuge was established in 1938 and consists of 4,589 acres of wetlands that provides a seasonal habitat for migratory birds. It is a critical locale in the Atlantic Flyway. Thousands of tundra swans, geese, and a large variety of ducks visit the refuge during fall and winter. Year-round, the refuge also provides food and shelter for threatened and endangered species such as the loggerhead sea turtle and piping plover.

Fishing is allowed in designated areas only, and a Virginia freshwater fishing license is required. Shad, herring, bluefish, and striped bass can be found here.

The Visitor Contact Station is located 9 miles from the Horn Point launch at 4005 Sandpiper Road on the southern end of Sandbridge. An entrance fee is required to enter the grounds there. Fees vary depending on whether you're entering in a car or on foot, but there are no fees from November 1 to March 31. Daily, yearly, and lifetime passes are available. The refuge offers more than 8 miles of hiking and biking trails as well as guided tram tours. The Dune Trail has a platform where you can see panoramic views of the ocean and the bay.

Another good place to launch nearby is from Lotus Garden Park at 1289 Sandbridge Road, which provides access to Ashville Bridge Creek, Muddy Creek, and North Bay. This small roadside park is on the south side of Sandbridge Road with launch points on both sides of the road.

58 | John H. Kerr Reservoir: Occoneechee State Park

Explore miles of scenic shoreline, watching for butterflies and a variety of waterfowl.

Location: Clarksville, VA
Maps: U.S. Army Corps of Engineers, www.saw.usace.army.mil
Area: 48,000 acres
Time: 2 to 3 hours or more
Average Depth: 30 feet
Development: Remote
Access: Park entrance fee and launch fee
Information: Virginia Department of Conservation and Recreation, Occoneechee State Park, 1192 Occoneechee State Park Road, Clarksville, VA 23927, 434-374-2210, dcr.virginia.gov
Camping: On-site: Clarksville Marine Rentals: 1192 Occoneechee Park Road, Clarksville, VA 23927, 434-374-2755, clarksvilleboats.com
Outfitters: On-site, at the main boat ramp
Take Note: Unlimited horsepower. Three boat launching ramps are available for access to John H. Kerr Lake for both motorized and nonmotorized boats. *Note*: the maps provided by the state park are not very detailed and can be difficult to follow. The signage on-site is correct, so stay alert and follow the signs.

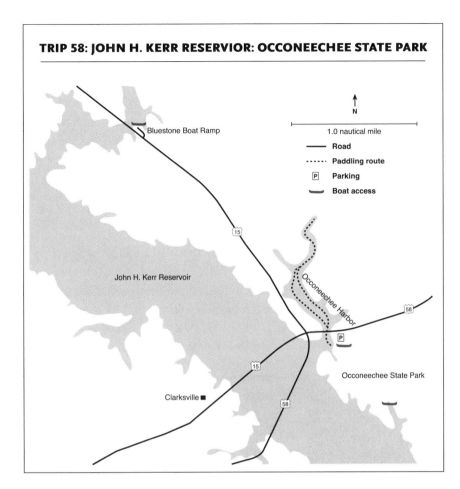

TRIP 58: JOHN H. KERR RESERVOIR: OCCONEECHEE STATE PARK

Bluestone Boat Ramp

N

1.0 nautical mile

—— Road
----- Paddling route
P Parking
⌣ Boat access

John H. Kerr Reservoir

15

Occoneechee Harbor

58

P

15

Occoneechee State Park

Clarksville ■

58

GETTING THERE

From I-85, take the exit to US 58 West at South Hill. Drive 26.4 miles, then turn left onto VA 364 South, 1 mile east of Clarksville. From this main entrance, turn right and follow VA 364 North (Occoneechee Park Road) for 0.5 mile to the main boat ramp. (36° 37.997′ N, 78° 32.073′ W)

WHAT YOU'LL SEE

The John H. Kerr Lake is a reservoir with more than 850 miles of shoreline and 50,000 acres. The lake is so massive that its creeks are located in three counties in North Carolina and three in Virginia. There are 30 boat launches around the lake as well as many day-use areas that are open to the public. The lake also offers an accessible fishing pier so all fishing enthusiasts can take part. With so many miles of shoreline, there are virtually endless waters to explore, with beautiful scenery and many opportunities to see bald eagles, ospreys, great blue herons, and other migratory birds.

The lake was artificially constructed from 1947 through 1952 as the result of a dam that was built to prevent flooding. It is named after the North Carolina representative who was successful in obtaining funding and approval for its construction. The area surrounding the lake was once inhabited by the Occoneechi native people, a tribe who played a major role in the deerskin and fur trades along the East Coast during the 1600s. In 1968, Occoneechee State Park was established here and designated for recreational use. The park is popular for fishing, boating, and aquatic recreation and has cabins, campsites, an equestrian campground, boat ramps, and a marina.

The main boat ramp, located at the Occoneechee Marina, provides good access to Occoneechee Harbor, where you can easily spend a few hours paddling. The boat ramp is triple wide and easy to launch from, although you should be aware of pontoon boats and other powerboats that may also be launching. There's also a single boat ramp that you can launch from just a short distance farther east of the marina. A second boat ramp is located on the park grounds in a less protected area continuing farther east.

Buttonbushes lining the coast of Kerr Lake attract butterflies.

After leaving the ramp, turn right and go underneath the bridge (US 58/VA 364). You will pass by a variety of houses and boat docks. You may notice that the homes all have riprap stones that create an embankment slope to prevent erosion along the waterfront. That is because this area has a huge variance in water level depending on the rainfall. With an average depth of 30 feet, it's one of the deepest waterways in the region and suitable for all kinds of boating. The boat ramps are also made of metal rather than wood and are adjustable to accommodate the regular changes in water depth.

The lake is great for fishing and anglers often catch striped bass, perch, and other freshwater fish. With the recent addition of fishing lights on the Clarksville bridge, you can now fish here at night, when it may be easier to lure the fish to the surface.

After you paddle past a variety of homes, you will eventually reach a forested area with oak, sweet gum, pine, maple, and beach trees. As the cove narrows, you will see lots of buttonbush, a low deciduous shrub that flourishes in wetlands and gets its name from round clusters of small white flowers that resemble pin cushions. Butterflies are attracted to the ball-shaped flowers and you will see dozens of them along the shoreline. At the end of the cove, keep paddling as far as you like through the narrow and shallow creek.

When you're ready, turn around and paddle back to the boat ramp or explore some of the smaller coves along the way. You can paddle along the shoreline of the park, but beware that these waters are more subject to currents and wake zones from boat traffic.

The park also has 20 miles of trails for hiking, biking, and horseback riding. Two self-guided interpretive trails introduce visitors to the Terrace Garden, the remains of the Occoneechee Plantation, and the Tutelo Birding Trail. The Joseph S. J. Tanner Environmental Education Center offers hands-on opportunities to learn about local bird and mammal species.

Located just across the reservoir and 4 miles from the state park, the lakeside town of Clarksville offers quaint shops, several restaurants, and a few hotels. A couple minutes up the road is the beautiful eighteenth-century Prestwould Plantation, the Kinderton Country Club, and the Three Sisters of Shiney Rock Winery.

Another good boat ramp to launch a kayak and enjoy easy paddling is at the Bluestone Wildlife Management Area, located just 3 miles northwest of the state park.

59 | Lake Anna

One of the largest freshwater lakes in Virginia, Lake Anna is a popular destination for paddling, sailing, swimming, water-skiing, and fishing.

Location: Spotsylvania, VA
Maps: Lake Anna Civic Association: lakeannavirginia.org; Sketch map of park trails available at the visitor center, with limited detail of the lake
Area: 13,000 acres
Time: 2 hours or more
Average Depth: 50 feet
Development: Rural
Access: Park entrance fee
Information: Virginia Department of Conservation and Recreation, Lake Anna State Park, 6800 Lawyers Road, Spotsylvania, VA 22551, 540-854-5503, dcr.virginia.gov; Lake Anna Business Partnership, P.O. Box 536, Mineral, VA 23117, visitlakeanna.org
Camping: On-site
Outfitters: Lake Anna Outfitters: 4634 Courthouse Road, Mineral, VA 22551, 540-894-3540
Take Note: Unlimited horsepower. Day-use parking areas near the beach and picnic areas fill up on weekends and holidays during the summer. The park entrance may be gated until enough parking spots have opened up. *Note:* the state park offers the best public access for launching your kayak; however, there are several marinas that also offer lake access.

GETTING THERE
From I-95, take Exit 118 at Thornburg and travel for about 5 miles west on SR 606 (Morris Road). Pass through the town of Snell, where the road changes names to SR 208 (Courthouse Road), and then continue for 10.7 miles (cumulative: 15.7 miles). Turn right onto SR 601 (Lawyers Road) and drive 3.3 miles (19 miles). Look for the state park sign on the left; turn onto State Park Lane. Follow the signs to Picnic Area B, where you will find parking and launching access. You can also launch at the boat ramp, which is busier in summer and subject to wake from larger watercraft. Kayak launch: (38° 7.055′ N, 77° 50.265′ W); boat ramp: (38° 6.811′ N, 77° 50.147′ W)

TRIP 59: LAKE ANNA

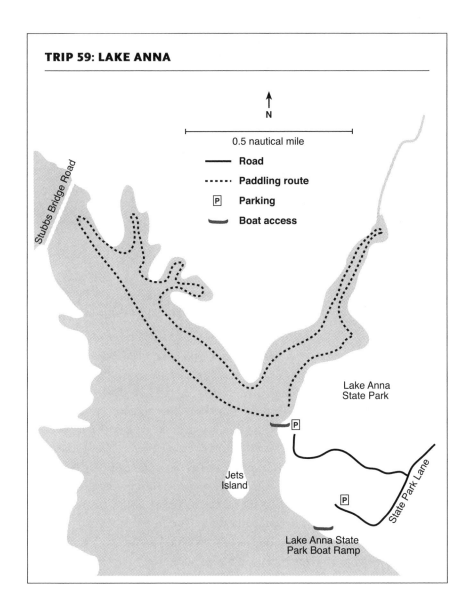

N

0.5 nautical mile

—— Road

····· Paddling route

P Parking

⌣ Boat access

Lake Anna
State Park

Stubbs Bridge Road

Jets
Island

State Park Lane

Lake Anna State
Park Boat Ramp

WHAT YOU'LL SEE

Lake Anna is the third-largest lake in Virginia and is located just 72 miles south of Washington, D.C. It has more than 225 miles of shoreline and 13,000 total acres, providing paddlers with endless waters to explore. The lake is just a half-hour drive from I-95, but along the way the landscape becomes very rural and you will feel like you are a world away.

As one of Virginia's most popular lakes, Lake Anna is a prime spot for sailing, water-skiing, and sport fishing. Public access to the lake is through Lake

Lake Anna is one of Virginia's most popular lakes, a perfect destination for the whole family.

Anna State Park and several marinas surrounding the lake. The southern portion of the lake is privately owned and does not allow public access. You must own or rent property to launch from the private areas. The state park is especially popular and fills to capacity on warm days in summer. The park has 10 miles of shoreline, a beach, a fishing pond, and a boat launch. Fishing is popular here and the park hosts various fishing tournaments throughout the year.

The land in Lake Anna State Park was a gold mine in the 1800s. In 1968, Virginia Electric and Power Company (now Dominion Energy) purchased 18,000 acres of farmland along the North Anna and Pamunkey rivers to build the dam to serve as a water coolant for Virginia Power's nuclear plant. Lake Anna State Park opened in 1983.

To launch your kayak from Picnic Area B, you will have to portage across the picnic area about 100 yards. Toward the right side, there is an opening in the rocks that provides an easy launch spot. At the time of this writing, the park has begun to clear an area to the right of this launch spot, where they will build an accessible kayak ramp. The picnic area is delightfully shady and has panoramic views of the lake. Starting your excursion here is ideal because it has a sheltered cove that leads directly into Ware Creek. This is one of the best places on the lake to see a variety of waterfowl.

Explore the coves and look for bald eagles, hawks, tundra swans, warblers, an assortment of ducks, and other birds. When you reach the duck blind, turn right and continue paddling into the narrow stretch of the creek until the waters get too shallow. Head back to the lake and then follow the shoreline north to explore more coves on the right side of the lake. Turning around at Stubbs Bridge gives you a trip of approximately 4 miles. Paddle as far as time and energy allow. It is easy to find the launch spot, as the picnic tables are visible from a distance.

After your paddling trip, enjoy a picnic or more than 15 miles of horseback riding, bicycling, and hiking trails. Try your own luck panning for gold, available year-round at Contrary Creek Prospectors.

Marinas you can launch from include:

- Anna Point Marina: 13721 Anna Point Lane, Mineral, VA 540-895-5900
- Duke's Creek Marina: 3831 Breaknock Road, Bumpass, VA 540-895-5065
- High Point Marina: 4634 Courthouse Road, Mineral, VA 540-895-5249
- Lake Anna Marina: 4303 Boggs Drive, Bumpass, VA 540-895-5051
- Rocky Branch Marina: 5153 Courthouse Road, Spotsylvania, VA 540-895-5475

The Lake Anna area is located just 30 minutes northeast of Fredericksburg where you can also paddle from the city dock along the Rappahannock River (see Trip 51: Rappahannock River).

60 | Lake Moomaw

Enjoy a quiet getaway with breathtaking scenery and endless paddling, fishing, hiking, and biking opportunities.

Location: Hot Springs, VA
Maps: U.S. Army Corps of Engineers: www.nap.usace.army.mil
Area: 2,530 acres
Time: 2 to 3 hours or more
Average Depth: 80 feet
Development: Rural
Access: Park entrance fee

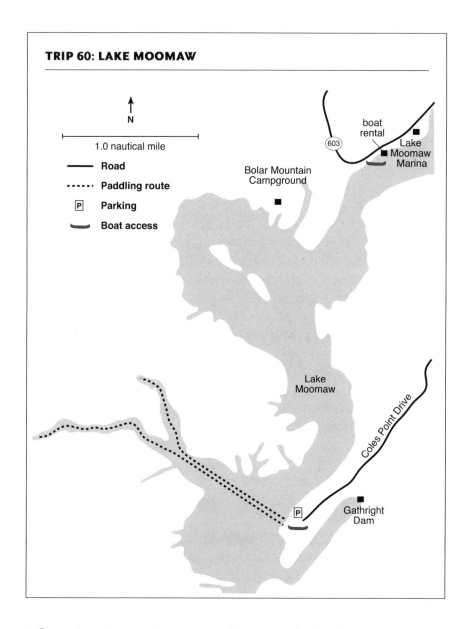

TRIP 60: LAKE MOOMAW

N

1.0 nautical mile

—— Road

····· Paddling route

P Parking

⌣ Boat access

boat rental

603 Lake Moomaw Marina

Bolar Mountain Campground

Lake Moomaw

Coles Point Drive

P Gathright Dam

Information: Virginia Department of Game & Inland Fisheries: dgif.virginia.gov; USDA Forest Service, Alleghany Highlands Chamber of Commerce: 110 Mall Street, Covington, VA 24426, 540-962-2178, ahchamber.com, visitalleghanyhighlands.com; Bolar Mountain Recreation Area, 756 Twin Ridge Drive, Warm Springs, VA 24484, 540-279-4144

Camping: Morris Hill Campsites, Bolar Mountain Campground, McClintic Point Campsites, Greenwood Point Campground, and Blowing Springs Campground (see Appendix A)

Outfitters: Bolar Mountain Recreation Area: 756 Twin Ridge Drive Warm Springs, VA 24484, 540-279-4144; Lake Moomaw Marina: 7368 A Bolars Draft Road, Warm Springs, VA 24484, 540-279-4144. *Note:* the only lakeside boat rentals are located on the west side of the lake.

Take Note: Unlimited horsepower. There is limited cell phone service. Be sure to map out your route ahead of time as you may not be able to use a GPS to find your way. While there are several boat ramps, the most convenient public kayak launch is from Coles Point Boat Launch. The lake is undeveloped and has no food concessions. There are no boat motor restrictions.

GETTING THERE

To Coles Point Boat Ramp: From I-64 at Exit 16A or 16B in Covington, follow signs to US 220 North and travel about 5.5 miles. Turn left on SR 687 (Jackson River Road) and drive for about 3.2 miles (cumulative: 8.7 miles). Turn left on SR 641 (Indian Draft Road), then after 0.6 mile (9.3 miles) bear right to continue onto SR 666 (East Morris Hill Road). Travel about 3.7 miles (13 miles) to a three-way intersection. Turn right on SR 605 (Coles Mountain Road) and travel 3.6 miles (16.6 miles) past the Morris Hill Campground entrance and across the Gathright Dam. Continue onto Coles Mountain Fire Trail and drive for 0.7 mile (17.3 miles). The beach and bathhouse will be on the left, and the boat ramp and parking lot are on the right. (37° 56.916′ N, 79° 58.120′ W)

    To Lake Moomaw Marina (near Bolar Mountain Recreation Area): From I-64 at Exit 16A or 16B in Covington, take US 220 North for 25.2 miles and turn left on SR 39. Drive for 11.1 miles (cumulative: 36.3 miles) then turn left onto SR 600 (Bolars Draft Road). Drive for 7.5 miles (43.8 miles). Continue onto SR 603 and drive for 1.1 miles (44.9 miles). The marina is on the right. (37° 59.657′ N, 79° 56.911′ W)

WHAT YOU'LL SEE

Lake Moomaw is a stunning 2,530-acre mountain lake located in Virginia's Allegheny Highlands with 43 miles of shoreline surrounded by the George Washington and Jefferson National Forests. This unspoiled locale offers a paradise for outdoor recreation experiences including boating, fishing, hiking, mountain biking, horseback riding, hunting, picnicking, and swimming.

The lake was formed by the Gathright Dam, which was constructed by the U.S. Army Corps of Engineers in 1979 to control flooding for the 345-square-mile drainage area of the Jackson River. Recreation facilities are now maintained by the U.S. Forest Service. The lake is surrounded by the Gathright Wildlife Management Area and several campgrounds. The setting is ideal for a peaceful paddling excursion. There is some boat traffic but it is generally very quiet here.

Lake Moomaw has three public boat ramps: Coles Point, Lake Moomaw Marina (Bolar Mountain), and Fortney Branch. Coles Point is most recommended for kayaking. It is located at the southeast end of the lake, has good access from I-64, and boasts a public beach and bathhouse. Bolar Mountain is located at the northern end of the lake and is an additional 45-minute drive from the dam. The launch at Lake Moomaw Marina is a good place to paddle from if you spend the night at the Bolar Mountain Campground. At the marina you can rent boats, pontoons, kayaks, and canoes, as well as park boats and trailers for the duration of your stay. There are also 11 miles of hiking trails from there that lead to two breathtaking scenic overlooks. Fortney Branch is located at the very southern tip of the lake and is not recommended as a kayak launch because it is the most popularly used ramp for power boats, which create choppy conditions.

Launching from Coles Point, you can paddle in any direction. The waters are deep and wide here, so you may want to paddle straight across the lake to reach a shoreline to follow toward a series of narrow coves. As you look back to your left, you will see a gorgeous red rock cliff which is where the stone was

Lake Moomaw features clear waters in a mountain setting in western Virginia.

quarried to create the dam. This cliff wall serves as a good marker to recognize the location of the boat ramp when you return. When facing the cliff, Coles Point is located just to your right (south). As you paddle along the west side of the lake, you will find some small inlets and marshes to explore. Look for great blue heron, ducks, and other waterfowl along the shoreline and in the smaller coves. You will also see sections of submerged dead trees that create a healthy fish habitat.

Lake Moomaw has clean fresh water and is a great fishery. The water is deep enough for both warm- and coldwater species. It has been stocked with large- and smallmouth bass, and many different varieties of trout.

The George Washington and Jefferson National Forests protect hardwood forests, dozens of species of mammals, and approximately 200 species of birds. Common wildlife here includes white-tailed deer, wild turkeys, red foxes, barred owls, pileated woodpeckers, great blue and green-backed herons, and several species of turtles. An occasional black bear may also be seen here.

The water in the lake is surprisingly warm in summer. The steep mountainous terrain prevents swimming on parts of the lake. There are two sandy beaches that are designated for swimming in addition to the island beaches in the center of the lake. One is located on the southern end of the lake at Coles Point, and the other is on the north end, near Bolar Mountain Campground.

The Alleghany Highlands has more than 100 miles of hiking and biking trails. The Jackson River Scenic Trail, a 14-mile multiuse gravel trail, was built on an old railroad bed parallel to the river, providing hiking and biking opportunities.

The Jackson River is also a popular kayaking and canoeing destination with class I and II rapids. Five canoe/kayak access points have been established below Gathright Dam. The first access point is just below the dam spillway, off VA 605; the second, Johnson Springs, is off VA 687; and the third, Smith Bridge, is off VA 721. The fourth, Indian Draft, is off VA 687, and the last, Petticoat Junction, is off VA 687. Note, that at the time of writing, there was no outfitter in the immediate area providing shuttle services. The Homestead and the Greenbrier resorts are located in the area and offer paddling trips on the Jackson River that include drop-off and pickup services. Alternatively, the access points are located along the Jackson River Scenic Trail, so you can leave a bicycle along the route to shuttle yourself between locations.

In addition to Lake Moomaw and the Jackson River, the Alleghany Highlands is also home to the Cowpasture River and Douthat Lake. With two lakes and two rivers, the region offers breathtaking scenery and endless boating and fishing opportunities.

Appendix A: Campgrounds

Campground	Address
NEW JERSEY	
Allaire State Park	4265 Atlantic Avenue Farmingdale, NJ 07727
AMC's Mohican Outdoor Center	50 Camp Mohican Road Blairstown, NJ 07825
Belleplain State Forest	County Route 550 Woodbine, NJ 08270
Bodine Field Campground	31 Atsion Batsto Road Hammonton, NJ 08037
Lake Lenape Park West	6303 Old Harding Highway Mays Landing, NJ 08330
Lazy River Campground	103 Cumberland Avenue #96 Estell Manor, NJ 08319
Mahlon Dickerson Reservation	955 Weldon Road Jefferson Township, NJ 07849
Parvin State Park	701 Almond Road Pittsgrove, NJ 08318
Pleasant Valley Family Campground	60 South River Road Estell Manor, NJ 08319
Spruce Run State Park	68 Van Syckels Road Clinton, NJ 08809
Turtle Run Campground	3 Cedar Lane Egg Harbor City, NJ 08215
Wawayanda State Park	885 Warwick Turnpike Hewitt, NJ 07421

Phone	Website
732-938-2371	njportal.com/DEP/NJOutdoors
908-362-5670	outdoors.org
609-861-2404	state.nj.us
609-561-0024	njparksandforest.org
609-625-8219	atlantic-county.org
609-476-2540	yellowpages.com
973-697-3140	morrisparks.net
856-358-8616	reserveamerica.com
609-625-1238	pleasantvalleycamping.com
908-638-8572	reserveamerica.com
609-965-5343	turtleruncampground.com
973-853-4462	reserveamerica.com

Campground	Address
PENNSYLVANIA	
Appalachian RV Resort	60 Motel Drive Shartlesville, PA 19554
Brandywine Creek Campground	1091 Creek Road Downingtown, PA 19335
Colonial Woods Family Camping Resort	545 Lonely Cottage Drive Upper Black Eddy, PA 18972
Don Laine Family Campground	790 57 Drive Palmerton, PA 18071
Eagle's Peak RV Park & Campground	397 Eagles Peak Road Robesonia, PA 19551
Gifford Pinchot State Park	2200 Rosstown Road Lewisberry, PA 17339
Mauch Chunk State Park	625 Lentz Trail Jim Thorpe, PA 18229
Nockamixon State Park	1542 Mountain View Drive Quakertown, PA 18951
Tohickon Family Campground	8308 Covered Bridge Road Quakertown, PA 18951
Tucquan Park Family Campground	917 River Road Holtwood, PA 17532
DELAWARE	
Big Oaks Campground	35567 Big Oaks Lane Rehoboth Beach, DE 19971
Brandywine Creek State Park	41 Adams Dam Road Wilmington, DE 19803
Cape Henlopen State Park	15099 Cape Henlopen Drive Lewes, DE 19958
Delaware Beaches Jellystone Park Camp	8295 Brick Granary Road Lincoln, DE 19960
Homestead Campground	Road 254 Georgetown, DE 19947
Killens Pond State Park	5025 Killens Pond Road Felton, DE 19943
Lums Pond State Park	3355 Red Lion Road Bear, DE 19701
Tall Pines Campground Resort	29551 Persimmon Road Lewes, DE 19958
Trap Pond State Park	33587 Baldcypress Lane Laurel, DE 19956

Phone	Website
610-488-6319	appalachianrvresort.com
610-942-9950	pacamping.com
610-847-5808	colonialwoods.com
610-381-3381	donlaine.com
610-589-4800	abcamping.com
717-292-4112	pennsylvaniastateparks.reserveamerica.com
570-325-3669	carboncounty.com
215-529-7300	pennsylvaniastateparks.reserveamerica.com
866-536-2267	tohickoncampground.com
717-284-2156	camptucquanpark.com
302-645-6838	bigoakscamping.com
302-577-3534	delawarestateparks.reserveamerica.com
302-645-8983	destateparks.com
302-491-6614	delawarejellystone.com
302-684-4278	homesteadde.com
302-284-4526	destateparks.com
302-368-6989	destateparks.com
302-684-0300	tallpines-del.com
302-875-5153	destateparks.com

Campground	Address

MARYLAND

Campground	Address
Annapolis Campground	46 Bennion Road Annapolis, MD 21402
Aqualand Marina and Campground	9610 Orland Park Road Newburg, MD 20664
Assateague Island National Seashore	7206 National Seashore Lane Berlin, MD 21811
Assateague State Park	6915 Stephen Decatur Highway Berlin, MD 21811
Bayshore Campgrounds	4228 Eastern Neck Road Rock Hall, MD 21661
Big Run State Park	10368 Savage River Road Swanton, MD 21561
Deep Creek Lake State Park	898 State Park Road Swanton, MD 21561
Goose Bay Marina and Campground	9365 Goose Bay Lane Welcome, MD 20693
Greenbelt Park	6565 Greenbelt Road Greenbelt, MD 20770
Horsepen Branch Campsite	Chesapeake and Ohio Canal Towpath Poolesville, MD 20837
Janes Island State Park	26280 Alfred Lawson Drive Crisfield, MD 21817
Joint Base Andrews Family Campground	4520 Wheeling Road Clinton, MD 20735
Little Bennett Regional Park Campground	23705 Frederick Road Clarksburg, MD 20871
Pocomoke River State Park: Milburn Landing	3036 Nassawango Road Pocomoke City, MD 21851
Pocomoke River State Park: Shad Landing	3461 Worcester Highway Snow Hill, MD 21863
Ramblin' Pines Campground	801 Hoods Mill Road Woodbine, MD 21797
Smallwood State Park	2750 Sweden Point Road Marbury, MD 20658
Taylors Island Family Campground	4362 Bay Shore Road Taylors Island, MD 21669
Tuckahoe State Park	13070 Crouse Mill Road Queen Anne, MD 21657

Phone	Website
877-628-9233	navymwrannapolis.com
301-259-2222	aqualandonthepotomac.com
410-641-1441	nps.gov
410-641-2918	parkreservations.maryland.gov
410-639-7485	bayshorecamping.com
301-895-5453	parkreservations.maryland.gov
301-387-5563	parkreservations.maryland.gov
301-932-0885	goosebaymarina.com
301-344-3944	recreation.gov
301-739-4200	canaltrust.org
410-968-1565	parkreservations.maryland.gov
301-981-3279	andrewsfss.com
301-528-3430	montgomeryparks.org
410-632-2566	dnr.maryland.gov
410-632-2566	dnr.maryland.gov
410-795-5161	ramblinpinescampground.com
301-743-7613	parkreservations.maryland.gov
410-397-3275	visitdorchester.org/taylors-island-family-campground/
410-820-1668	dnr.maryland.gov

Campground	Address
VIRGINIA	
Algonkian Regional Park	47001 Fairway Drive Sterling, VA 20165
Blowing Springs Campground	7698 Mountain Valley Road Warm Springs, VA 24484
Bolar Mountain Campground	756 Twin Ridge Drive Warm Springs, VA 24484
Chichahominy Riverfront Park	1350 John Tyler Highway Williamsburg, VA 23185
Chincoteague Island KOA	6742 Maddox Boulevard Chincoteague Island, VA 23336
Davis Lakes Campgrounds	200 Byrd Street Suffolk, VA 23434
Ed Allen's Campground	13501 Campground Road Lanexa, VA 23089
False Cape State Park	4001 Sandpiper Road Virginia Beach, VA 23456
First Landing State Park	2500 Shore Drive Virginia Beach, VA 23451
Fredericksburg VA/ Washington DC South KOA	7400 Brookside Lane Fredericksburg, VA 22408
Greenwood Point Campground	Hot Springs VA 24445
Indian Cove Resort	1053 Sandbridge Road Virginia Beach, VA 23456
Lake Anna State Park	6800 Lawyers Road Spotsylvania, VA 22551
Leesylvania State Park	2001 Daniel K. Ludwig Drive Woodbridge, VA 22191
McClintic Point Campsites	8446 Bolars Drive Road Hot Springs, VA 84445
Morris Hill Campsites	Coles Mountain Road Hot Springs, VA 24445
North Bay Shore Campground	3257 Colechester Road Virginia Beach, VA 23456
Occoneechee State Park	1192 Occoneechee Park Road Clarksville, VA 23927
Pine Grove Campground	5283 Deep Hole Road Chincoteague Island, VA 23336
Pohick Bay Regional Park	6501 Pohick Bay Drive Lorton, VA 22079

Phone	Website
703-450-4655	novaparks.com
540-839-2521	fs.usda.gov
540-279-4144	recreation.gov
757-258-5020	jamescitycountyva.gov
757-336-3111	koa.com
757-539-1191	davislakescampground.net
804-966-2582	edallens.com
757-426-7128	reserveamerica.com
757-412-2300	reserveamerica.com
540-898-7252	koa.com
800-342-2267	fs.usda.gov
757-426-2601	indian-cove.com
540-854-5503	reserveamerica.com
703-730-8205	reserveamerica.com
540-279-4144	recreation.gov
540-279-4144	recreation.gov
757-426-7911	northbayshorecampground.com
434-374-2210	reserveamerica.com
757-336-5200	pinegrovecampground.com
703-339-6104	reserveamerica.com

Campground	Address
Prince William Forest	18100 Park Headquarters Road Triangle, VA 22172
Riverside Camp	18496 North Fork River Road Abingdon, VA 24210
Rockahock Campgrounds	1428 Outpost Road Lanexa, VA 23089
Shenandoah Valley Campground	168 Industrial Park Road Mount Jackson, VA 22842
Toms Cove Park	8128 Beebe Road Chincoteague Island, VA 23336

Phone	Website
703-221-7181	nps.gov
276-623-0340	riversidecampground.org
804-966-8362	rockahock.com
540-477-3080	shenandoahfamilycampground.com
757-336-6498	tomscovepark.com

Appendix B:
Further Reading

PADDLING EQUIPMENT AND TECHNIQUE

Web sources: canoekayak.com; paddling.com; outdoorplay.com

Burch, David, and Burch, Tobias. *Fundamentals of Kayak Navigation: Master the Traditional Skills and the Latest Technologies*, 4th ed. Guilford, CT: The Globe Pequot Press, 2016.

Dunn, Leslie. *Quiet Water Kayaking: A Beginner's Guide to Kayaking.* Amazon Digital Services, LLC., 2016.

Foster, Nigel. *The Art of Kayaking: Everything You Need to Know About Paddling.* Guilford, CT: Falcon Guides, 2017.

Parsons, Scott. *How to Paddle a Kayak: The 90 Minute Guide to Master Kayaking and Learn to Paddle Like a Pro.* Amazon Digital Services, LLC., 2012.

FLORA, FAUNA, AND THE ENVIRONMENT

Alden, Peter, and Cassie, Brian. *National Audubon Society Field Guide to the Mid-Atlantic States: New York, Pennsylvania, New Jersey, Maryland, Delaware, West Virginia, Virginia.* New York: Chanticleer Press Inc., 1999.

Roman, Charles T., and Burdick, David M. *Tidal Marsh Restoration: A Synthesis of Science and Management.* 2nd ed. Washington, D.C.: Island Press, 2012.

Thompson, Bill. *Mid-Atlantic Birds: Backyard Guide.* Gloucester, MA: Cool Springs Press, 2013.

White, Christopher P. *Chesapeake Bay Nature of the Estuary: A Field Guide.* Atglen, PA: Schiffer Publishing, 2009.

CAMPING AND CAMPGROUNDS

Web sources: gocampingamerica.com; www.reserveamerica.com; gorving.com

Jacobson, Cliff. *Canoeing & Camping Beyond the Basics: 30th Anniversary Edition.* Guilford, CT: Falcon Guides, 2007.

Louderback, Jeff. *The Unofficial Guide to the Best RV and Tent Campgrounds in the Mid-Atlantic States.* New York: Hungry Minds, 2002.

HIKING

Adach, Jennifer, and Martin, Michael. *AMC's Best Day Hikes in the Shenandoah Valley: Four-Season Guide to 50 of the Best Trails from Harpers Ferry to Jefferson National Forest.* Boston: Appalachian Mountain Club Books, 2015.

Charkes, Susan. *AMC's Best Day Hikes Near Philadelphia: Four-Season Guide to 50 of the Best Trails in Eastern Pennsylvania, New Jersey, and Delaware.* Boston: Appalachian Mountain Club Books. 2010.

Martin, Michael. *AMC's Best Backpacking in the Mid-Atlantic: A Guide to 30 of the Best Multiday Trips from New York to Virginia.* Boston: Appalachian Mountain Club Books, 2014.

Rails to Trails Conservancy. *Rail-Trails Mid-Atlantic: The definitive guide to multiuse trails in Delaware, Maryland, Virginia, Washington, D.C., and West Virginia,* 2nd ed. Birmingham, AL: Wilderness Press, 2015.

Sklarew, Renee, and Cooper, Rachel. *60 Hikes Within 60 Miles: Washington, D.C.* 3rd ed. Birmingham, AL: Menasha Ridge Press, 2017.

Willen, Matt. *Best Hikes of the Appalachian Trail: Mid-Atlantic.* Birmingham, AL: Menasha Ridge Press, 2016.

Appendix C:
Other Resources

PADDLING CLUBS AND ORGANIZATIONS
AMC Delaware Valley Chapter: amcdv.org
AMC New York–North Jersey Chapter: amc-ny.org
AMC Potomac Chapter: outdoors.org/chapters/potomac
Baltimore Canoe and Kayak Club: baltimorecanoeclub.org
The Blue Ridge Voyageurs (Reston, VA): blueridgevoyageurs.org
Canoe Club of Greater Harrisburg: ccghpa.com
Canoe Cruisers Association (Washington, D.C.): ccadc.org
Chesapeake Bay Kayak Anglers: chesapeakebaykayakanglers.com
Chesapeake Paddlers Association (Greenbelt, MD): cpakayaker.com
Coastal Canoeists (Fredericksburg, VA): coastals.org
Conewago Canoe Club (York, PA): conewagocanoeclub.org
Jersey Shore Sea Kayak Club: jsska.org
Monocacy Canoe Club (Frederick, MD): monocacycanoe.org
Pennsylvania Kayak Fishing Association: pkfa.org
Philadelphia Canoe Club: philacanoe.org
Potomac River Paddlers: groups.yahoo.com/group/Potomac_River_Paddlers
Richmond Canoe Club: richmondcanoeclub.com
Tidewater Kayak Angler Association (Eastern VA): tkaa.org
Washington Canoe Club: washingtoncanoeclub.org
Washington Kayak Club: washingtonkayakclub.org
Wilmington Trail Club: wilmingtontrailclub.org

OTHER ORGANIZATIONS
AMC Mid-Atlantic Conservation Office: 100 Illick's Mill Road, Bethlehem, PA 18017;
    610-868-6915; outdoors.org
American Canoe Association: 503 Sophia Street, Suite 100, Fredericksburg, VA
    22401; 540-907-4460; americancanoe.org

Chesapeake Bay Foundation Philip Merrill Environmental Center: 6 Herndon
Avenue, Annapolis, MD 21403; 410-268-8816; cbf.org
National Audubon Society: 225 Varick Street, Seventh Floor, New York, NY 10014;
212-979-3196; audubon.org
The Nature Conservancy: 4245 North Fairfax Drive, Suite 100, Arlington, VA 22203;
703-841-5300; nature.org
Potomac Conservancy: 8403 Colesville Road, Suite 805, Silver Spring, MD 20910;
301-608-1188; potomac.org
Sierra Club: 2101 Webster Street, Suite 1300, Oakland, CA 94612; 415-977-5500;
sierraclub.org

OUTFITTERS
New Jersey
AMC Mohican Outdoor Center: 50 Camp Road, Blairstown, NJ 07825; 908-362-
5670; outdoors.org
Cowboy Mike's Canoe Rental: 510 Park Boulevard, Cherry Hill, NJ 08002;
609-332-5065; cowboymikescanoerental.com
Clark's Canoe Rental: 201 Hanover Street, Pemberton, NJ 08068; 609-894-4448;
clarkscanoe.com
Wawayanda State Park: 885 Warwick Turnpike, Hewitt, NJ 07421; 973-853-4468;
state.nj.us
Yellow Dog Paddle, Van Syckles Road, Clinton, NJ 08809; 908-310-3742;
yellowdogpaddle.com

Pennsylvania
Beltzville State Park: 2950 Pohopoco Drive, Lehighton, PA 18235; 610-377-0045;
dcnr.pa.gov
Blue Marsh Rentals: 5097 Bernville Road, Bernville, PA 19506 610-488-5540;
bluemarshoutdoors.com
Core Creek Park: 901 Bridgetown Pike, Langhorne, PA 19047; 215-757-0571;
buckscounty.org
Gifford Pinchot State Park: 2200 Rosstown Road, Lewisberry, PA 17339;
717-432-5011; friendsofpinchot.org
Marsh Creek State Park: 675 Park Road, Downingtown, PA 19335; 610-458-5040;
marshcreeklake.com
Nockamixon State Park: 1542 Mountain View Drive, Quakertown, PA 18951;
215-538-1340; nockamixonboatrental.com

Delaware
Killens Pond State Park: 5025 Killens Pond Road, Felton, DE 19943; 302-284-4526;
destateparks.com

Lums Pond State Park: 3355 Red Lion Road, Bear, DE 19701; 302-368-6989; destateparks.com

Trap Pond State Park: 33587 Baldcypress Lane, Laurel, DE 19956; 302-875-5153; destateparks.com

Wilderness Canoe Trips: 2111 Concord Pike, Wilmington, DE 19803; 302-654-2227; wildernesscanoetrips.com

Maryland

Annapolis Canoe and Kayak: 222 Severn Ave. Bldg. #2, Annapolis, MD 21403; 410-263-2303; annapoliscanoeandkayak.com

Assateague Outfitters: 13002 Bayside Drive, Berlin, MD 21811; 410-656-9453; mdcoastalbays.org

Ayers Creek Adventure:, 8628 Grey Fox Lane, Berlin, MD 2181; 443-513-0889; ayerscreekadventures.com

Atlantic Kayak: 108-A Mattingly Avenue, Indian Head, MD, 301-292-6455; atlantickayak.com

Black Hill Regional Park: 20930 Lake Ridge Drive, Boyds, MD 20841; 301-528-3490; montgomeryparks.org

Blackwater Paddle and Pedal Adventures: 2524 Key Wallace Drive, Cambridge, MD 21613; 410-901-9255 blackwaterpaddleandpedal.com

Bladensburg Waterfront Park: 4601 Annapolis Road, Bladensburg, MD 20710; 301-779-0371; outdoors.pgparks.com

Calleva Outdoors: 13015 Riley's Lock Road, Poolesville, MD 20837; 301-216-1248; calleva.org

East Neck Boat Rental: 2981 Eastern Neck Road, Rock Hall, MD 21661; 410-639-7100; eastneckboatrental.com

Janes Island State Park: 26280 Alfred J Lawson Drive, Crisfield, MD 21817; 410-968-1565; dnr.maryland.gov

Kayak Annapolis:Truxton Park, Annapolis, MD 21403; 443-949-0773; kayakannapolistours.com

Piney Run Park: 30 Martz Road, Sykesville, MD 21784; 410-795-3274; pineyrunpark.org

Pocomoke River Canoe Co.: 2 River Street, Snow Hill, MD 21863; 410-632-3971; pocomokerivercanoe.com

Pocomoke River State Park Shad Landing: 3461 Worcester Highway, Snow Hill, MD 21863; 410-632-2566; dnr.maryland.gov

Tuckahoe State Park: 13070 Crouse Mill Road, Queen Anne, MD 21657; 410-820-1668; dnr.maryland.gov

Ultimate Watersports Dundee Creek: 7400 Graces Quarter Road, Middle River, MD 21220; 410-335-5352; ultimatewatersports.com

Wisp Resort Deep Creek Lake State Park: 296 Marsh Hill Road, McHenry, MD 21541; 301-859-3159; wispresort.com

Washington, D.C.

Anacostia Watershed Society (guided tours only): The George Washington House, 4302 Baltimore Avenue, Bladensburg, MD 20710; 301-699-6204; anacostiaws.org

Fletcher's Boathouse: 4940 Canal Road Northwest, Washington, D.C. 20007; 201-244-0461; boatingindc.com

Key Bridge Boathouse: 3500 Water Street Northwest, Washington, D.C.; 202-337-9642; boatingindc.com

Thompson Boat Center; 2900 Virginia Avenue Northwest, Washington, D.C. 20037; 202-333-9543; boatingindc.com

Virginia

Adventure Kayak Tours: Virginia Beach, VA; 757-237-8776; adventurekayaktours.net

Algonkian Regional Park (guided tours only): 47001 Fairway Drive, Sterling, VA 20165; 703-450-4655; novaparks.com

Assateague Tours: 712 East Side Road, Chincoteague Island, VA 23336 ; 757-336-6176; assateaguetours.com

Bell Haven Marina: George Washington Memorial Parkway, Alexandria, VA 22307; 703-768-0018; saildc.com

Bolar Mountain Recreation Area: 756 Twin Ridge Drive, Warm Springs, VA 24484; 540-279-4144; recreation.gov

Clarksville Marine Rentals: 1192 Occoneechee Park Road, Clarksville, VA 23927; 434-374-2755; clarksvilleboats.com

First Landing State Park, Narrows, 64th Street, Virginia Beach, VA 23454; 757-465-2216; first-landing-state-park.org

Front Royal Outdoors: 8567 Stonewall Jackson Highway, Front Royal, VA 22630; 540-635-5440; frontroyalcanoe.com

Kayak Nature Tours: 89th Street, Virginia Beach, VA 23451; 757-480-1999; kayaknaturetours.net

Lake Anna Outfitters: 4634 Courthouse Road, Mineral, VA 23117; 540-894-3540; lakeannalife.com

Lake Moomaw Marina: 7368 a Bolars Draft Road, Warm Springs, VA 24484; 540-279-4144; moomaw.lakesonline.com

Lake Ridge Marina: 12350 Cotton Mill Drive, Woodbridge, VA 22192; 703-494-5565, pwcgov.org

Leesylvania State Park: 2001 Daniel K Ludwig Drive, Woodbridge, VA 22191; 703-730-8205; dcr.virginia.gov

Pohick Bay Regional Park: 6501 Pohick Bay Drive, Lorton, VA 22079; 703-339-6104; novaparks.com

River Rock Outfitter: 915 Sophia Street, Fredericksburg, VA 22401; 540-372-8708; riverrockoutfitter.com

Route 11 Outfitters: Woodstock, VA; 540-459-8823; route11outfitters.com

Skyline Canoe Company: 541 South Royal Avenue, Front Royal, VA 22630; 540-305-7695; skylinecanoe.com

Surf & Adventure Co.: 577 Sandbridge Road, Virginia Beach, VA 23456; 757-721-6210; surfandadventure.com

Virginia Outdoor Center: 3219 Fall Hill Avenue, Fredericksburg, VA 22401; 540-371-5085; playva.com

Appendix D:
Launch Permits by State

Requirements for boat registrations and launching vary from state to state. Note that fees are subject to change; check online for current information.

NEW JERSEY

In New Jersey, non-powered kayaks and canoes are exempt from licensing and registration. However, any vehicle used to transport or launch a vessel at the boat ramps at the New Jersey Wildlife Management Areas must have either a Boat Ramp Maintenance Permit or a photocopy of a valid hunting, fishing, or trapping license showing the Conservation ID Number. Permits may be purchased for $15 from any license agent or the New Jersey Division of Fish & Wildlife. Visit njfishandwildlife.com for details, call 908-637-4125, or email njfishandwildlife@dep.nj.gov.

PENNSYLVANIA

For most lakes and reservoirs in Pennsylvania, canoes, kayaks, and non-powered boats must display one of the following: boat registration from any state, a launching or mooring permit from Pennsylvania State Parks, or a launching permit from the Pennsylvania Fish and Boat Commission.

State parks are governed by the Department of Conservation and Natural Resources. Their launch permits are $10 per year for residents and $15 for nonresidents, with discounts available for two-year permits. Permits can be obtained from any state park office or online at theoutdoorshop.state.pa.us.

Many other reservoirs and lakes are governed by the Pennsylvania Fish and Boat Commission. You can purchase a launching permit online at fishandboat.com. Some county parks have their own permits, which you can obtain from the park office at the location.

DELAWARE

Non-powered kayaks and canoes are exempt from licensing and registration in the state of Delaware. A daily or seasonal fee is required at some areas administered by the Division of Parks and Recreation. For more information, visit the website for the State of Delaware Division of Fish & Wildlife at dnrec.delaware.gov.

WASHINGTON, D.C.

According to D.C. law, any vessel operated primarily on waters in the District of Columbia must be registered annually with the D.C. Boat Registration Office. This includes kayaks and canoes. New vessels to D.C. or change of ownership of D.C. boat users should contact Harbor Patrol at 202-727-4582. To obtain a title, you must show proof of ownership and pay an initial $2 title fee and titling tax. The Certificate of Number issued stays with the boat as long as it is registered in the District of Columbia. The certificate itself is pocket-sized and must be on the boat and available for inspection by law enforcement personnel whenever the boat is in operation. In addition, validation stickers are issued each year that must be placed within 6 inches of the number. For registration details, visit mpdc.dc.gov. Kayak launches operated by Boating in D.C. charge a $5 fee.

MARYLAND

Non-powered kayaks and canoes are exempt from licensing and registration in Maryland. However, the majority of public water access sites in Maryland are managed and maintained by the local jurisdictions in which they are located. Fees, permits, and regulations vary by jurisdiction, so it is highly recommended that you contact the managing entity to clarify requirements before you go. The Maryland Department of Natural Resources provides contact information for the waterways in each county at dnr.maryland.gov.

In Maryland, kayaks and canoes may launch from boat ramps, but you are encouraged to use a separate soft launch area if one is provided at the same site.

VIRGINIA

Non-powered kayaks and canoes are exempt from licensing and registration in Virginia. An Access Permit is required when using any wildlife management area or fishing lake owned by Virginia's Department of Game and Inland Fisheries. A permit is not required for any person holding a valid hunting, freshwater fishing, or trapping license or a current certificate of boat registration issued by the department or for any persons 16 years of age or younger. The Access Permit requirement does not apply to department-owned boat ramps or segments of the Appalachian Trail on department-owned land. The permit fee is $4 for a daily permit or $23 for an annual permit and may be purchased online or at any license agent. For more information, visit dgif.virginia.gov.

List of Waterways

About the Author

Rachel Cooper is a freelance writer with extensive knowledge of Washington, D.C., and the Mid-Atlantic region. Her other books include *60 Hikes Within 60 Miles: Washington, D.C.* and *Images of Rail: Union Station in Washington, D.C.* Rachel has written travel-related articles for local and regional publications, including About.com (now TripSavvy.com), *Washingtonian*, the Montgomery County parks department, *Conde Nast Traveler*, and other regional media. Rachel especially enjoys kayaking, stand-up paddleboarding, hiking, biking, and skiing. To learn more about her writing, visit rachelqcooper.com.

AMC's Delaware Valley Chapter

AMC's Delaware Valley Chapter offers a wide variety of hiking, backpacking, climbing, paddling, bicycling, snowshoeing, and skiing trips each year, as well as social, family, and young member programs and instructional workshops. The chapter also maintains a 15-mile section of the Appalachian Trail between Wind Gap and Little Gap, as well as trails at Valley Forge National Historical Park. The Water Gap is also home to AMC's Mohican Outdoor Center, a frequent base for AMC's outdoor leadership workshops. A 90-minute drive from New York City, Mohican offers front-porch access to the Water Gap, with self-service cabins, comfortable bunkrooms, and the river, wetlands, and Appalachian Trail a stroll away.

To view a list of AMC activities in Pennsylvania, central and south New Jersey, northern Delaware, and other parts of the Northeast and Mid-Atlantic, visit activities.outdoors.org/search/.

AMC Book Updates

At AMC Books, we keep our guidebooks as up-to-date as possible to help you plan safe and enjoyable adventures. After publishing a book, if we learn that trails have been relocated, or that route or contact information has changed, we will post an update online. Before you hit the trail, check outdoors.org /bookupdates.

While hiking or paddling, if you notice discrepancies with a trip description or map, or if you find any other errors in the book, please submit them by email to amcbookupdates@outdoors.org or by letter to Books Editor, c/o AMC, 10 City Square, Boston, MA 02129. We will verify all submissions and post key updates each month. We are dedicated to making AMC Books a recognized leader in outdoor publishing. Thank you for your participation.

APPALACHIAN MOUNTAIN CLUB

At AMC, connecting you to the freedom and exhilaration of the outdoors is our calling. We help people of all ages and abilities to explore and develop a deep appreciation of the natural world.

AMC helps you get outdoors on your own, with family and friends, and through activities close to home and beyond. With chapters from Maine to Washington, D.C., including groups in Boston, New York City, and Philadelphia, you can enjoy activities like hiking, paddling, cycling, and skiing, and learn new outdoor skills. We offer advice, guidebooks, maps, and unique lodges and huts to inspire your next outing. You will also have the opportunity to support conservation advocacy and research, youth programming, and caring for 1,800 miles of trails.

We invite you to join us in the outdoors.

YOUR CONNECTION TO THE OUTDOORS

AMC's Best Sea Kayaking in the Mid-Atlantic

Michaela Riva Gaaserud

Explore 50 coastal paddling adventures, from the New York City Water Trail to beautiful Virginia Beach at the mouth of the Chesapeake River. This new guide features an at-a-glance trip planner, descriptions and maps of the routes, and information on launches, tide and currents, and nearby attractions.

$18.95 • 978-1-62842-031-9

AMC's Best Day Hikes near Philadelphia, 2nd Edition

Susan Charkes

No matter your experience or ability level, there are hikes for you in this fully updated second edition covering Pennsylvania, New Jersey, and Delaware—from less-traveled mountains and gorges to stretches of the Appalachian Trail, all hikeable a day or less.

$18.95 • 978-1-62842-090-6

Quiet Water Massachusetts, Connecticut, and Rhode Island, 3rd Edition

Alex Wilson & John Hayes

Discover 100 of the best flatwater pond, lake, and river trips for all skill levels in southern New England. This fully updated guide features an at-a-glance trip planner, GPS coordinates for parking, improved maps, and new planning and safety information, handy for locals and visitors alike.

$19.95 • 978-1-62842-000-5

AMC's Best Backpacking in the Mid-Atlantic

Michael R. Martin

Whether you're seeking a quick overnight trip or a challenging weeklong trek, you'll find suggested routes of all levels within easy reach of New York, Philadelphia, and Washington, D.C., in this three-season guide covering thousands of miles of trails.

$19.95 • 978-1-934028-86-5